Sleepless in Sin City

Sleepless in Sin City
Tales from the Graveyard Shift

Randy Rutecki

Sleepless in Sin City: Tales from the Graveyard Shift
Randy Rutecki

Published by: Neon Veil Press
Las Vegas, Nevada

© 2025 Randy Rutecki

ISBN 979-8-9988184-3-1
$32.99

Design & production: Tanya Maynard

Cover design and layout: Randy Rutecki
Certain graphic elements created with AI assistance and edited by the author.

Cover Roulette photo: ID 51140420 | © Cornelius20 | Dreamstime.com

For permissions or inquiries, contact:
info@neonveilpress.com
SleeplessinSinCity.com

All rights reserved. No part of this publication may be reproduced, distributed, or transmitted in any form or by any means, including photocopying, recording, or other electronic or mechanical methods, without the prior written permission of the publisher, except in the case of brief quotations embodied in critical reviews and certain other noncommercial uses permitted by copyright law.

This is a work of nonfiction. Some names and identifying details have been changed to protect the privacy of individuals.

Dedication

To the night workers—the dealers and doormen, the cabbies and cooks, the newspaper carriers and donut makers—who live their lives while the rest of the world dreams.

Author's Note

For 35 years, I watched the roulette ball spin, dealing to everyone from downtown grinders stacking 10-cent chips to billionaires wagering more on a single hand than most people make in a lifetime. This book is my attempt to capture a Las Vegas that's mostly gone now—transformed as dramatically as the city's famous neon skyline.

The stories in these pages are true, though I've changed some names and reconstructed dialogue from memory. After thousands of graveyard shifts, some details may have shifted like chips on a busy layout, but the heart of each story remains exactly as I lived it.

From break-in joints downtown to the Strip's most exclusive high-limit salons, I had a front-row seat to human nature at its most extreme. I dealt to billionaires who threw tantrums when they lost and media moguls who tipped $100,000 on a single hand. But this isn't just about high rollers and their excesses; it's also about the dealers who came from every corner of the world, all of us united by the flow of the games and the peculiar democracy of the casino floor.

I wrote this book partly because the Las Vegas I knew is disappearing, but also because I kept hearing people share casino stories, amazed by someone betting $1,000 on a cruise ship or at a local casino. I listen to how riveted everyone was by these tales and while I never wanted to be the guy who played the "oh, that's nothing" game, I realized I was sitting on thirty-five years of stories that needed to be told. Stories about a world most people never see, where $1,000 bets were so common they barely registered and where I watched people win and lose life-changing money without blinking.

If you've never set foot in a casino, don't worry; I'll guide you through. If you're a veteran of the tables, I hope these stories bring back memories. Either way, pull up a chair. The wheel's spinning and I've got stories to share.

No more bets, please.

—Las Vegas, 2025

Table of Contents

Author's Note i

Chapter 1: One Night on the Graveyard Shift 1
Million-Dollar Spins Before Sunrise

PART I
Breaking In

Chapter 2: The Journey West 15
From Nickel Games to Nevada Dreams

Chapter 3: Baptism by Fire: Breaking in Downtown 25
Learning the Ropes on Fremont Street

Chapter 4: Golden Nugget Days 41
Ten-Cent Roulette and the Rhythm of Downtown Nights

Chapter 5: The Tipping Point 55
Inside the Economy of Gratitude, Luck, and the Occasional George

Chapter 6: Sacred Tools of the Trade 67
How Cards, Dice, and Wheels Are Treated Like National Treasures

PART II
The Transformation

Chapter 7: The Golden Nugget Reborn 79
When Downtown Went Upscale

Chapter 8: Mirage: The Revolution Begins 91
The $630 Million Gamble That Changed Vegas Forever

Chapter 9: Mirage: Where Art Meets Avarice 101
Monet on the Walls, Money on the Tables, and Chaos All Around

Chapter 10: Mirage: Madness, Mayhem, and Markers 121
From Behind the Table: High-Stakes Hijinks and Vegas Absurdities

Chapter 11: Bellagio: Welcome to the Show 137
When Luxury Redefined Las Vegas

Chapter 12: Bellagio: The Glamorous Circus 145
An Insider's Take on Where Fortune, Fame, and Folly Intersect

Chapter 13: The Wynn Blueprint: Luxury, Loyalty, and a Second Act 165
Building Another Empire from the Ground Up

Chapter 14: Encore: Back for One More Round 185
A High-Stakes Afterparty

Contents

PART III
Behind the Curtain

Chapter 15: Behind the Velvet Rope 201
Inside Jobs, Outside Cons, and the Eternal Cat-and-Mouse Game

Chapter 16: Dangerous Players 211
Dealing to Killers, Kingpins, and Crime Bosses

Chapter 17: The Melting Pot 223
Stories of Survival, Hustle, and the Long Road to the Table

Chapter 18: Ever-Changing Las Vegas 235
From Cigar Smoke to Sushi Bars: Three Decades of Sin City Evolution

Epilogue 245
Glossary of Casino Terms 249
Further Reading 257

Chapter 1
One Night on the Graveyard Shift

Million-Dollar Spins Before Sunrise

It's 3:55 a.m. and the white ball spins as I approach a game where one mistake could cost the house $80,000 or cost me my job. An hour ago, I was asleep. Now I'm alert and ready for the mental precision required when a single spin might move over a million dollars in chips.

There's no easing into it. You're either alert or you're a liability. "Sorry, I'm not awake yet" doesn't fly when the stakes are this high.

Minutes earlier, I'd slipped through the service entrance, weaving between delivery trucks loaded with supplies for the hotel kitchens. The concrete floor vibrated under my feet from the rumbling engines, the air thick with diesel fumes and kitchen prep smells. One moment you're navigating the industrial maze that keeps the place running, the next you're in a world where a single hand could buy one of those trucks outside.

I cross the casino floor, moving from the chaotic noise and flashing lights past the two crystal peacocks that guard the high-limit entrance. Usually, stepping into the high-limit room feels like entering a cathedral of money, all hushed reverence and quiet tension.

But tonight, the rarified air carries something different entirely. The room is buzzing with energy: champagne bottles, laughter, and the kind of electricity that only comes when someone's on a hot streak.

My route tonight takes me between three roulette wheels, starting with SR1 and SR2, the single-zero games. As a relief dealer, I typically rotate among three games. The routine is simple: twenty minutes on each game I relieve, followed by a twenty-minute break, then repeat the cycle throughout the shift.

SR1 is my first stop. The table is full, with a crowd stacked behind it, though only four players are actively betting.

At chair one, a well-dressed man in his mid-50s bets with $1,000 blue chips, about $40,000 stacked in front of him. Next to him in chairs two and three, a younger Asian couple is betting $100 chips, stacking four or five on individual numbers. Each has about five full stacks, each worth $10,000.

Chair four belongs to Mr. Big, a regular I've nicknamed for his wild bets and wilder energy. Confident and in his 20s, he's flanked by an entourage of admirers who hype his wins as he gambles with a mix of $1,000 and $5,000 chips. A quick glance tells me he's got around $300,000 on the felt. His cheer squad spills into nearby seats and extra chairs dragged up behind him, turning that end of the table into a champagne-fueled party zone. A bottle of Cristal chills in a stand beside him and a forest of cocktail glasses, some full, some abandoned, lipstick prints on the rims, makes it feel more like a private club than a casino game. I stay alert, ready to catch any drink that threatens to spill.

My stint here is just twenty minutes before Tom, the primary dealer, returns from his break. The energy is high, but I stay sharp with each spin, watching both the crowd and the chips as much as the wheel.

Conversation drifts up from Mr. Big's crew. A few women mention being at XS Nightclub earlier. They're stunning; two look familiar from other high-rolling groups. Their confident camera-ready vibe hints they might work at one of the local gentlemen's clubs. But it's past 4 a.m. now and even the most polished professionalism has limits; one starts to nod off until Mr. Big tosses a pair of $1,000 chips her way, encouraging her to play. That perks her up. She trades them in for hundreds, places a few quick bets, then discreetly pockets the rest.

After a few spins, the table hits a lull, until I drop the marker on number 17.

Mr. Big had bet $1,000 straight up on it, plus another $1,000 on each of the four splits. Payout: $103,000. He flicks a $500 chip my way and tosses $100s to his entourage. Cheers, high-fives, and applause erupt across the table, drawing the attention of everyone in the room. For a brief moment, all eyes are on SR1, the spotlight firmly on Mr. Big, glowing with pride that says this win is secondary to being watched winning.

The couple at chairs two and three are also riding a hot streak. Their stacks grow steadily and they share the occasional knowing smile. Eventually, as dawn creeps in and fatigue settles over the room, they nod to me, ready to call it a night. I cash them out: pockets heavier, smiles wider, and clearly ahead for the night. Right on cue, the cocktail waitress clears away a few stray glasses, lightening my load.

Between spins, I take a breath and scan the room. Despite the hour, the place still hums with the quiet intensity of serious money in motion.

A few spins later, I see Tom approaching from his break. He walks up to the end of the table to scan his ID badge into the computer, signing into the game. Glancing down at the acrylic box attached to the end of the table, used to hold our tokes, our term for tips, he notices the pink $500 chip and a few black $100 chips.

Tom's mood is upbeat as he sees we're off to a promising start.

As he taps me on the shoulder, I turn to the players and say they're in good hands, claiming, with a grin, that Tom's been on a streak lately, giving away money. It's just a touch of dealer showmanship, keeping the table loose and the optimism flowing. Before stepping away, I thank Mr. Big, loud enough for Tom to know where the tip came from.

A few feet away, SR2 hums with a different kind of energy entirely. While Mr. Big's table buzzes with champagne and celebration, this game belongs to one of our regulars—and those small plastic lammers scattered around the rim of the roulette wheel represent $450,000 in call bets. I scan my badge and tap out the dealer, stepping into a world where the real money moves in whispers rather than cheers.

This game is reserved for Pedro, a billionaire from Brazil. He's also absorbed in a $100,000-per-hand mini-baccarat session at the table in front of mine. He's requested privacy and is so focused that he hasn't noticed the dealer change at roulette.

Call bets mean no chips on the felt, just Pedro's booming voice announcing wagers that the previous dealer tracked with these plastic markers. When a player calls out, "One hundred forty thousand complete middle dozen!" my job is to grab a lammer, mark the amount, and place the bets before the ball drops. It's like balancing a checkbook in your head while the numbers keep changing, except each error could cost tens of thousands.

Pedro speaks English well, but his heavy Portuguese accent means I'm always hoping that what he says and what I hear match exactly. Add overlapping bets to the mix, including complete bets on numbers, neighbor bets, and section bets, and the math becomes a beat-the-clock challenge every spin. A complete bet on number 32 would cost him $80,000, but pay $864,000 if it hits.

Then there's tracking what he has left. The computer shows $600,000 available, but subtract the $450,000 riding on the rim and he's really down to $150,000. If he starts calling out more huge bets, I might have to stop him. The nightmare: refusing his bet on 32, then watching it hit.

Pedro's baccarat session is going well. He spots me and walks over with a handshake, saying he's happy to see me. He remembers his previous trip when he had a very profitable visit while I was dealing to him.

He glances at the rim. "How much?" he asks. I tell him: "Four hundred and fifty-thousand." Without hesitation, he jogs back to the baccarat game, grabs eighteen $25,000 chips, and drops them on the layout in front of me. With a quick nod, he spins on his heel and heads straight back to baccarat.

I notify the floor supervisor, then stack the chips and cut them into neat groups of four, with two singles spread clearly to show $450,000. Then I remove the lammers from the wheel head and line them up beside the chips. The supervisor and I confirm the rim is now zero and he logs the transaction. With thousands of surveillance cameras throughout the property, I'm sure that at least five or six are simultaneously observing my every move. If needed, the eye in the sky can verify everything from multiple angles.

The rest of my 20-minute stint passes with Pedro still glued to his baccarat game. I knew he wouldn't be back at the roulette game until it was time to shuffle the baccarat cards. He likes to stay in action; he has no time to sit and watch the shuffle.

Around me, the high-limit area hums with action. Players betting $50,000 per hand, others $100,000. After all these years, I barely blink at the numbers. Still, I keep an eye on the other games, not just out of habit, but because every tip goes into our shared pool. Whether you're dealing to millionaires or standing over an empty table, we all benefit from nights like this.

My final stop takes me deeper into the casino's inner sanctum: the salon. Well past the crystal peacocks, the ambience shifts again.

The atmosphere here is different, no crowds or celebrations, just empty tables waiting for players wealthy enough to reserve entire rooms with private dining and personal butlers. Tonight, one of those tables sits ready for Sir Philip Green, whose triple-limit roulette game means a complete bet on his favorite number 5 costs $120,000—and pays over a million if it hits.

The salon sits empty, but we must staff the tables while the player's in town. I'm relieving a private roulette game reserved for Sir Philip Green, the UK retail billionaire.

Over the years, I've dealt private roulette games for Sir Philip at the Bellagio, Wynn, and now the Encore. The standard limit on our single-zero games is $1,000 straight up on a number. A few of our players, like Pedro, negotiated special limits of double that amount. But Sir Philip took it one notch higher, securing triple the limits.

It's a bold style of play with wild swings. Every spin can mean a massive loss or a seven-figure win.

For now, we wait. These reserved rooms often sit idle all night, but we stay ready. The salons have televisions, so we often watched sports or played Trivial Pursuit to pass the time. More than once, the floor supervisor had to scramble to hide the game or change the channel when the player showed up unexpectedly, sometimes at 5 a.m., ready to gamble. She quickly stashed the trivia cards and switched the TV from Seinfeld to Bloomberg or a Manchester United match, whatever fit the VIP's tastes. Everything in these rooms was tailored to the client's comfort.

Twenty minutes of watching an empty table, waiting for a billionaire who might or might not show up. It's part of the job: Sometimes you deal millions in minutes, sometimes you stand guard over nothing. Time for my break. I head downstairs to the dealers' lounge, trading the casino's eternal twilight for fluorescent lights and the comfortable chaos of the back-of-house world.

My break routine is simple: coffee and one of those oversized

One Night on the Graveyard Shift

chocolate chip cookies from the employee dining room on my first break. Sometimes, I squeeze in a 10-minute walk through the sprawling service corridors behind the resort's scenes. These back hallways even connect us to Wynn Las Vegas next door via a network of corridors at the basement level.

Despite these walks, my Armani tuxedo seems to be shrinking. Must be the dry cleaning or the cookies on my break. I mentally note to swing by uniform control and see if the seamstress can work her magic again. If not, I might need to swap this tux for a larger size. But that can wait; right now, I need my break.

After my break, I return to SR1. The players from earlier have cleared out, replaced by a familiar face from Nigeria. He told me he was from the Ministry of Petroleum Resources. Impeccably dressed even at this early hour, he always wore a perfectly tailored suit with a colorful pocket handkerchief that somehow looked dignified rather than flashy.

He's visited several times recently, likely here for business meetings. He stops by for coffee and a little roulette before his day begins. He's soft-spoken but personable and usually comes in for a couple of hours in the mornings. Whether he's an early riser, avoiding crowds, or simply following Nigerian time, he's here when the casino is quietest.

While dealing to him, I often wonder about contrast. His play isn't anything too wild, but he is betting $2,000 a spin, which could equal a year's salary back home for many. I picture someone in Lagos or the Nigerian countryside, working 12-hour days in the heat, on a tight budget, while this man casually pushes forward what would be their entire year's hope for survival. The chips make their familiar click as I sweep away another lost bet, the sound of someone's annual wages disappearing in 15 seconds of a ball spinning. However, that thought applies to just about every player I deal with, regardless of their nationality. The numbers might differ, but the gap between their bets and the average person's paycheck is always staggering.

Looking over at the next table, I see Pedro has wrapped up for the night. I expect he'll return with his wife and other family members in a few hours. Typically, around 9 a.m., the butler in his villa calls down to let us know they're finishing breakfast. Shortly after, we get the heads-up that they're on their way. When the family joins him, the game slows down a bit. But Pedro remains the main player; his relatives place much smaller bets, more for the fun than the stakes.

Despite his wealth, Pedro and his family remain remarkably down to earth. Once between trips, a friend of his, who also gambles here regularly, approached my table and handed me the phone. I can't recall another time someone handed me a phone on the game. I picked it up and immediately recognized Pedro's voice. He was calling from Brazil to say hello and let me know the family would be in town in a couple of weeks.

On his last visit, Pedro had an exceptional run, winning a couple of million. One moment stood out: He noticed the porter emptying the trash near the game during that hot streak. Pedro called him over and handed him two $1,000 chips. His generosity wasn't reserved for dealers or waitresses; it extended to everyone. That shift, he toked me $87,000. Sure, it was split amongst the dealers, but it still made for a *very* good day.

I check in on my third game, but there's still no sign of Sir Philip Green. The supervisor touches base with the crew over at the Wynn, but there is no sign of him there either. Still, we wouldn't dare shut the game down. Not until we're absolutely sure.

It's happened before. A player's been presumed gone, only to reappear unexpectedly. That's when the scramble starts: dealers rushing in, floor staff scrambling to open the game, all while trying to make it look seamless. These players don't like to be kept waiting. And they don't have to be. Hosts constantly watch, track movements, and stay ready to accommodate any request immediately.

Of course, the opposite can happen too. Sometimes a player reserves a game for a six-day stay and four days in, you're still waiting. Then you read an article in the paper saying they were just in a meeting in San Francisco. You wait anyway.

The butlers and casino hosts always have the best intel. I remember one boss who refused to close a game until the player's plane was wheels up. Others used to joke that they wouldn't close the game until the guy was out of U.S. airspace.

The sequence continues throughout the shift: an hour on, then a 20-minute break. I head to the quiet room to read the newspaper for this one. It's a separate space within the dealers' lounge, furnished with the same comfy chairs, but with an extra door to keep things hushed. That buffer helps block out the typical break-room chatter: recipes, world news, or uniquely Vegas, how to get scorpions out of your garage.

In one corner, the usual group grumbles about coworkers, players, or bosses. I do my best to steer clear and retreat to the quiet room. Unfortunately, the lights are off this time, and a chorus of snoring greets me. Occasionally, someone commandeers the room for a nap. It's the graveyard shift, after all. You'd think a 20-minute break, minus five minutes for the round-trip hike from the pit, wouldn't cut it for a nap. But we made it work. The real culprits are often the supervisors, who get fewer but longer breaks. They're always a little jumpy about the clock, especially if they're alone. You don't want to wake up thinking you've been left behind.

As 10 a.m. approaches, the casino begins to stir. Early-rising guests begin to appear. The once-quiet halls fill with conversation and the electronic chirping of slot machines.

The energy builds just in time for the day shift to take over. Noon hits and the graveyard shift fades out.

One of the perks of working overnight is having your days free. Whether it's golfing, running errands, or squeezing in a tennis match, graveyard can't be beat. Plus, the commute is easy, with no rush-hour stress on the way in.

But what sets the graveyard shift apart is the camaraderie. There's something special about working through the night while the rest of the city sleeps. The quiet hours lead to closer bonds, personal conversations, and lasting friendships. The hours are unconventional and the sleep schedule isn't for everyone. But the lifestyle works for those of us who prefer a cadence outside the norm.

Three decades of dealing, starting downtown and moving to the most glamorous casinos on the Strip, have given me more stories and memories than I could have imagined when I first walked onto a casino floor.

How did I end up in this line of work? Not through any childhood dream or family tradition. I wasn't raised around gambling and this career certainly wasn't planned. It was part opportunity, part timing, and decisions that seemed logical in the moment. Looking back, it all fits together, though it felt more like instinct than strategy.

In fact, it all started in the most unlikely place: a college library in Buffalo, New York, where a dusty book about card counting would change the entire direction of my life.

The automatic doors slide open, releasing me from the casino's eternal twilight into the blazing Nevada sun. After eight hours under artificial light, the brightness forces me to fumble for sunglasses. The dry Nevada heat accompanies my walk to the car.

As I head up Flamingo out of the valley, the Strip shrinking in my rearview mirror, I can already feel my body switching to day mode. By the time I pull into my driveway, the adrenaline has faded, replaced by the familiar pleasant exhaustion that comes from another night of managing millions.

PART I
BREAKING IN

Downtown Dreams and Learning the Game

From a college kid with a card-counting book to a seasoned dealer navigating downtown Las Vegas's gritty reality. These are the foundational years—learning the ropes, understanding the economics of tips, and discovering the sacred rituals that protect the games.

Chapter 2
The Journey West

From Nickel Games to Nevada Dreams

My high school guidance counselor never mentioned it. Among all the career paths she suggested—doctor, lawyer, teacher—*casino dealer* wasn't on the list. I wouldn't have known what that meant anyway. Working in Las Vegas casinos was never something I pictured as a kid. I grew up in a household where gambling wasn't glamorized or even really discussed. Our exposure to betting came in the most innocent forms. At family gatherings, the deck of cards came out for games filled with laughter, not wagers. I can still hear the rhythmic *riffle* of cards being shuffled, the smell of my grandmother's homemade pizza drifting in from the kitchen, and the loud knock my grandfather gave the table when he was ready to wrap up one of our nickel games. And the rare trip to church bingo, with its modest prizes and friendly banter, offered no hint of the heart-pounding high-stakes action that later defined my career.

My first brush with gambling came around the age of 15, while I was working as a paperboy. With a bit of pocket money for the first time, I found a new pastime: flipping coins. It wasn't formal, just a schoolyard game where two players each flipped a coin a nickel at first, though it didn't take long to escalate to quarters. You flipped the coin onto your opposite wrist and covered it quickly. Your opponent then called out "match" or "no match." If both coins showed the same face, whether heads or tails, it was a match, and the caller took the pot.

A quarter was serious loot for a teenager in the '60s. You could get a Coke and maybe a slice of pizza. It felt like you were rolling high.

Simple as it was, that game taught me two of the most essential precepts in gambling, which I'd revisit often in my years behind the felt.

The first was the danger of chasing losses; later in casino life, I learned the Martingale system. Sometimes after a loss, a kid suggested "double or nothing." At first, that sounded like a quick road back to even, or better. A quarter could turn into 50 cents, then a buck, then two. Pretty soon, you're five flips away from either cleaning up ... or being cleaned out. The thrill of the win wore off fast the moment you hit "nothing." It was a valuable early lesson: When you keep doubling bets without a stop limit, especially when your opponent has deeper pockets, you're just gambling on borrowed time.

The second lesson came courtesy of the neighborhood loan sharks-in-training. As the stakes crept up to a couple bucks, so did the tension. If I wanted to end the game, sometimes the other guy wouldn't let me. "One more, double or nothing," he'd say, especially if he was losing, and suddenly I was negotiating with someone twice my size who didn't take "no" for an answer. I learned quickly that some people get creative about debt collection when money's on the line. The message stuck. If you can't collect, it's not a bet; it's a donation.

Looking back, that short-lived coin-flipping phase did more than

The Journey West 17

lighten my pockets. It introduced me to the basics of risk and reward, the rush of chance, and the human flaws that surface when money's at stake. And while I didn't know it then, it was my unofficial apprenticeship for a future in Las Vegas, minus the lunch-money losses and awkward wrist bruises.

As I got older, my fascination with gambling didn't fade; it just took a few unexpected turns.

While working at a restaurant as a student at the University at Buffalo, I struck up a conversation that quietly redirected my life. The owner and his son, Joey, had just returned from a trip to Las Vegas and they were still riding high off the glow of the blackjack tables. I'd never heard the game's rules, but their enthusiasm was contagious. During slow moments at the bar, Joey grabbed a deck and walked me through a few hands, showing me the basics. It didn't take long before I was hooked, not on the cards themselves, but on the idea that strategy was behind the shuffle.

This was long before the Google era, when "research" meant squinting at microfiche and hunting through dusty stacks, not typing a question into a search bar. I spent more hours in UB's Science and Engineering library than in the student union. One afternoon, hidden on a back shelf, I discovered gold: *Beat the Dealer* by Edward O. Thorp.

The title practically dared me to open it. Inside? Pure blackjack sorcery. This guy wasn't just gambling. With charts, math, and memory tricks, he was *calculating*. He claimed you could actually beat the house. Not just hold your own, but win. For someone raised on nickel games and bingo nights, it was like discovering a blackjack Bible hidden between physics textbooks.

That book flipped a switch in my head. I wasn't just curious anymore; I was obsessed. I dove into card-counting systems, memorizing values, running drills in my head, and practicing at every chance. The fact that you could use logic and discipline to tilt the odds in your favor, just slightly, felt like discovering a loophole in the universe.

Little did I know that dusty library book was planting the seed for what would eventually become my career. The casino floor started to feel less like a mystery and more like a destination. I couldn't shake the idea that I might belong in that world, a mix of chance and calculation, adrenaline and control.

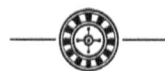

After graduating from UB, I had a half-baked plan to head west. There was some vague talk about establishing residency in California and maybe attending grad school at Berkeley. But mostly, I was looking for an adventure and a break after years of lectures and exams. A lot of people assumed I'd be back in a month. I wasn't so sure.

By the summer of 1974, I was practicing card counting each evening. I'd never stepped into a casino, but on paper, I was getting good. When August rolled around, I packed up my '72 Chevy Vega and hit the road with a buddy, Paul. The car burned oil at an impressive rate, so I brought a five-gallon can along for the ride. I had to top it off at nearly every gas stop. With fingers crossed and a plan held together by optimism and fumes, we rolled toward Las Vegas.

I had just over $500 to my name and a precious $50 carved out specifically for my first live blackjack session. This was a mix of hope, strategy, and maybe a little youthful delusion. Stepping into the casino felt like walking into another dimension. The place buzzed with energy: Flashing lights pulsed from every direction, bells chimed like victory songs, coins clanged into metal trays, and the air was thick with cigarette smoke, cologne, and adrenaline. It was sensory overload and I loved it. My heart pounded as I approached the blackjack table, convinced that the strategies I'd studied in a dog-eared book weren't just theory. I wasn't just there to try; I was there to win.

Two hours later, reality cashed me out. My $50 vanished, as if the casino hid a vacuum beneath the felt, specifically for overconfident card counters. I just sat there, stunned. How could this be? According to the simulations, I was supposed to break even at least or lose slowly. Not be wiped out in time for an early dinner.

The real world hit like a ton of bricks. The math hadn't lied, but the game had layers I hadn't anticipated: shuffling patterns, table conditions, distractions, pressure. It wasn't just a numbers game. It was a people game. And I still had a lot to learn.

Deflated but not defeated, I left the table lighter in the wallet, but heavier in respect for the house edge. I half-expected a pit boss to hand me a coupon for a free buffet and a book titled *Why You Won't Beat Us*. Instead, I walked away knowing I needed to sharpen not just my skills, but my instincts.

That first loss didn't scare me off; it did the opposite. It locked me in. This world, chaotic and glittering, was where I wanted to be. I wasn't sure whether I'd be playing, dealing, winning, or watching, but I knew I'd return.

Even though I was still fascinated by blackjack, it had to take a back seat. I needed to make some money. Fast. At that moment, gambling wasn't going to pay any bills and I had rent, groceries, and motor oil to think about.

I stayed in California for a few years, steadily climbing the retail management ladder at Wherehouse Records. Dealing with demanding customers taught me a valuable skill: staying calm under pressure, even when someone screamed about a warped record or missing liner notes. Later, this emotional judo helped when gamblers blamed their dealer for everything from bad streaks to slow cocktail servers.

But corporate politics soon wore thin and I realized I wanted nothing to do with middle or even upper management. Meanwhile, I couldn't help noticing dealers had a sweeter schedule: an hour of work, followed by a 20-minute break, and typically an eight-hour shift. That lifestyle started looking a lot better than the corporate grind.

Around then, I bought my first computer: a Radio Shack TRS-80. It was incredibly basic by today's standards, with limited memory and simple graphics, but it was enough for me to learn some basic programming. I managed to write programs to simulate dealing cards and track card values, effectively running thousands of blackjack hands. My living room became an early blackjack lab, where I tested card-counting strategies straight from Thorp's book. Despite its limitations, that rudimentary setup fueled my growing fascination. Vegas kept calling, not just for the gambling, but something deeper.

When the opportunity arose, I decided to pursue my passion for card counting full-time. If that didn't work out, I planned to try my hand at dealing. To the surprise of many, I walked away from my management position and headed to Las Vegas, ready to embark on a new chapter.

When I finally committed to card counting, I quickly learned that while it didn't require me to be Rain Man, it was still a mentally taxing pursuit. After an hour at the tables, I felt like I'd just taken the SATs twice. To avoid drawing too much attention, I developed the "paper route" method. I mapped out a circuit of casinos with favorable rules and betting limits and hit a few each day, moving on before anyone got suspicious.

Card counting was legal, but not exactly welcome. If you were spotted, the best-case scenario was a polite invitation to leave. The worst-case scenario was a less-than-polite one.

Despite my best efforts, the reality set in: Hard work was not always profitable. After a while, I decided it was time to try my hand on the other side of the table.

Getting a job at the more prestigious joints like Caesars, Sands, the Dunes, and Desert Inn wouldn't happen overnight. Those spots were reserved for folks with connections, seniority, or charm. I had none of the above. Downtown was the more likely starting point, the same as it had been for so many others before me.

Even that required considerable effort. I knew the math. I knew the games. But I didn't know the first thing about dealing procedures. Even being an expert blackjack player didn't automatically qualify me to deal it. That's where the local dealing schools came in. Casinos occasionally called these schools when they needed new blood, so I signed up at the Valley School of Dealing, dropped a couple of hundred bucks, and got to work.

The classes were surprisingly fun. We drilled nonstop on chip handling, card shuffling, cutting checks, and the nuances of various blackjack game types: single deck, double deck, shoe games, face up, face down, and hand-pitching. After a few days, we started dealing to one another.

At first, it felt awkward. My hands didn't know where to go. Just handling the chips, especially cutting checks, was clumsy to say the least. That simple-looking drill, taking a stack of 20 chips and slicing them cleanly into stacks of four or five with one fluid motion, was a basic but critical skill. It was like trying to juggle quarters with oven mitts at first. But eventually, muscle memory kicked in, at least for me. Some students never quite got the hang of it.

The math wasn't complicated. A winning hand pays even money and a blackjack pays 3 to 2, but even basic payouts could trip people up. Ask someone to calculate 1.5 times a $187 bet and you'll see some panicked blinking.

We drilled nonstop, taking turns dealing to get lots of repetition with simple straightforward bets. Of course, there was always a wise guy eager to complicate things, not satisfied with beginner-friendly bets of $5, $10, or $20. Instead, these bozos would toss out a stack of about 30 chips in multiple denominations—known as a 'rainbow bet' because of the various colors involved. To make matters worse, the chips were randomly mixed, slowing everything to a crawl. If your goal was practice through repetition, this definitely wasn't helpful.

What struck me most, though, was the mixture of the students. There were folks from every walk of life: truck drivers, college students, single moms, retirees, and even former Air Force pilots. It was my first real glimpse into the crowd I'd soon be working alongside.

One guy stood out immediately. Jim, a good ole boy from Tennessee, drove a hearse for the county and had endless stories. My favorite? The time he got called into work after enjoying some ... powerful recreational drugs. His emergency call was to retrieve the remains of a recently deceased individual. Every intersection he stopped at, Jim swore the body sat up and looked around. After dealing with passengers who wouldn't stay dead, handling the zombies of the graveyard shift seemed like a step up

While at dealer's school, I took a couple of casino courses at UNLV out of curiosity. One, taught by a former head of surveillance at the Frontier, was part security briefing, part con-artist exposé, full of real-world war stories. The other, Mathematics of Casino Games, explained the probabilities behind every game, showing how odds shifted with rule tweaks or deck changes.

These classes didn't guarantee me a job, but they made the inner workings of casinos feel less mysterious, more attainable. The more I learned, the more I wanted in.

The Journey West

Armed with my newly minted dealer skills and a head full of probability theory, I hit the streets looking for my first real casino job. The Strip seemed like a pipe dream; those positions were locked up tighter than the casino vaults. But downtown? Downtown was where dreamers and hustlers went to prove their worth. It was time to see which one I was.

Chapter 3

Baptism by Fire: Breaking in Downtown

Learning the Ropes on Fremont Street

Once I felt confident in the basics, I was eager to begin my new career. But as I waited for job opportunities, it quickly became apparent that the school hadn't received any calls from casinos looking to hire. Determined not to sit around any longer, I took matters into my own hands. I headed downtown to Las Vegas alone, ready to audition, showcase my skills, and prove I had what it took to become a professional dealer.

Back then, break-in joints like the El Cortez and Lady Luck were the go-to spots for aspiring dealers. These places were a rite of passage, a baptism by fire. Downtown had around 10 casinos clustered together in a neon jungle, each a potential stepping stone or a dead end. The conditions were anything but glamorous, more *Apocalypse Now* than *Ocean's Eleven*. I knew I'd be dealing to a motley crew: some friendly, some downright menacing. I remember one regular who'd stare you down like a hawk, ready to pounce at the first mistake. It was like being thrown into the deep end of a pool filled with sharks, while wearing a suit made of chum.

My plan was simple: start at one end of Fremont Street and apply at every casino on one side, then work my way back on the other side the next day. I'd keep at it until someone hired me or got tired of seeing my face. At the time, you'd typically claim to know one game well and be familiar with a second. The main games were blackjack, craps, and roulette, with the occasional Big Six wheel or chuck-a-luck. At dealer's school, I'd focused on blackjack and had a bit of roulette under my belt, so blackjack became my go-to for auditions.

An "audition" usually meant putting on your black-and-whites, black pants and white shirt, and walking into a casino to ask for a job. If they agreed, sometimes they sent you right into a live game, with the regular dealer standing next to you. It was a different ballgame from dealer school, where you thought you knew it all after a few weeks. On a live table, everything happened faster, with higher stakes and less margin for error. Mistakes weren't an option—if you wanted the job.

Before asking if they were hiring, you casually strolled around the pit to get a feel for the procedures. Each house did things a little differently. You didn't want to be too obvious, but the black-and-whites usually gave it away. Other variables were out of your control, like the players. Would you get a friendly crowd or a table full of jerks trying to rattle you just because they could tell you were green? It wasn't for the faint of heart, especially on that first go-around.

The regular dealers standing by during auditions were generally supportive, but not in a "let me show you the ropes" kind of way. They mostly babysat the table, ensuring you didn't crash and burn while the bosses watched from a distance. Still, a subtle nod or a slight shake of the head was all the feedback you needed to know if you were on track or not.

Some break-in joints offered free dealing classes, but there was a catch: You had to sign a contract committing to six to 12 months

Baptism by Fire: Breaking in Downtown

of work afterward. These were places with revolving doors. Once you got a taste of the action and gained some experience, the urge to move on to better games and better tips was hard to resist.

As I started making the rounds, I walked into casino after casino with a blend of anticipation and anxiety. Responses varied. Some bosses barely looked up from their paperwork before grunting, "We're not hiring." Others were a bit warmer, handing me a form to fill out or telling me to come back at a specific time to see the "audition master." Each interaction was a mini-adventure, another small but meaningful step in my quest to become a dealer in the heart of downtown Las Vegas.

The moment I stepped into the Las Vegas Club, I was met with an immediate invitation to audition, right then and there. The place was in chaos, to put it mildly. Dealers were being cycled through at a pace that suggested desperation. The casino was mid-renovation, a construction zone disguised as a gaming floor. Buckets hung from the ceiling to catch rogue raindrops, the carpet was more patchwork than flooring, and the air had a scent that could only be described as … unique. Still, amidst all the chaos and disrepair, something about it whispered, "This is your starting line."

The building itself had history. It sat on one of the oldest hotel sites in Las Vegas, the former home of the Overland Hotel, established in 1905. In the mid-1940s, a group of partners bought it, one of them the legendary Benny Binion.

By 1962, Jackie Gaughan and Mel Exber had taken over and transformed the property into the sports-themed Las Vegas Club, a fixture at the corner of Main and Fremont. Its facade was designed to resemble Ebbets Field, the famed home of the Brooklyn Dodgers. Mel and his brother Marty ran the place; it was Marty, the casino manager, who greeted me for the audition. Marty looked like he'd stepped off a movie set: gruff, no-nonsense, and not exactly warm and fuzzy. Maybe he was a teddy bear at home, though I wouldn't bet on it. He played the tough guy on the casino floor and he played it well.

I passed the audition. Now all I had to do was head to the sheriff's office at the far end of Fremont Street to get my Sheriff's card. Back then, it cost about $35. They snapped your photo, took your fingerprints, and supposedly ran a background check. There were no drug tests at the time, which was probably a blessing, because if there had been, at least half the dealers I worked with would've been out of a job.

When I returned to the Las Vegas Club, they told me I'd start the next day at 2 a.m. I'd landed a spot on the graveyard shift, 2-10 a.m. Not exactly banker's hours. But I didn't care. I was officially in and couldn't wait to get started.

The '70s in downtown Las Vegas were a spectacle of light and color. Neon signs towered over the streets, each one a masterpiece, a dazzling display of artistry and engineering. It may have been 2 a.m., but you felt like you needed sunglasses on Fremont Street.

The first few nights on the job were like warm-up laps, dealing mostly with players betting silver dollars. Real Eisenhower dollars, clunky and worn. Most players tossed out one or two at a time, maybe a red chip worth five bucks if they were feeling bold. It was a perfect pace for a rookie, slow and steady, letting me get my sea legs without capsizing. I was settling in, building confidence hand by hand.

Then came the moment that jolted me fully awake.

Out of nowhere, a guy strolled up, cool as could be, and slapped a crisp hundred-dollar bill down on the layout like it was pocket change. My brain stalled. My heart kicked into overdrive, my palms turned clammy, and my voice cracked as I shouted, "Money plays, one hundred!" louder than I meant to. Heads turned. I was officially

Baptism by Fire: Breaking in Downtown

in over my head.

After days of slow-motion action, it felt like someone hit fast-forward. My adrenaline spiked. For a split second, that table felt like center stage and I was the only one who hadn't rehearsed my lines. My hands moved faster than my brain, eager to prove I could hang with the big kids.

Sure, I'd go on to deal stacks of hundreds, chips worth more than most people's cars, and roulette bets that hit like lottery wins. But that first hundred-dollar bill? It's etched in my memory like a tattoo.

It wasn't just the money. It was what it represented. That single bill flipped a switch, from playing casino to being the casino. In that moment, I wasn't practicing anymore. I was in the game, for real.

What makes that hand unforgettable isn't just the money. It's the rookie mistake I made right after. The player had 19. I showed a ten. I flipped over a face card—20. "Twenty," I said, half-thrilled, half-crushed. Then I broke protocol. Instead of settling the hands in proper order, I lunged for the hundred and stuffed it straight into the drop box, ignoring the other bets. It was a clear breach of procedure, but no one said a word, since the casino got its money.

A few mornings later, we marched into the pit like soldiers heading into battle. The air was thick with the smell of musty carpet and worn felt. Chips clacked, gamblers murmured, and the usual downtown chaos unfolded around us. But I was too amped to notice. The adrenaline of being the new guy was still shielding me from the grungier side of graveyard hours. As we lined up for our game assignments, I had my eye on a $10 table in the corner. It looked like the hottest game in the pit and I silently hoped I'd land it.

I walked up to Johnny, the "pencil." He stood there like a pit sentry, a cigarette in one hand and a Styrofoam cup of coffee in the other. Johnny wasn't big on words, but he didn't need to be. One glance from him and your fate was sealed. "The pencil" wasn't just a scheduler; he was part matchmaker, part tough guy with the air of a mob boss. Some games went to pals, some to pretty faces. I was neither, so I was just hoping for a decent table.

"Take table fourteen, kid," he mumbled in a gravelly New York accent.

My heart leapt. That was it, the $10 game I'd been eyeing, the busiest one on the floor. It felt like I'd hit the mini-lottery. My wish came true. I was stepping into the arena.

I hit a groove right away. The players were loose, the chips were flowing, and the mood was upbeat. The table was winning, nothing major, but a few hundred bucks here and there kept everyone happy. As I was settling into the flow, I felt a tap on my shoulder. Another dealer stood behind me, ready to take over. I was confused. It wasn't time for my break.

The players noticed, too. "What's going on?" one of them asked. "He just got here. We're just warming up!"

The shift boss called out from across the pit, "He's not feeling well."

I turned, caught off guard. "No, I feel fine, actually."

The boss didn't miss a beat. "He's not feeling well," he repeated, this time with more authority.

After pulling me off the table, he leaned in and said, "From now on, when I say you're not feeling well, you're not feeling well. Got it?"

It didn't take long to figure out what was really going on. He thought I was unlucky. Superstition ran deep back then. I later learned I'd been placed on the game because I was new. They called it "break-in luck." They didn't care if you were green or shaky. They wanted rookie luck. Luck trumped talent every time.

Baptism by Fire: Breaking in Downtown

Back then, the bosses who ran those joints looked like they came straight out of *Guys and Dolls*, flashy sports coats that looked like horse blankets, pinky rings, and the occasional cigar.

Most didn't know the first thing about the games' math. They didn't need to. They believed in streaks, hunches, and gut feelings. One boss wouldn't even let dealers play cards on their breaks. Said he didn't want them using up their luck.

Early one morning, while dealing roulette at the Las Vegas Club, in walked this blind guy who said his name was Lou. Now, Lou might not have been able to see the wheel, but it sure seemed like Lady Luck was whispering in his ear. He tapped his way up to my table, cane clicking like he was tapping out Morse code for the winning numbers.

"Put me down for eight, seventeen, twenty-three and the corner— one, two, four, and five,," he said, grinning like he'd just been handed the universe's secrets.

I started placing his bets, calling out results, and sliding his winnings over to him, doing my best to help without being obvious. After about 30 minutes, Lou's stack was growing faster than a mob-funded Vegas construction site.

That was when my shift boss, Joe, came storming past. His face was beet red and he was muttering just loud enough for me to hear. "Are you gonna let this blind guy beat you?!"

I'm pretty sure Joe wasn't serious about doing anything shady— but back then, if I had accidentally swept up some winning bets, I doubt he'd have lost sleep over it.

Still, I kept dealing it straight. I watched Lou's stack grow and Joe's blood pressure right along with it. When Lou finally tapped away from the table, his pockets jingling like a piggy bank on payday, I couldn't help but smile. Sometimes, justice really is blind.

Don't get me wrong. Some of those old-timers weren't bad guys. They were just ... characters. One time, a fellow dealer on the game behind me looked genuinely ill, pale as a ghost, and sweating. I turned to the floor supervisor and asked, "Is Bill okay?"

His reply: "Waddaya, a docta? Dummy up and deal."

Another classic: If you asked too many questions, you'd get hit with, "Waddaya, writin' a book?"

Today, that might sound awful. People would ask how you could work under those conditions, or why you'd take that kind of abuse. But honestly, I loved it. That stuff cracked me up. Of course, I kept my amusement to myself. I also knew the right time to laugh, especially if the boss was telling the joke.

Like everything else at the Las Vegas Club, nothing was top of the line. Not even close. The surveillance system was a relic: just a network of catwalks above the casino floor. Every so often, dust drifted down from the ceiling as someone crept around up there. The rest of their "security system" consisted of walls lined with mirrors. Low-tech to say the least, but they made do.

While the surveillance left much to be desired, the place offered a few perks. Employees got a 10% discount at the snack bar or for the more adventurous, there was always the option of venturing out onto Fremont Street during our 20-minute hourly breaks. Each option had its own peculiar charm.

Wandering Fremont between 3 and 6 a.m. was like walking through a Fellini film. You got a glimpse of Vegas that few tourists ever see. You could indulge in downtown's finest culinary delights, like the 25-cent shrimp cocktail just across the street, and cross paths with some of the most colorful characters.

Baptism by Fire: Breaking in Downtown

I remember one guy who stopped me and asked for a couple of bucks for food. Despite looking well-fed, I played along and asked how I knew he wouldn't spend it on gambling. He tapped his pocket and grinned. "Oh no, I've got gambling money right here." I gave him a couple of bucks.

If you chose to stay in and eat at the snack bar, you'd meet Delia. She ran the place on the graveyard shift. Middle-aged, full of energy, scatterbrained, and always a spectacle. She usually had some kind of condiment on her face and a cigarette with a dangling half-inch of ash permanently affixed to her lips. At least she wore the required hairnet.

The snack bar itself looked like something out of a forgotten diner scene. A long counter was flanked by round red (or were they pink?) vinyl stools that spun with a satisfying squeak. The air always carried the mingled scent of fryer oil, old coffee, and burnt toast. Behind the counter was the usual lineup: shelves stocked with chips and candy, a small refrigerated case with premade sandwiches, and a flat-top grill that sizzled away with burgers, grilled cheese, and the occasional breakfast burrito. It wasn't fancy, but it was ours—a kind of smoky oasis from the neon chaos just outside its swinging door.

But what made Delia special wasn't her cooking. It was her stories. Between grilled cheese orders and breakfast burritos, she spun tales from her wild past with the flair of a vaudeville performer. That dingy snack bar was a refuge, a place to catch your breath and get lost in Delia's latest saga.

One story stuck with me more than the rest. Delia told me about her mother's illness, how one night, her mother called her to the hospital bedside to say she didn't expect to make it. She instructed Delia to go to her apartment after she passed, where she'd find a shoebox with $2,400 to split with her brother.

Delia left the hospital, went straight to her mother's closet, found the box, and disappeared for 36 hours. She hit every casino she could. She gambled away the entire $2,400.

Three days later, her mother made a miraculous recovery and was released from the hospital, only to come home to an empty shoebox.

Delia wasn't the only one with a cautionary tale. Sid, our shift boss, reminded me of a character out of "Eleanor Rigby." He was thin, elderly, and lived alone in a tiny apartment near the casino. His life followed a strict pattern: save money all month, blow it on craps, then repeat. He never broke the cycle and I don't think he ever tried.

Then there was Tommy, a fellow dealer who knew his way around a craps table. He was just days away from marrying his fiancée, Mary. Her father, wanting to help, gave Tommy the cash to pay for the reception hall, the catering, and the band. All he had to do was drop off the deposits.

Instead, Tommy hit the tables, fueled by booze, bravado, and impaired judgment. He lost everything. The wedding was canceled, Mary was devastated, and her father and brother were ready to kill him. Tommy vanished for a few weeks, lying low to avoid the fallout. Looking back, Mary probably dodged a bullet, but that didn't make the betrayal sting any less.

For tourists, gambling is a short-term thrill. They come with a budget and a return ticket. But for locals, the danger is different. You live in it. It'll swallow you if you don't let the novelty wear off or learn to keep it in check.

After about eight months at the Las Vegas Club, I was in a reflective mood one evening. The neon lights of Fremont Street had become a familiar backdrop and the faces at my blackjack table had started to blur into one continuous stream of tourists, drunks, and dreamers. I'd grown comfortable dealing blackjack and even picked up some roulette experience. The early jitters had faded, replaced by a steady confidence and a sense of control over the games. I'd learned a lot about the mechanics of dealing, the quirky rituals of old-school

Baptism by Fire: Breaking in Downtown

bosses, and the late-night weirdness of downtown gamblers.

Graveyard shift came with its eccentricities. Some were funny, some frustrating, and all part of learning how to live on Vegas time.

Working the graveyard shift takes some adjustment, especially regarding the hours. Whether your start time is 2 or 4 a.m., you've got to be in bed by 6:30 or 7 p.m. if you want any chance at real sleep. With blackout curtains and a quiet room, it's manageable. But no matter how prepared you are, that fear of oversleeping always lurks in the back of your mind.

Almost every newbie on graveyard has at least one panic attack while adjusting. It usually happens during those weird times of year when dusk can easily be mistaken for dawn. You'll be dead asleep for about 45 minutes, roll over, and see 7:45 on the clock. Your heart jumps. Light seeps through the curtains. You bolt upright, convinced you've already missed half your shift.

I've heard the same story a dozen times: Someone frantically calls the casino scheduler, breathless and apologizing, swearing they'll be right in, only to have the calm voice on the other end say, "Your shift doesn't start for another five hours."

The relief hits first. Then the embarrassment. You hang up sheepishly, hoping they forget about it. But don't worry, they won't. It's practically a rite of passage. Just like your first 8 a.m. "lunch" break or learning to sleep through the sounds of kids playing outside and neighbors firing up their barbecues.

Eventually, your body adjusts. You start knowing what time it is without even checking a clock, though most of us still set two or three alarm clocks, just in case.

Getting ready for the graveyard shift wasn't all that different from prepping for any other shift, except you had to do everything in near silence to avoid waking the rest of the house. For me, one unique part of the routine was the dog walk. We had beagles—three at one point—and taking them out at 3 a.m. brought its own special brand of chaos.

Our neighborhood backed up to the desert and if those dogs caught sight or even a whiff of a rabbit, all hell broke loose. Nothing shattered the stillness of a sleeping neighborhood quite like a chorus of howling beagles echoing through the streets at three in the morning.

But noise aside, those early walks had their moments. Occasionally, I spotted a pack of coyotes watching us from across the open desert, curious but keeping their distance. Now and then, I came across a tarantula inching its way across the road or a rattlesnake stretched out on the warm asphalt, soaking up the last heat from the day.

Oddly, those walks became my morning meditation before the madness of the casino floor. From our vantage point in the hills, I could see the Strip glowing 10 miles away, a flickering neon ribbon in the valley. The contrast was surreal: quiet sidewalks under the stars followed by tables full of tourists still riding high from midnight drinks and dice rolls.

It was a strange way to start a workday, but somehow, it fit.

One of the more amusing questions I used to hear back when I was first breaking into dealing, when the Las Vegas metro area barely topped 400,000 people, was, "Do you live here?"

It always gave me pause. I never knew quite how to take it. Did they think we lived in dorms beneath the casino, like some subterranean tribe of dealers? Or maybe they pictured us commuting in daily from Los Angeles, crossing the desert like nomadic card slingers.

That question said a lot about how tourists saw Las Vegas back then: a fantasy island in the middle of nowhere, a neon playground, not a real city. To many, it was hard to picture Vegas with schools, supermarkets, or suburban life. Their mental map stopped at the Strip and downtown on Fremont.

Baptism by Fire: Breaking in Downtown

Today, with nearly two and a half million people calling the Las Vegas Valley home, that question's gone extinct. The city's grown into a full-blown metro with pro sports, luxury shopping, and sprawling suburbs. But back then, we were still trying to convince people we existed outside the pit.

You might assume that working the graveyard shift, I've seen a dealer or two nod off during a slow night—and you'd be right. Even though I did catch the occasional dealer falling asleep on his feet at the Vegas Club, it wasn't limited to just break-in joints. Nearly every graveyard shift I ever worked came with at least one moment of someone drifting off, sometimes subtly, sometimes spectacularly.

A particularly memorable one happened at the Nugget. April, a fellow dealer, was posted at a dead game, standing idle with one hand on the layout and the other on the plastic discard rack. As she started to doze, her weight shifted to the right, and startled awake, she accidentally snapped the discard rack clean off the table.

But the gold standard of graveyard dozing came from Juan, a baccarat dealer I worked with at Bellagio. From my game across the pit, I had a front-row view of his uncanny ability to power-nap in one-minute bursts right in the middle of a hand.

Seated at the baccarat table, Juan waited for the dealer with the shoe to call the totals and outcome. While he waited? Eyes closed. Dozing. The moment he heard, "Bank wins," his eyes opened and without missing a beat, he paid the bets, marked the commission, and closed them again. Like nothing happened.

And these weren't low-stakes hands, either. He was handling $5,000 and $10,000 bets like he was on autopilot.

That didn't last long, of course. Juan was soon promoted to a host for Latin American players, where he presumably got a little more sleep.

Graveyard dealers saw it all—good, bad, and just plain disgusting. Even the most upscale Strip properties had their moments, but the most memorable incidents of questionable behavior always seemed to happen downtown. The booze was cheaper, the security more relaxed, and the line between impulse and action often vanished by sunrise.

Take this gem from a fellow dice dealer. He once noticed a liquid pooling in the chip rail, the raised ledge around the craps table where players keep their chips. Assuming it was just spilled beer, he leaned in to wipe it up, only to be hit with the warm temperature and unmistakable ammonia smell. It might've started as beer, but it was now being recycled. A player, too busy gambling to bother with a restroom, had made his own deposit.

And then there was my personal favorite. Around 6 a.m. on a quiet weekday, a man in his mid-30s, clearly hammered, asked me where the bathroom was. I pointed him around the corner, gave him clear directions, and watched him shuffle off. A few minutes later, a voice crackled over security's radio. The guy had made a wrong turn and ended up in a deserted bank of slot machines.

In his fogged-up state, he mistook them for urinals. He was mid-stream, steadying himself with one hand on the handle, about to "flush" the coin tray.

They got to him just in time and promptly escorted him out.

Looking back, these stories are funny in the way war stories are funny, once the danger (or the smell) has passed. But they also underscore how unpredictable the job could be during graveyard hours. Between sleep-deprived dealers and blackout-drunk gamblers, sometimes the most surprising part of the shift was what didn't happen.

But it wasn't just bodily functions that made graveyard dealing unpredictable. Sometimes, it was life and death.

I witnessed my share of medical emergencies over the years of working in crowded casinos. Heart attacks, fainting spells, seizures—you name it. Most of the time, people responded with

Baptism by Fire: Breaking in Downtown

concern, even kindness. But one incident still sticks with me for all the wrong reasons.

It was a busy night and the craps table was packed. The energy was electric, players shouting, chips flying, that frenzied beat of downtown gambling in full swing. Then, in the middle of it all, an elderly man clutched his chest and collapsed right next to the table.

Security rushed over and within seconds, CPR was underway. They brought oxygen, called for paramedics, everything handled quickly and professionally.

But what happened around the table? That I'll never forget.

Instead of backing up or showing any concern, several players started complaining.

"Come on, let's keep it rolling!" one guy shouted, clearly annoyed that someone was dying next to his dice game.

Another muttered about losing his momentum, as if the dying man was just delaying his hot streak. A few of them even kept tossing chips in, trying to place bets. Some were actually reaching to roll the dice while this poor guy was being pumped on, gasping for life.

I was stunned. Furious. I wanted to scream, *Are you kidding me? A man might be dying and you're worried about missing a roll?*

The lack of humanity was staggering. The contrast between the gravity of the moment and their blind obsession with the game felt surreal. It was like they weren't seeing a human being, just another obstacle between them and their next payout.

I've seen plenty of emergencies over the years and in most cases, people react like you'd hope: concerned, maybe even shaken. But this one was a harsh reminder that the casino, for all its flash and fun, could also reveal just how far some people will go to disconnect from basic decency, especially when there's money on the line.

But comfort can be a double-edged sword. It was easy to let the days melt into nights, to lose track of time in a haze of cards, chips, and cigarette smoke. I knew I had more in me, more to learn, more to earn. The real prize was the Strip, where the stakes were higher and the money better. But getting in? That was like trying to win the lottery. It took connections, timing, and a whole lot of luck. Usually, someone had to retire, or die, for a seat to open up. And when one did, a line of seasoned dealers was waiting to pounce.

So I set my sights on something more within reach, but still a step up: the Golden Nugget.

It was still downtown, but classier. Moving there felt like upgrading from a bench seat to a window spot in the *Ben-Hur* rowing galley. The vibe was sharper, the clientele slightly more polished, and the tips noticeably better. After nearly a year at the Las Vegas Club, I felt ready for something sharper, faster, and better-paying.

With a mix of excitement and a touch of nostalgia, I gave my two-week notice at the Las Vegas Club, a professional courtesy I thought was standard. Management thought otherwise. "Thanks—and don't bother coming in tomorrow." Apparently, in casino lingo, "notice" translates to "don't let the door hit you on the way out."

It was a surprise ending, but in some ways, fitting. The Las Vegas Club had been my proving ground, for all its grit and grime. The abrupt exit only confirmed what I already knew. I'd learned what I needed to there and it was time to climb the next rung, carrying those hard-won lessons forward.

Walking away from the Las Vegas Club, I thought I was just changing jobs. I had no idea I was about to discover what Vegas could really be when someone with vision got hold of it. The Golden Nugget was about to teach me that downtown didn't have to mean down and out and that a young guy named Steve Wynn was about to turn the whole city upside down.

Chapter 4
Golden Nugget Days

Ten-Cent Roulette and the Rhythm of Downtown Nights

Rumor had it the Golden Nugget was hiring and I wasn't about to miss my shot.

In the days leading up to the audition, I sharpened every edge of my game. I practiced pitching cards like I was auditioning for the Vegas dealer Olympics, knowing the double-deck setup would require more finesse than the shoe games I was used to. I also brushed up on roulette payoffs, still a little shaky there, and hoped I wouldn't embarrass myself too badly if they tested me. At that point, "not getting laughed out of the pit" was a perfectly acceptable goal.

On audition day, I suited up in my signature black-and-whites and marched into the Nugget trying to look like I belonged. Just walking through the doors felt like leveling up in a video game. The process was light years ahead of what I'd experienced at the Las Vegas Club. There, I walked in off the street and they handed me a deck of cards. At the Nugget, I had to fill out paperwork, sit through an interview, and wait for a callback like a real job.

The audition wasn't quite as nerve-wracking as my first, since I had some experience under my belt. I did pretty well on a blackjack shoe game and some roulette, but I was sweating the double-deck test. We didn't deal that at the Las Vegas Club, so it was new territory for me.

Even though the double deck had me a little rattled, I managed to pull it off and made it through the audition. The unfamiliar style threw me at first, but my basics from the Club were solid enough to get me by.

A few days later, the call came: I was in. Even better, they let me pick my shift. After months of working graveyard, the idea of "normal hours" sounded fantastic, so I chose day shift.

I didn't know it yet, but the Golden Nugget wouldn't just be another casino gig. It would be a game-changer. Not that I could see that from the audition table. I was just hoping my tie was straight and my hands didn't shake when I cut checks.

The Golden Nugget wasn't just any casino. It had roots. It opened in 1946 under Guy McAfee, a former LAPD vice cop turned speakeasy kingpin. When a new mayor in L.A. started cleaning up City Hall and cracked down on cops taking envelopes, McAfee read the writing on the wall and got out. He brought his talents and his flair for bending rules to the desert instead. He even named the Strip, borrowing the name from Sunset Boulevard back home.

But the real turning point came in 1973, when a 31-year-old mover and shaker named Steve Wynn stepped in, took over the Golden Nugget, and started making waves. He was the youngest casino owner in town and wasted no time stirring things up. By '77, he'd added a gleaming hotel tower and a level of polish downtown had never seen.

I didn't know any of that when I started there. I was just a rookie in a fresh uniform, clocking in and hoping I didn't butcher a roulette payoff. I didn't even know who the guy signing my paycheck really was. But looking back, it's clear I'd walked into a crossroads between the old Vegas of wise guys and cigarette smoke and the new Vegas

Golden Nugget Days

of vision and five-star restaurants.

The Nugget felt like a different galaxy, despite being only two blocks away. The energy was sharper. The clientele dressed better. And most importantly, the tips blew away anything I'd seen at the Las Vegas Club. A few days in, we broke $100 for a shift. At the Las Vegas Club, that kind of haul was a fantasy. Here, it was just another Saturday.

The crew at the Nugget, dealers and players alike, were an eccentric bunch, but definitely a notch classier than the crowd back at the Las Vegas Club. I was thrilled to finally escape the sometimes mind-numbing pace of blackjack and land a regular spot on roulette. The wheel game fascinated me. It was chaotic and meditative all at once. Every spin felt like a new puzzle. It kept my brain firing. I was still a hungry young dealer at that point, always sharpening my skills and proud to be mastering something more intricate.

And those ten-cent chips? They were the secret sauce. Dirt cheap for players, just a dime each, but pure madness for dealers. That low denomination drew people in like insects to a porch light. They stacked chips by the hundreds across the layout and every spin brought a fresh avalanche.

After each roll, I swept the losers, sorted out the winners, and rebuilt mountains of chips like some caffeinated mason. It was part math, part muscle memory, and a full-body workout. The non-stop pace was brutal, but it made me sharper.

Once the payoffs were done, I swapped out high-value chips for more fresh dimes, then cut and stacked each color back into tidy rows of 20, resetting for another round of chip bedlam.

On busy nights, we sometimes got a "chip racker"—also called a mucker—to help sort through the disarray. But more often than not, it was just me and the table.

Even between spins, I couldn't relax. I handled change requests, watched for sneaky hands drifting near the wheel head, and kept a mental tally of who had what where. I quickly learned to work fast and stay alert, priding myself on maintaining a Zen-like calm as gamblers slapped down chips and hollered numbers. And I always had one eye on bet limits, which at the time were no more than $25 on a single number.

The roulette wheel didn't need much—a soft push, and it would spin like butter. The prank wasn't played on me, but later on, we loved messing with the new guys. We sent them off to find a "wheel crank" from another pit, sometimes even a "left-handed" one. Most fell for it. But once in a while, a sharp rookie played along, took a slow lap around the casino, and came back looking refreshed. More than once, the prank backfired and ended up giving someone an unofficial break. Not quite the lesson we were trying to teach.

Even without the rookie gags, roulette could turn into pandemonium fast.

One night, Mike was dealing a packed game when a couple wandered over from the slots, arms full of silver dollars. He gave them the basic rundown—pick a number, put a chip there, and hope for the best. But something got lost in translation, because the next thing we knew, they were yelling numbers and hurling silver dollars directly into the spinning wheel. Those things ricocheted like shrapnel. It was like a coin-operated war zone.

Another time, Julie, the cocktail waitress, got bumped mid-stride and launched an entire tray into the layout, including a Bloody Mary, which detonated like a tomato grenade inside the wheel: glass, vodka, tomato juice, and one very confused roulette ball. I'm not sure what won that spin, but I think it was celery.

But the all-time roulette horror story belonged to my buddy Jim, who was dealing at a small joint near Sparks. One Friday night, a cowboy already deep in the beer leaned in a little too close to the spinning ball. This was back before the plexiglass shields we use today, so nothing stopped players from getting right up on the game.

Golden Nugget Days

Jim gently nudged him back. A few minutes later, the guy leaned in again … and this time, unloaded the full contents of his stomach—burrito, nachos, and all—right across the wheel and down Jim's arm.

Jim went home to change, thinking he'd get reassigned. Instead, the boss handed him a rag and pointed back at the table. That pretty much ended his glittering Truckee career. Vegas was calling.

The Golden Nugget's dealers' lounge felt like Versailles compared to the glorified closet back at the Las Vegas Club. We had actual furniture. Dedicated restrooms. Vending machines that worked. It even smelled better, unless you walked in right after someone's "herbal" break.

Call me square, but I preferred to calculate chip payouts without being stoned. Plenty of others disagreed. The lounge had its regular crew of mellowed-out mathematicians and a few more took their smoke breaks outside.

My buddy Mark, who had just joined us at the Nugget after working at the Marina, an old joint on the south Strip where the MGM Grand now stands, used to talk about a favorite smoking spot he and his crew had there. They found a big ventilation duct they swore was perfect—hidden, breezy, and safe from detection. Too bad the duct fed straight into the security office. That might've played a role in Mark's job hunt in the first place.

Some dealers took a more liquid approach to their breaks, slipping into bars across the street to help rival casinos meet their liquor quotas. Others headed over to play slots, doing their part to boost someone else's gaming revenue while risking their own.

I've got no problem with a little recreational gambling. Live and let live. The problem came when someone actually hit a jackpot. A thousand-dollar payout might've made their day, but it also meant the rest of us were stuck waiting for a slot attendant to pay them out. Then they showed up late with a grin, acting like the hero of their own break-room legend. Funny how the biggest winners on break were always the last ones back from it.

The sportsbooks were a classic break destination for a different kind of action. These weren't the slick operations you see now with walls of LED screens. The old-school betting shops were tailored for horse and sports bettors, not dealers. Picture a Runyonesque scene: odds scrawled in grease pencil on whiteboards, clerks scribbling bets on carbon-paper dupe pads, the air thick with cigar smoke and shouted opinions.

Three of the old-timers—Leroy's, The Derby, and Hollywood—were just steps from the Nugget. Leroy's was directly across the alley and a favorite of mine on breaks. Ron, a floor supervisor at the Nugget, was a regular, too. He headed over, bet a horse "for him and Sue," then returned, shaking his head and telling her she owed him twenty bucks. Apparently, their horse usually didn't cooperate.

Navigating the alleys between casinos downtown was part of the lifestyle. Shady? Sure. Convenient? Absolutely.

Years later, when the Union Plaza opened a sportsbook, the shift boss occasionally asked me to cash winning tickets for him on my breaks. No big deal, just strolling through a sketchy alley at 4 a.m. with several hundred dollars in my pocket. What could go wrong?

In hindsight, probably not the wisest move.

Sal, one of the dice dealers, learned that lesson harder than most. One night on his break, he found a guy in the alley selling VCRs out of his trunk. Hundred bucks. A steal. Sal bit, rushed back to the lounge, grinning like he'd hit a slot jackpot.

Until he opened the box. Just rocks.

He sprinted back to the alley, but the "salesman" had vanished like a ghost in a smoke cloud. Let's just say Sal learned the hard way that if it seems too good to be true, it is.

The blocks around us had their own flavor—bars, pawn shops, and a fading collection of "adult theaters," complete with private booths. The internet eventually bulldozed that entire business model, but in the early days, those spots still clung on. Marvin, one of our dice dealers, was one of their more loyal patrons.

One day, Marvin didn't return from break. When he finally shuffled in the next day like nothing had happened, everyone already knew the story. Word had spread that the place he'd ducked into during break, the one with the private viewing booths, had been raided. Rumor was he'd been caught enjoying more than just the movie. He never said a word about it. Just picked up his apron and went back to work like nothing had happened.

The daily parade of gamblers at the Nugget was a cross-section of humanity. Most came and went with little fanfare, but now and then, real characters wandered in.

There was this elderly couple who showed up every morning. Not to play, just to stand near the roulette table, scribbling down the winning numbers and timing the wheel like they were running a lab experiment. After a few days of watching them, curiosity got the best of me.

"You two planning to write a book or something?" I asked with a grin.

The husband chuckled. "Just doing a little research. I used to work down the street at the Bingo Club, back when Vegas was still figuring itself out."

"Two bucks a day," his wife chimed in, "and a guaranteed jackpot every shift. Twenty dollars, like clockwork."

I raised an eyebrow. "You mean you hit a jackpot every day?"

He leaned in, lowering his voice. "It was part of the job. House made sure one of us 'won' every shift. Good for business."

That kind of luck? Yeah, let's just say the game might've been a little ... guided.

They came in daily for nearly a year, tracking patterns, scribbling in notebooks. Then one morning, they finally brought cash to play. I asked the husband if they'd cracked some system.

He gave me a wink. "We think we've found a pattern."

Five minutes later, they were down ten bucks. They left without a word and never came back.

So much for beating the house with all that "research."

Not everyone came in with notebooks. Some brought … other baggage.

One guy in his 20s wandered up, silent and twitchy, clearly not tracking the wheel. He started swatting at the air, freaking out about spiders crawling on his arms. I asked if he was okay, but he just mumbled something and drifted off. I'm guessing the roulette ball wasn't the only thing spinning that morning.

Then there was a family of four—Dad, Mom, two grown kids—who placed group bets, huddled in a circle, chanting and swaying like they were summoning something. I don't know what they were invoking, but they walked away a couple of hundred bucks richer. It seemed to work like a charm, literally maybe.

Another time, a woman with purple hair and enough facial piercings to set off TSA started casting spells at the wheel. She flicked her fingers and whispered incantations at the ball every spin. Sadly, her magic wasn't working. Maybe her crystals were out of alignment.

And then there were the Japanese players.

In the '80s, with Japan's economy booming, groups of tourists began showing up regularly. I'll never forget the Tokyo Roulette Club, marching into the pit in perfect formation behind a guide waving a logo flag like they were on a school trip.

Because of chip limitations, many had to use the same color chips. Normally, that causes total confusion, with five players claiming the same winner. Not with these guys. If one of them won, he'd point to the chip and tap his nose. That was it. No arguing. No confusion. Just clean respectful play.

Compared to the spider guy and the spell caster, it was like dealing to a Zen monastery.

In Las Vegas, hot sports tips flew around as often as cards. Everyone had an inside scoop—boxing, football, baseball, you name it. As a dealer, you learn to take those "locks" with enough salt to rim a margarita glass.

But then there was the Horse Whisperer from Northern California.

Rumors started trickling over from the dice pit. This guy, let's call him Bay Area Bob, showed up every so often with horse picks that felt like they came from the horses themselves. Bob didn't talk much. He didn't offer advice. But every now and then, he leaned in, whispered the name of a horse, and walked away like he'd just passed along state secrets.

At first, it sounded like nonsense. But the record? Six-for-six. All long shots. All winners.

The craps dealers started guarding his tips like classified intel. They lowered their voices, spoke in code, stopped sharing with anyone outside their circle. But one day, I got lucky. I caught the name of a horse and placed a small bet.

It won.

After that, Bob's handicapping tips went underground. The dice crew clammed up. He might've stopped giving them. Maybe they got greedy. Maybe he just vanished, like a desert legend.

Whatever happened to him, Bay Area Bob never showed up again. Or if he did, no one talked.

Then there was the guy with the Grover Cleveland bill.

It was a quiet night at the Nugget and I was dealing blackjack to a guy whose chip stack was shrinking. It looked like he was about to make his final "case bet." Instead, he reached into his wallet and pulled out a $1,000 bill, folded, from deep in one of those spy-movie compartments no normal wallet actually has.

I'd never seen one in play. Most people hadn't seen one, period.

The front had Grover Cleveland, sure, but the back looked so plain it could've been printed at Kinko's.

Nobody wanted to be the guy who took a fake and dropped it in the box. So we did the smart thing: sent it to the cage.

Those folks are like currency crime-lab techs—ultraviolet lights, reference charts, probably a red phone to the Treasury. They took their time.

Eventually, the call came back: It was legit. As I later learned, the U.S. Mint stopped printing $1,000 bills in 1945. The Fed pulled them in 1969, but they're still legal tender.

The best part? The guy won the hand. He casually tucked Grover back into his wallet, right into that secret slot, like he was saving it for another high-stakes flex.

After about a year on day shift at the Nugget, working noon to 8 p.m., I realized it wasn't quite the perfect banker's hours I'd envisioned. I've always been more of a morning person, and honestly, 4 a.m. wasn't as brutal as the 2 to 10 a.m. shift I'd worked at the Las Vegas Club. Plus, they needed someone to deal roulette on graveyard. The wheel was a harder spot to land on day shift.

Each shift had its own personality.

Swing shift? That was the party crowd. It was the busiest shift, full of people young enough to work eight hours and party for another four. And in Las Vegas, you can do that seven nights a week and many of my coworkers did.

Day shift attracted a more career-oriented crowd. Plenty of folks wanted to be seen by the higher-ups, maybe move up the ranks. Others had families and worked it to keep a "normal" routine.

Graveyard? That was a different breed entirely. Unique is the polite way to put it. Most of us weren't chasing promotions or brownie points. We just wanted to do our jobs and go home. I'd come from management and was thrilled to clock in, clock out, and never attend a meeting. Graveyard suited me just fine.

Golden Nugget Days

One of the perks of the overnight shift was the commute—smooth sailing, no traffic. One particular morning, I pulled into the Horseshoe parking garage and parked up on the fourth floor, as always. Next to the elevator for easy access and to avoid forgetting where I'd left the car.

It was 3:20 a.m. I was barely conscious as I rode the elevator down to the street level. The doors slid open, and I stepped out into ... six police officers with guns drawn, all pointed right at me.

For a split second, I wondered if I'd forgotten to pay a parking ticket. Was I being hunted for an overdue library book?

Nope.

The show's real star was the guy parked directly in front of the elevator. Turned out he'd been in a high-speed chase with the police and was making his last stand right in front of the elevator I happened to be stepping out of. I casually sidestepped the entire standoff and made my exit, stage right. Just another routine morning in the life of a graveyard dealer.

Navigating Fremont Street often felt like an obstacle course, but the benefit of working graveyard was that I usually strolled through around 3:30 a.m., long after the sidewalk congestion died down.

Usually.

One Sunday morning, my commute turned biblical. I walked into what can only be described as a plague of locusts—okay, technically grasshoppers, but it might as well have been Exodus. Drawn in by the lights like every other tourist, these bugs were everywhere. And I mean everywhere. The sidewalks were covered. Every step made a crunch. They jumped on clothes, clung to hair, and swarmed the air.

Later, I learned this kind of swarm can number up to 45 million and show up on radar. It's a rare desert event that happens once every decade or so after a wet winter. But if this was a divine warning for Vegas to clean up its act, it didn't work. People kept strolling along, crunching away, totally unfazed. It was Sin City, after all. We'd seen worse.

By the time I got to the entrance, I had to pick half a dozen hoppers off my uniform before I could even clock in. So much for graveyard being quiet. Still, I'll say this: At least the grasshoppers were more polite than the average Fremont foot traffic. And after the swarm passed, the sidewalks had never looked so clean.

Working at the Golden Nugget, I had more than my share of celebrity encounters. Being a dealer in Las Vegas turns you into a sort of accidental stargazer. You spot celebrities as often as you shuffle cards. I was never the autograph-seeking type, but if you log enough hours in the high-limit rooms, you're bound to deal a hand or two to faces you've seen on TV, in movies, or on the sports highlight reel.

The Nugget was a magnet for stars, even back in the '70s and '80s.

I remember Willie Nelson's band hitting the roulette table after a gig in the lounge. Willie stood nearby, whiskey bottle in hand, giving me a wink and saying, "Take care of my boys." As if I had a secret button under the table to make them win.

Kenny Rogers came through during his "Gambler" heyday. He sat down at the blackjack table next to mine and casually asked for a $10,000 marker. Vince, an old-school floor supervisor, wandered over—not to gush about Kenny's music, but to ask for ID. "He puts his pants on one leg at a time, just like everybody else," Vince muttered afterward.

When the Nugget opened its new ballroom and tower, Frank Sinatra headlined the launch alongside Willie Nelson. Ol' Blue Eyes himself occasionally dabbled in blackjack and baccarat.

Not every celebrity moment happened on the job. I once attended a heavyweight fight at the Hilton. Afterward, I ducked through the casino to avoid the mob exiting the arena. As I weaved between slot machines, a crowd came toward me, led by none other

Golden Nugget Days

than Muhammad Ali. As we crossed paths, he reached out his hand. I shook it and couldn't help but think about the sheer destructive power it had once delivered in the ring.

While it's fun to reminisce about celebrity sightings, the real stars for us dealers were the *crowds* those big names brought in. When someone like Sinatra, Willie Nelson, or Kenny Rogers performed in the showroom, it was like hitting the jackpot—for the casino and for us. Management shelled out serious money to book those acts, knowing they'd reel in the high rollers. And high rollers meant more action at the tables. More players. More tips. It was a win-win.

Of course, not every dealer had the same luck. I remember Al, a fellow dealer who had previously worked at the Riviera. I asked him how the tips were there and he told me a story I still laugh about.

Out front of the Riviera, they had an "entertainer," a guy with an organ and a monkey. The monkey wore a tiny outfit, complete with a hat, and held a little cup to collect tips from passersby. Apparently, if someone was stingy, the monkey would give them a dirty look. Al, meanwhile, was grinding away inside, making about $50 a day. The monkey? Bringing in $200 to $300 a night.

Al wasn't just upset. He was *jealous*—of a monkey. Only in Vegas.

Al's story stuck with me, not just because he got out-earned by a monkey in a vest, but because it nailed the absurd truth of our business. We were professionals handling thousands, sometimes millions, of dollars a night, but our paychecks lived or died on the whim of a tip. No rules. No logic. Just casino justice, where sometimes the monkey wins.

Chapter 5
The Tipping Point

Inside the Economy of Gratitude, Luck, and the Occasional George

After a few years of dealing, you start to see patterns—not just in the games, but in the money. The tips that keep us afloat, the ones that make the graveyard shifts bearable, each tells its own story. And like everything else in Vegas, that story is more complicated than it looks from the outside.

Back in 1979, a dealer's paycheck might cover rent, if you had roommates and a taste for ramen. The real money came from tips, or "tokes" in casino speak. It wasn't just etiquette. It was the economy. It was survival. I recall earning $7 in tokes during some of my earliest days on the job, compared to later years on the Strip when a single shift could bring in over $1,000.

Tipping wasn't just a side note to the job. It shaped the culture, the money, and the unspoken dance between dealers and players.

One of the most common questions from players was, "Do you get to keep that?" The answer? It depends. Some casinos ran on a "table-for-table" system, where you kept what you made at your game. In craps, the crew split tips four ways. Other places pooled tips by shift and a few pooled across the entire 24-hour day.

That 24-hour system smoothed out the highs and lows, but the day of the week still made a difference. Some dealers tracked this religiously. They could tell you, down to the dollar, how much more you'd make working a Saturday night versus a Tuesday.

At the Golden Nugget, we worked under a shift-by-shift pooling system. Every dealer on the same shift got an equal cut, whether the tips came in hot or barely trickled at all.

It was fair. And more importantly, it was a safety net.

On a dead Tuesday graveyard, maybe only two dozen of us were on the schedule. If just one big tipper walked in, it could turn the whole shift into a mini–New Year's Eve. You might not deal a single hand all night and still walk out with a solid share, thanks to someone else's action across the pit.

Of course, getting the money was only half the game. Holding onto it? That was the trick.

Plenty of dealers weren't exactly masters of delayed gratification. I can't count how many times I heard about someone "calling in rich" after a big night. You'd spot them the next morning over at the Horseshoe, still in yesterday's clothes, at the slot machines or playing keno, already halfway through their tip money.

There are basically two different ways dealers are tipped: either directly with tips handed in or by betting for the dealer.

When a bet is made for the dealer on a game like blackjack, the dealer's bet is generally placed in front of the player's bet. This is a standard way of letting everyone know that these chips are for the dealers. When a bet wins and is paid, the dealer thanks the player and "locks up the toke." Most casinos don't allow the bet to ride.

The other method is for players to toss in a chip, usually after a hand or at the end of play. Occasionally, a player will attempt to hand a bet to the dealer. When this happens, the dealer asks the player to place the tip on the table, as direct hand-to-hand tip transfers are a no-no. To acknowledge the tip, the dealer taps the chip or chips against the table's edge or the chip rack, letting the floor supervisor and surveillance know it was indeed a tip and not swiped from the rack.

In the early days, dealers temporarily stashed their tipped chips in their shirt pockets. During each break, usually every hour, these chips were moved to a locked communal box in the pit. I recall, on at least a couple of occasions over the years, the heart-stopping moment of finding a chip still in my pocket after I got home and the relief of returning it the next day.

Later, plexiglass boxes were attached to each table for collecting tips, which ended the use of shirt pockets for this purpose. While this change boosted security, it also phased out a charm associated with the process, especially when a female dealer invited a generous tipper to slip the tip directly into her pocket.

Even though the house mostly avoided tip management, procedures were still in place to handle tokes, ensuring transparency and accountability from the moment a player handed over a tip to when it ended up in the dealer's possession. At the end of each shift, a designated crew of dealers, known as the toke committee, made the rounds, collecting all the chips from the locked tip boxes in each pit. We then gathered in the dealer's room, looking more like a band of accountants after a heist than casino workers, sorting through thousands of dollars in chips by denomination. The math was straightforward, total tips divided by the number of dealers, but the sorting and counting could take some time.

Once the totals were in, we headed to the cashier's cage to get the appropriate denominations needed to pay out everyone's share. Then came envelope duty. Each dealer got a sealed packet with their cut. Some picked theirs up right away, while others waited until the next day. A few hung out at the bar, expecting delivery. As we delivered their tokes, we usually showed up to a cold one waiting for us as a thank you.

Any unclaimed envelopes were locked in a strongbox and stored in the cage until the following day. But early in my time at the Golden Nugget, something happened that still baffles us. Someone managed to break into that supposedly secure strongbox and cleaned it out. This, despite it being under the watchful eye of the cage.

It was a jarring reminder that even in a place built around security, vulnerabilities could and did exist. Unfortunately, with only a few envelopes left in the box at the time, the rest of us had to make up the shortfall ourselves. Just one of those unexpected hits that came with the job and a reminder that the casino floor wasn't the only place risk lived.

The security breach was another indication that everyone wanted a piece of the pie. Back when we pooled tokes shift by shift, the routine was pretty straightforward: We gathered the racks of chips at the end of the shift and took them to the cage. The cage crew cashed them out, breaking everything down into the denominations we requested, so it could be distributed to the dealers. The folks in the cage were just doing their job, but in appreciation, we usually gave them a little something, maybe a set amount like $50 or the equivalent of one share.

But when the tokes started getting better—this was during the Nugget's transformation in the mid-'80s—the cage crew decided their cut should get better too. What had been a simple thank-you gesture suddenly became a negotiation. Things got a little sticky. Suddenly, what used to be a five-minute process was taking 30. They were "busy." The racks sat untouched, while we stood around waiting. We got the message.

Eventually, we gave in and bumped up their share. Not because we wanted to, but because we needed the cash and they were the only ones who could turn our chips into spendable money. It was one of those classic standoffs, tough negotiations even though we were the ones holding all the chips.

When I migrated over to the Mirage in 1989, I was chosen to represent the graveyard shift on the toke committee. That's when I realized: The days of passing out cash envelopes were numbered.

Some dealers didn't set aside anything for taxes. Others needed a real income on a paycheck to get a loan, buy a house, or contribute to an IRA. No pension meant we had to plan for retirement ourselves and paper trails mattered.

I met with Valley Bank and reps from other shifts to explore options. But management wasn't exactly eager to intervene. Not our call, they said. Dealer vote, they said.

That vote stirred up a hornet's nest.

Plenty of dealers liked their tips in cash and off the record. Some wanted to gamble with it. Others didn't want their spouses to know what they made. A few just liked keeping the IRS guessing.

I pushed for the change anyway. And I paid for it. I lost friends, people I'd worked alongside for years. The vote failed.

A few years later, management pushed the change through anyway. Paychecks replaced envelopes. And with that, dealer pay stepped into the modern age, whether we liked it or not.

Looking back, I understand their resistance better now. For many dealers, that daily cash wasn't just income, it was freedom, independence, and in some cases, the fuel for their gambling dreams. By pushing for paychecks, I was asking them to change not just how they got paid, but how they lived.

When I started at the Nugget, there were no official sick days, but there was an unofficial rule for tips. Bring in a doctor's note and you would still get your share of the tokes while you were out. Nobody knew where the rule came from. It wasn't written down. It was just how we did things. A trust-based safety net for when you were truly down for the count. And like most trust-based systems, it worked—until it didn't.

A few slick operators figured out they could keep collecting toke shares without ever dealing a hand. Phantom illnesses, recycled doctor's notes, one-week flus that stretched into months. While the rest of us worked the floor, they stayed home and still got paid.

Eventually, we had to shut it down. A system built to help each other, undone by greed. Another lesson in casino math: It takes only a few bad bets to ruin the whole run.

When a George (our name for a top-tier tipper) hit the high-limit tables, everything changed. You didn't just deal. You were in the spotlight. If the player started tipping, the buzz spread fast. During breaks, dealers swarmed you.

"How much did you drop?" They were dying to know the running total. Dealers across the casino were already figuring out their potential cut and dreaming up ways to spend it.

"Is he still there?"

"Keep it going. Don't let him cool off."

You could be a hero for dumping the rack, losing money to a big player who tipped like a king.

But screw it up? Let him walk after a quick cold streak? You were the one who "scared off our George." Dealers who weren't even in the pit suddenly had opinions. You could feel the shift, like you'd just clanked a free throw in the fourth quarter. It was part casino math, part schoolyard politics.

Of course, not all players were super high rollers. Most of the day-to-day income came from the regular grind, with average Joes happy to share their winnings. Some dealers had a knack for getting players to toss in chips, with a talent for schmoozing—or maybe just good old-fashioned BS. These dealers had what's called a "soft hustle," gently coaxing tips from players through smooth talking. Since outright begging for tokes was a no-no, these dealers walked a

The Tipping Point

fine line, living on the edge of casino etiquette.

One night Suzie, one of our more ambitious dealers, tried to upgrade her tip. A baccarat player was about to leave the table with several stacks of flags ($5,000 chips) and he tossed her a $500 chip, already a generous toke by any standard.

Suzie looked at the chip, then let her eyes drift to his stacks of flags. With a practiced smile, she said, "Gee, I wish I had one of those."

Her gaze lingered just a beat too long.

The player paused, then said very slowly, "Oh, you'd rather have one of these?" He picked up the $500 chip, slipped it back into his pocket, and walked away without leaving a dime.

The table went dead quiet. No lectures, no smirks. Every dealer there knew exactly what had just happened.

To be fair, Suzie's boldness had paid off plenty of times before. Her risky comments often turned into extra money for all of us. But that night, she flew a little too close to the sun and we watched the tip melt away right in front of us.

Tipping also changed depending on who the player was with. A guy playing solo or with his buddies was often more generous than when he had his wife with him. If he was trying to impress a girlfriend, that was a different story altogether.

One night at Bellagio in the early 2000s stands out. Ben Affleck, who had a reputation for being a solid tipper, was on a hot streak at the roulette table. After a big win, he casually tossed a $1,000 chip toward the dealer. Smooth move. Nice gesture. Exactly what you'd expect from a movie star in a good mood.

Enter Jennifer Lopez, the other half of one of Hollywood's golden couples at the time. She saw the chip and intercepted it like a defensive back. Without missing a beat, she swapped it for a $100 chip and handed that over instead. "That's enough," she said flatly.

The whole table froze like we'd just watched a magic trick.

The dealer nodded politely, took the hundred, and we all silently recalibrated our expectations for some A-list generosity.

We'd seen it before. Generous tokes downgraded once a significant other raised an eyebrow. In some cases, a person reached into their pocket with one hand, while receiving the death stare with the other. You learned to spot it coming. The hesitation, the glance sideways, the subtle retreat from black chip to green.

It wasn't personal. Just economics. Emotional economics.

Bottom line, I was just thankful for any tip and knew it wasn't mandatory. Unfortunately, not everyone shared that attitude. Some dealers expected a cut from every win, which is a slippery slope. That kind of thinking can turn a friendly dealer into someone sour and tight-lipped, watching every payout like it's coming out of their own pocket.

And besides, that big win you just witnessed? It might not even put a dent in whatever the player lost at the last table—or the one before that. Assuming every winner is ahead is a fast track to frustration. It's not healthy for the dealer, and it's not good for the house or player either.

In the past, in the days of toke envelopes when dealers divvied up tips among themselves, there was a common belief that paying taxes on these tips was optional or that you only had to report a small portion. Some dealers were convinced that these tips were gifts and, therefore, not subject to taxation. Throughout the late '70s and early '80s, it seemed like the IRS was on a mission to make sure dealers were reporting their tips accurately.

Their plan of attack was to focus on one casino at a time, starting with the big boys on the Strip. The IRS offered an amnesty deal to dealers at the targeted casinos: agree to report 100% of your tips from then on and you were off the hook for audits for the past few years. Turn it down and your chances of getting audited went through the roof. This method, while slow, worked like a charm. As more dealers took the deal, ensuring a known amount of daily tips, those who hadn't signed on were faced with hard evidence during audits, thanks to their cooperative colleagues.

Audited dealers who didn't play ball were made an example of. They got slapped with hefty bills for back taxes, including penalties and interest, amounts most couldn't afford. As a result, their wages were garnished and those handing out tokes could only give them $15 a day, barely enough for gas and lunch, with the rest going straight to the IRS. This strict enforcement made it crystal clear: The IRS meant business regarding tip reporting, turning what many dealers considered a gray area into a black-and-white requirement.

Some dealers, faced with garnished wages, simply quit. In contrast, others who had taken the amnesty deal jumped ship to other properties, including ours, giving the IRS the data they needed from these individuals. By this time, many of us at the Golden Nugget had already gotten on board with compliance. My compliance was triggered by an IRS audit for 1981 and 1982. Those of us working the graveyard shift had a bit of an advantage, as our tips, divided by shift, were significantly higher than those of other shifts. However, because the day and swing shifts had more dealers, the baseline amount the IRS expected was much lower than our actual earnings. So, when I got audited, the IRS hit me with a figure for a surprisingly low adjustment, and I quickly settled the slight increase.

The following year, the IRS shifted its focus from the bigger Strip casinos to the downtown joints, including ours. At that time, I was one of the four people in charge of toke distribution. An IRS agent once stopped by our casino, demanding to observe our process for splitting up that day's tokes. While I would have instinctively gone along with it, Tammy, the head of our toke committee, put her foot down and refused, and the agent left. Her defiance made her a bit of a legend among the dealers, at least until a week later, when the four of us on the toke committee got a scary legal notice from Washington. The document, with the ominous title "US Government VS" followed by our names, set off major alarm bells.

The dealers banded together in response, pooling resources to hire a lawyer. He quickly responded to the intimidating notice and then we waited. The expected fallout never happened; there was no further communication or action from the IRS. We braced for fallout that never came—but the anxiety hung around longer than any audit notice.

The players I dealt with came from all over the world, bringing a wide range of cultural norms and practices. This diversity often extended to attitudes toward tipping Not everyone was used to, or comfortable with, the idea of tipping. What might be considered polite or expected in one culture could be seen as offensive or unnecessary in another. For example, while tipping is a common practice in North America, it's not the norm in many Asian cultures, where giving a tip to casino dealers can sometimes be seen as rude or disrespectful. Yet many travelers from Asia to Las Vegas are slowly adopting more Western-style tipping habits.

European attitudes toward tipping have also been changing. Back in the '80s and '90s, I chatted with other dealers who had worked in the UK, where tipping wasn't only uncommon, but actually against the law. This changed in 2005 when a new law was passed making it legal to tip dealers in the UK, even though it wasn't enacted until 2007, showing a clear sign that tipping culture was going global, even in places where it was once taboo or even illegal.

Through the ups and downs of big wins and slow nights, the

challenges of managing windfall tip nights, and the uncertainties of relying on the generosity of others, tipping has remained a constant presence, defining the unique culture and atmosphere of the casino industry. It's a world where a single tip can change the course of a night, where the bond between a dealer and a player can be forged over a shared moment of triumph or disappointment, and where the camaraderie among colleagues is strengthened through the shared experience of the tipping rollercoaster.

Over my three decades in the casino, I watched tipping evolve from cash-in-pocket freedom to computerized accountability. But one thing never changed: that moment of anticipation when a big player pushed chips your way, the silent calculations running through every dealer's head, and the camaraderie (or conflict) that those tips could stir up among us. In a world built on chance, tips were the one bet where we all had skin in the game.

And then there was the thrill of the unknown, the buzz in the air when a big player was in town, especially one known to be generous. You'd come in for your shift hoping they were still at it or that your crew had caught the tail end. But sometimes, the magic happened while you were off the clock, fast asleep, dreaming of anything but roulette balls and baccarat shoes. Then you walked in the next day and heard about it: Some high roller showed up out of nowhere, dropped a fortune, and toked like it was going out of style.

That was the best kind of surprise. Your name wasn't on the game, but it was still on the envelope, like waking up to a bonus you never saw coming, like Christmas morning with your name on the gift tag, even if you hadn't been in the room when Santa showed up. It made every shift feel like a scratch-off ticket. You could be showing up for a slow Tuesday and walk away with your share of someone else's magic.

Chapter 6

Sacred Tools of the Trade

How Cards, Dice, and Wheels Are Treated Like National Treasures

After decades of dealing to everyone from downtown grinders to billionaire high rollers, I'd learned that the real magic in a casino wasn't just in the games themselves, it was in the intricate systems designed to protect them. Throughout my career, I witnessed just how obsessive casinos are about their equipment.

With staggering amounts of money circulating through a casino, safeguarding that cash is a top priority. However, many people might not realize that casino equipment requires equal, if not greater, levels of security and protection. Once the integrity of the equipment is compromised, the casino stands to lose a considerable amount of money in the blink of an eye.

Let me start with the most basic tool of our trade, the cards themselves. You might think a deck of cards is just a deck of cards, but in a casino, they're treated like currency.

The cards used in a casino's blackjack game aren't something you can casually order online. You might wonder, "Why not?" The last thing a casino wants is for someone to sneak in a couple of cards, say an ace and a jack, on their max bet at a blackjack table, or even worse, switch out an entire shoe. Such actions could cost the casino a fortune. That's precisely why casinos drill holes in used cards or cut off a corner before giving them away or selling them in the gift shop.

Control over the cards starts with the manufacturer and continues until the moment they're introduced into the game. Every step of the way, these cards are monitored— logged, secured, and verified—as if they were gold bars en route to Fort Knox.

On graveyard at the Wynn, I watched pit managers inventory every single deck, used and unused, before calling in security for the card room run. To get access, they passed through a man trap, a series of interlocked doors straight out of a spy movie. Surveillance had to be notified. The inventory had to match. If it didn't? The search was on.

We weren't just protecting plastic rectangles. We were protecting the game itself. You lose a card, you lose control. And in this business, control is everything.

Once they established the number of new cards they needed, they called for a couple of security guards to escort them to the card room, meeting them outside the man trap, which was designed to secure access to the cards. After notifying surveillance ("the eye in the sky") about their intentions and the quantities they'd be moving, they were buzzed in by security personnel watching from the eye. They conducted an inventory of all cases and cross-verified the total count with the cards on the casino floor. Any discrepancies could trigger a major search; the numbers had to align perfectly.

Just how seriously casinos take card security became crystal clear to me during one unforgettable morning at the Wynn.

During my shift, word spread quickly through the pit: Two decks were missing from a swing-shift game. What followed was a full-scale investigation that showed me just how vigorously the casino took even the smallest discrepancy.

This particular pit also supplied cards to the outdoor poolside games. Management initially searched the pool area, thinking the cards might still be there. No luck. Surveillance combed through hours of video footage, trying to piece together what had happened. Teams were dispatched to search every nook and cranny of the casino, hoping against hope that the cards would turn up. They didn't. The mystery was solved the next day. Gail, a swing-shift pit manager, had mistakenly thrown away two decks of cards while changing out double decks during a hectic moment.

By the time that was discovered, the trash had already been removed from the building. That didn't stop the search. The garbage truck was tracked down and followed to the disposal site, where a brave (and probably very smelly) team of employees suited up and dove into the dumpsters, sifting through piles of rubbish in search of the missing decks.

Despite their valiant efforts, the cards were never found. And Gail? Well, whether she was unaware of her mistake or too afraid to admit it, the damage was done. In the end, she lost her job over those two missing decks.

Hearing about Gail's termination the next day was sobering. Twenty years of casino experience, gone over two decks of cards. The rest of us walked on eggshells for weeks, double-checking every procedure. It was a harsh reminder that in this part of the business, there's no room for even innocent mistakes.

But it wasn't just complete decks we had to worry about. Even individual cards required meticulous tracking.

Not only do cases, boxes, and full decks need to be meticulously accounted for, but individual cards must also be tracked. For instance, if a card gets bent during play, it's replaced from a designated replacement deck, then torn in half to prevent reuse. Another scenario that might not immediately come to mind is what happens if a card gets blood on it. Whether it's from a dealer or a player with a cut finger, a card stained with even a tiny dot of blood can't continue in play.

Aside from the obvious issue of a blood-marked card potentially giving an unfair advantage, there's also the health concern. No one wants to handle a card that's been contaminated with someone else's blood. This was especially true during times when fears about diseases like AIDS were more widespread. Such a card can't simply be tossed into a used deck or discarded. The solution? A hazmat kit equipped with a special biohazard bag is designated for items like these.

But the process doesn't end with sealing the card in a biohazard bag. Surveillance must be notified and a team member collects the bag. A note is then made in the inventory log to document this special card's removal, ensuring that every card, down to the individual level, is accounted for.

When new cards are introduced to a game, the dealer has a specific routine to follow. First, they must review each deck to ensure all cards are present. Fortunately, the cards come in order, which speeds up this process. Next, the dealer flips the cards over to inspect the backs. This isn't so much to catch any subtly marked cards—those would be hard to spot in a quick scan—but more to identify glaring manufacturing errors.

One day at the Nugget, I'd just begun a game with a fresh deck, following the steps I've just outlined. We didn't have scanners to check the dealer's hole card back then. I had a king showing and peeked at my hole card, only to find it was blank! It was as if Houdini had paid a visit to the game. Upon closer inspection, I realized that

Sacred Tools of the Trade

two cards had been stuck together during my initial check, and one of them was blank.

Another memorable moment occurred at the Nugget while I was dealing from a six-deck shoe. I hadn't been dealing much blackjack for a while, as I was primarily focused on roulette. During my time away, the casino had switched to a new type of card with an ultra-slick plastic coating. When I tried to load the six decks of cards into the shoe, a task akin to loading a Pez dispenser, the cards went airborne, scattering all over the table and onto the floor. It was another clumsy attempt at magic, courtesy of yours truly.

The roulette wheel isn't just a piece of equipment; it's a shrine. As dealers, we learned to treat it with a mix of respect and caution. After enough years behind the apron, you develop a feel for when something's off. Maybe a loose fret, an odd ping on the bounce, or just a spin that doesn't sound right.

Beneath the polished wood and brass is a perfectly balanced machine: cone, spindle, frets, deflectors, all built for precision and unpredictability. Even the landing apron plays its part, guiding randomness with just enough order.

On the Strip, roulette wheels were treated like high-performance machines, precision-calibrated, perfectly balanced, and maintained like race cars. One odd bounce, one squeaky spin, and it got pulled for inspection.

Downtown? Let's just say the standards were looser. Some of those wheels looked like they'd been hauled in on the back of a pickup and tuned up with WD-40 and prayer. You learned to work around the quirks, because nobody else was fixing them.

Roulette balls may look identical, but they're not. Most are made from materials like synthetic ivory (Ivorine), Teflon, or phenolic resin—each with its own bounce, sound, and personality. Ivorine balls ping like pinballs; Teflon ones land soft and straight. Sizes vary, usually 5/8 or 3/4 inch, just big enough to see, just small enough to surprise. Subtle differences, but they matter, especially when the ball has other plans.

For all the precision engineering that goes into the roulette wheel, it's often that tiny bouncing sphere that causes the biggest headaches. As any experienced dealer will tell you, the roulette ball has a mind of its own, sometimes launching itself across the table or veering into unexpected territory. Let me share a few tales of rogue spins and wayward balls from my years at the wheel.

Take one night at the Golden Nugget. I was swamped, juggling stacks of chips and trying to keep the game flowing. The table was full and I was working fast. Maybe too fast. In my haste, I gave the ball a little extra zip, hoping to buy the players and myself a few extra seconds to catch up. But I didn't set it properly in the track. Instead of nestling into the groove as it should, I accidentally released it from the very edge of the wheel.

The result? A high-speed misfire.

Then came the unmistakable "CRACK!"—not from the wheel, but from the head of a woman sitting right in front of it.

I was mortified. She was startled, clearly embarrassed, but to her credit, incredibly gracious. Even as a noticeable red mark began to form on her forehead, she waved off the attention and tried to laugh it off, saying something like, "Well, that's one way to wake up at the tables."

She stayed for a little while longer, still playing, making light of it all, as if she'd caught a fly ball at a baseball game rather than a rogue roulette ball to the head. I kept apologizing between spins.

These days, in our lawsuit-happy world, I imagine there might've been paperwork, maybe even a lawyer's card discreetly passed across the table. But back then? She handled it like a champ.

Sacred Tools of the Trade 73

No drama. No demands. Just a good sense of humor and the kind of grace you don't forget. I got lucky that night, but not in the way the players hoped to.

One of my rogue spins once made a beeline for a woman sitting mid-table, this time aiming for a more ... personal zone. The ball skipped the wheel entirely and dove straight down the front of her low-cut dress, vanishing like a coin in a fountain.

I froze. The table howled. Before I could react, Bruce, my floor supervisor and master of bad timing, was already halfway over, clipboard in hand and grin locked in place.

"Need a hand retrieving that?" he said, only half-joking.

The woman raised a finger. "I've got it, boys." She fished out the ball and set it on the table like a magician pulling a coin from behind your ear.

She stuck around, laughing with the players and tossing out zingers like a regular. Grace under pressure, or maybe just Vegas experience.

Then there's Troy, a fellow dealer, who swore he set a record at the old Mint, just across the street. His mishap might still hold the title for "farthest-traveled roulette ball" in Vegas history.

His table sat near an elevator to the rooftop restaurant. One night in the middle of a rushed game, he gave the wheel a strong spin, but botched the ball release completely. It launched like a marble from a slingshot, bounced off the rim, ricocheted off a chip tray, and just as the elevator doors were closing sailed cleanly through them like it had somewhere to be.

The players just stared. Silent. Mouths open. Then the elevator dinged, and the doors slid shut, sealing the ball's fate.

When the supervisor came rushing over and said, "Where's the ball?" Troy didn't flinch. "Upstairs," he said, pointing skyward.

No one ever figured out where it landed. In a diner's soup, under a booth, or maybe still up there, collecting dust. But that spin?

Definitely one for the books.

But the most shocking ball incident I ever witnessed didn't involve where the ball went—it was about where it ended up.

Saturday nights bleeding into Sunday mornings were always a spectacle on the graveyard shift. We clocked in just as the die-hard revelers were hitting their stride, or stumbling, as the case may have been. Some looked like they were on the verge of keeling over, making it easy to gently suggest they call it a night and return later, much later, considering it was usually around 6 a.m. when we'd have this chat. But not everyone took the hint.

Troy's ball vanished most unexpectedly, but this next one took disappearance to a whole new level.

One night, while still downtown, a pair of young guys appeared, clearly enjoying themselves a bit too much. Physically functional despite their intoxication? Sure. Mentally sharp? That's debatable and not just because of the booze. They weren't exactly high rollers, but as their energy and cash started to wane, one of them dramatically slapped a $20 bill on the table and bellowed, "RED! Money plays!"

As they stood by the wheel, eyes glued to the spinning ball, it landed on a BLACK number. The taller of the two did the unthinkable: He reached into the wheel and snatched the ball. A major faux pas, to say the least. But what came next was even more astonishing. He examined the ball briefly and then swallowed it, washing it down with a swig of beer!

I stood there stunned, watching this guy chase a beer with a roulette ball like it was a bar snack. In all my years of dealing, I thought I'd seen everything. The duo dashed across the bustling casino floor, vanishing into the night. Had they been caught, I'm not exactly sure what the protocol would've been. The casino would definitely want that ball back, though I doubt it would ever see play again. The logistics of its retrieval, however, would've been ... complicated, to say the least.

Sacred Tools of the Trade

Cards, dice, wheels, and balls—our sacred tools—might seem simple, but after 30 years in the business, I learned that protecting them required constant vigilance, detailed procedures, and sometimes a good sense of humor when things inevitably went wrong. In a world built on chance, even our equipment occasionally reminds us that nothing is entirely predictable.

PART II
THE TRANSFORMATION

When Vegas Reinvented Itself

The Steve Wynn revolution that transformed Las Vegas from a gambling town into a luxury destination. From the Golden Nugget's rebirth through the Mirage, Bellagio, Wynn, and Encore—witness the creation of modern Vegas from behind the table as history unfolded.

Chapter 7
The Golden Nugget Reborn

When Downtown Went Upscale

I came to the Golden Nugget thinking it was just a stepping stone on my way to the Strip.

But Steve Wynn had other plans. He brought the Strip downtown.

During my years at the Nugget, the place underwent a complete transformation, from a classic downtown joint into a property that could hold its own against anything on the Strip: better restaurants, world-class entertainment, and serious high-limit action. And with that shift came serious money: bigger players, bigger tips.

What impressed me most was the attention to detail. Even the temporary construction walls were polished: clean, sleek, designed to impress. At the Las Vegas Club, you were lucky if the plywood didn't have splinters. At the Nugget, the construction barriers looked better than some casinos' lobbies.

You could feel the pride radiating off the staff. There was a buzz in the air, like we were all part of a secret the rest of the city hadn't caught on to yet. It wasn't just a remodel, it was a rebirth. And we all knew it.

In 1983, every employee got a gift: shares of Golden Nugget

stock. At the time, I thought it might be the start of a real stock-option program: finally, a casino giving back to its workers. But it didn't last. Most employees cashed out right away and rumor had it Mr. Wynn wasn't thrilled. The stock program vanished almost as fast as it appeared.

Then things really took off. In 1984, a new tower and state-of-the-art showroom were added. Willie Nelson and Frank Sinatra headlined the grand opening. High-limit baccarat rolled in and hosts were brought in from across town, bringing their whales with them. Strip-level action had arrived, no more chasing it.

And for those of us on the floor, everything shifted. The job used to be a routine of regulars and predictable games. Now, it felt electric. Every shift came with a possibility. You never knew who might walk in, what surprise was coming, or how fast the night might turn into a story.

It felt like holding a backstage pass to a casino in metamorphosis. And we weren't just watching it unfold; we were part of the show.

It seemed like almost everyone I dealt to had some sort of system, even if it was just birthdays or favorite jersey numbers. Others swore by elaborate strategies—complex formulas, charts, and notepads full of wheel-tracking data. I never quite understood the logic. If red comes up six times in a row, does that mean red is hot and you should stay on red ... or that black is due and you should jump ship?

Einstein is famously credited with saying, "You cannot beat a roulette table unless you steal money from it." The quote reflects his view that roulette is purely a game of chance, governed by the laws of physics and mathematical probabilities.

Mathematicians will tell you: Each spin is an independent event.

The wheel doesn't remember what came before. But try explaining that to a guy who just remortgaged his confidence on the next spin.

The most common "can't-miss" system was the Martingale. Double your bet after each loss, so that you recoup everything, plus one unit of profit when you win. Sounds simple. But the problem is always the same: money—yours, and the casino's limits.

Let's say you're at a $5–$5,000 table. In each sequence, you're trying to win just five bucks on red. Not bad, until red doesn't come up for 10 straight spins. That 10th bet would be $2,560. And if that loses, your next bet would be $5,120, over the table max. Even if the casino allowed it, losing that bet means you've just dumped $10,235 trying to win $5.

I can't count how many times I've seen the display board show nothing but red or black, for 10, even 15 spins. When the first board was first introduced, some of the old-school floor supervisors hated them. They thought it was giving away secrets. The reality? It was catnip for gamblers. They saw patterns where there weren't any and chased them hard.

Speaking of house wisdom, I was occasionally told to swap out the roulette ball during a hot streak. Every game had at least two balls, usually slightly different in size. One was just a little smaller, subtle, but enough to change the bounce and roll.

One night, Vince, the gruff old-school supervisor who sweated every dollar, was hovering at my table. The game was packed, chips stacked across the layout, and one number, 20, had a mountain of action on it.

Sure enough: bam. Twenty hit. Four different players had straight-up bets. The payout was huge. Vince wasn't thrilled. He drifted up behind me, gave me a little kick in the heel, and muttered, "Change the ball," with a few choice expletives mixed in.

I nodded, stayed cool, and casually swapped in the smaller ball.

Same players, same number. They pressed their bets, still riding twenty.

I spun.

And wouldn't you know it? Twenty hit again. A repeater.

I marked the number, looked straight at Vince, and said loud enough for everyone to hear, "Twenty winner! Must be that lucky ball he asked me to use," while pointing right at him.

He didn't say a word, but I swear I saw smoke coming out of his ears.

The players? They couldn't have cared less. I could've swapped in a bowling ball and they'd have cheered. They were too busy high-fiving strangers, scooping up chips, and riding the high of their lucky number.

One night, I walked into the dealers' room and checked the schedule. I was assigned to a reserved roulette game, never a boring sign. This one came with some unusual rules. The betting limit was bumped to $1,000 per number and one of the zeros was barred. If that specific zero hit, the spin was void and I would re-spin. The player had the option to choose which one to ban at the start of play.

I figured it would be anarchy, stacks of $25 and $100 chips flying everywhere. But instead, the guy calmly placed five straight-up bets, every spin. Same five numbers. Always $1,000 each.

When one hit, I pushed out $35,000. In between? Just steady losses and silence.

The player was Billy Walters, the legendary sports bettor often tied to something called the Computer Group. Word was, he used advanced models to exploit soft betting lines around the country.

That caught my interest. At that time, I was writing a column for *Gaming Today* called "Computer Gambling" and dabbling in handicapping software of my own. But Walters wasn't in a talking mood, especially while he was stuck, and I got the strong sense he didn't want any questions. He was already under some federal heat.

Spin after spin, he kept taking out markers as the losses piled up.

The Golden Nugget Reborn

By the time Percy came to tap me out, Walters was in for $400,000.

Then Percy, my relief dealer, took over. And everything changed.

He started hitting Walters's numbers—7, 10, 20, 27, and 36—again and again. Walters caught fire. Instead of leaving, he asked Percy to stay another complete shift. Percy agreed.

When I came in the next day, I heard Walters hadn't just gotten even; he finished up $50,000. Percy's run had flipped the night. And thanks to some generous tipping, the entire shift was rewarded for his overtime efforts.

Not long after, word spread that Walters had done something similar at the Golden Nugget in Atlantic City, but with even higher stakes. That time, he started with a $2 million deposit in the cage and played at a $2,000-per-number limit. By the time he walked out, he'd turned that $2 million into $5.8 million.

According to Walters, he had identified biased wheels—subtle mechanical flaws that caused specific numbers or sections to hit more often. His team had tracked results across multiple wheels, feeding everything into a computer program to isolate patterns and correlations.

The Vegas Nugget got the message.

Shortly after, a group of us dealers were given a special new assignment: log every spin of every wheel around the clock. Players or not, the wheels kept spinning. We tracked every result by hand: no auto-scanners, no digital displays. Just notepads, ink, and tired eyes.

Some wheels were even pulled from the floor and moved upstairs to a special room, where they were spun and logged 24/7. It wasn't glamorous work—but it was clear the casino wasn't taking any more chances.

Today, the process is automated. Casinos use sensors to track every spin in real time. Any bias, any pattern, gets flagged immediately. The wheels themselves have changed, too: shallower pockets, extra deflectors, more erratic bounces. Some properties even rotate wheels between pits to prevent "familiarity."

More maintenance. Less magic. And a lot fewer Billy Walters moments.

But Billy's story didn't end with roulette wheels and betting systems.

Years later, I learned the federal scrutiny I'd sensed at the table was more serious than I realized. Walters was well known not just for his betting, but for his philanthropy and political connections, especially his close relationship with Senator Harry Reid.

In 1985, he was arrested and charged with illegal bookmaking as part of the Computer Group, a sophisticated sports gambling syndicate. He was acquitted, but the feds never stopped watching.

He kept betting big—and winning bigger. On a typical game day, he reportedly wagered $20 million. In 2010, he scored $3.5 million on a single Super Bowl bet when the Saints beat the Colts. ESPN called him "the greatest sports gambler ever."

But in 2017, Walters was convicted of insider trading, far from the roulette wheel. He'd used stock tips from a corporate board member and turned them into millions. Despite his political clout, he was sentenced to five years in federal prison. Because of the pandemic, he was allowed to serve the remainder of his sentence under house arrest in Southern California. Still, he pushed for a full presidential pardon. He got close. Very close.

In the final hours of Donald Trump's presidency, Walters received a commutation, but not the full pardon he wanted.

According to Walters's autobiography, one man blocked it: Steve Wynn.

Walters claims Wynn, his sworn enemy, used his influence to shut down the pardon. Why? Supposedly, Wynn never got over Walters's $3.8 million roulette win at the Golden Nugget in Atlantic City, which followed the win I'd witnessed in Las Vegas. After that Atlantic City run, Walters kept pressing his edge, continuing to beat

The Golden Nugget Reborn

the house with biased-wheel strategies.

Wynn, according to Walters, didn't just take it personally; he took it all the way to the White House.

Looking back, it's wild to think my small role at that Las Vegas roulette table was connected to a story involving federal investigations, Wall Street crimes, decades-long grudges, and influence with the president of the United States. Wynn's sudden obsession with tracking every spin makes more sense now. He wasn't just trying to protect the casino; he was settling a score.

Of course, Billy Walters wasn't the only sophisticated player trying to beat our wheels. The game had a funny way of attracting system players: some scientific, some just hopeful.

Over the years, I occasionally saw nerdy-looking groups huddled at the table with clipboards, charts, and whispered conversations. A few even admitted they were students from California universities, testing out a "theory."

One group of three guys stands out. They fit the mold perfectly: serious faces, data sheets, and a strange calm even as their chips vanished. After a few hours and a few thousand in losses, I overheard one say, "Time to call for more funds."

The floor supervisor and I exchanged a look and joked, "System working. Send money."

At the time, I didn't think much of it. I assumed they were like the rest, convinced they'd cracked the code, destined to leave broke. But I later learned that a group of physics students from UC Santa Cruz actually did pull something off.

They built one of the world's first wearable computers, right around the same time the original Apple desktop launched. It fit under the armpits or inside a shoe. One partner timed the spin with toe taps and the other received vibrational signals telling them where to bet.

Their goal was simple: time the wheel, time the ball, and narrow the point of impact. With enough precision, they could reduce the randomness and tilt the odds just slightly in their favor. They tested it live in casinos in the early '80s and the Golden Nugget was one of their proving grounds.

I can't say for sure, but I wouldn't be surprised if that clipboard-carrying trio I dealt to was part of it. The timing matched. So did the quiet confidence and the lack of panic, even while losing.

Their story ended up in a book called *The Eudaemonic Pie*, a wild blend of science, math, and casino surveillance.

Funny enough, the group credited much of their inspiration to Edward Thorp, the same guy whose book *Beat the Dealer* I'd stumbled across years earlier in the UB library. That same book flipped a switch in my brain and launched my journey into card counting and casino life.

I can't help but smile at that coincidence: different coasts, different games, but the same spark. Turns out, the future of gambling didn't start in a lab. It began under someone's armpit. Long before AI or smartwatches showed up, these guys were already betting on technology.

Not all high rollers relied on physics or wearable computers. Some preferred brute force: emotional, financial, and occasionally, literal.

As the Nugget evolved, so did the players. The stakes got higher, the games sharper, and the stories more memorable. But not all of them happened on the table.

Although swing was known as the party shift, graveyard dealers found plenty of reasons to celebrate too—just in the afternoon, instead of the late-night hours. I remember one dealer's birthday when Donna, a blackjack dealer and part-time rodeo barrel racer, rode a horse down Spring Mountain Road to the casino.

Traffic was lighter back then. So were the rules.

While I occasionally joined those gatherings, I wasn't as

dedicated to the social scene as some of my coworkers. One party I skipped was hosted by my friend Bill up in Kyle Canyon, a scenic stretch about 40 minutes up Mt. Charleston. He said it would have a "greaser" theme, with leather jackets, Fonzie hair, and a few people riding motorcycles up the hill.

Bill really wanted me there, but I passed. Even back then, the idea of drinking at altitude and navigating mountain curves on the way down didn't sit right with me. A DUI, or worse, just wasn't worth the risk.

The next morning, halfway through my shift, the news hit like a gut punch. Word was spreading through the pit: Bill hadn't made it home. At first, I thought it had to be a rumor—someone got the story wrong or he just stayed the night.

But then came the confirmation.

Search crews had spotted sunlight glinting off the chrome of his Harley, at the bottom of a ravine. One of those steep turns had taken him. He'd died instantly. Broken neck.

The shock hit all of us like a silent wave. Bill wasn't just another dealer, he was one of the good ones. Easy-going. Dependable. Never stirred up drama. Just solid.

People came back from break red-eyed and quiet. Some hugged. Others stared into space. And still the roulette wheel spun. Dice bounced. Slots chimed. There was no pause button for grief. No moment of silence. The show went on, but the air had changed. There weren't any high-fives. No loud celebrations. Even the usual dealer banter turned soft. We were all just trying to hold it together long enough to make it through the shift.

Another tragic story from my time at the Nugget almost sounds too unbelievable to be true, but I can vouch for every word.

Ronnie was a fellow roulette dealer, always upbeat, sharp on the game. What most of us didn't know was that he had a long battle with alcoholism. He'd claimed five years of sobriety. Then one afternoon, while his wife was out of town, he relapsed.

That evening, he headed to the Santa Fe casino, not far from his home in Desert Shores, and started drinking and gambling heavily. By nightfall, he'd lost a few thousand dollars. Then, he made the worst decision of his life: He got behind the wheel.

Drunk and disoriented, Ronnie entered the freeway going the wrong way and slammed head-on into another car. He had to be airlifted to the hospital. The other driver had only minor injuries, a broken arm. But here's the twist: That driver was the vice president of the Southern Nevada chapter of Mothers Against Drunk Driving.

After Ronnie recovered, he was arrested and sentenced to prison. He lost his job, his house, his marriage. A brutal fall from grace.

Some of us stayed in touch during his time inside, catching up through short phone calls on the prison's public line. I'll never forget one moment that was equal parts ironic and crushing, when he told me who his cellmate was —a guy doing time for cheating at roulette.

We spent our shifts on the casino floor, but life happened everywhere else: in the canyons, on the roads, in the silence between spins. And sometimes, the toughest losses didn't show up on a layout; they showed up off the clock.

Downtown itself was getting a makeover. The gritty charm was still there, but slowly, the rough edges were being sanded down. Pawn shops and adult bookstores began to disappear, replaced by something glossier and more family-friendly.

Carson Street, which once ran parallel to Fremont, didn't just get shut down; it got absorbed. The city handed it over for the Nugget's expansion. A new tower went up and the Carson Street Café was built right on top of what used to be a working street. A restaurant where a road once was—that's how fast downtown was changing.

Around that same time, the Golden Nugget's sister property in Atlantic City had launched and quickly became the place to be on the East Coast. That buzz carried west, drawing more high rollers to

The Golden Nugget Reborn

Las Vegas.

I still remember Steve Wynn holding an electrified staff meeting where he laid out his vision for a new resort on the Strip, something that could stand toe to toe with Caesars Palace. I remember thinking, if he pulls off even half of what he's describing, he'll change the face of Las Vegas.

Wynn also made a point that stuck with me: If the company thrived, so would we. Someone asked how we'd know if things were going well. He smiled and said, "Watch the stock." I took that advice seriously. Based on what I was seeing, the momentum, upgrades, energy—I bought in.

But Wynn wasn't just transforming real estate. He was trying to change the culture, too. One subtle but important shift: He encouraged dealers to actually talk to the players. Not just deal. Not just smile. But engage.

Signs in the dealers' room urged us to "Talk to the Player." Of course, some wiseass eventually changed it to "Talk to the Animals," but the message was clear and it marked a real shift.

At most casinos back then, especially downtown, you were expected to deal fast, stay quiet, and keep your eyes down. Interacting with players? That was frowned upon; some bosses treated small talk like a crime against game protection.

But Wynn wanted something different. He encouraged conversation, connection, and actual rapport with the people across the felt. It wasn't just about moving chips, it was about creating an experience. That idea, simple as it sounds, was revolutionary at the time.

Those quick exchanges didn't just make the shift go by faster, they sometimes turned into something more, interesting bits of knowledge along the way. I remember talking in the mid-'80s with a gentleman who was in town for meetings about a proposed bullet train linking Las Vegas and Los Angeles. It was exciting at the time, especially since many of us loved making quick weekend trips to the beaches of L.A. on our days off. Over the years, I saw him occasionally, always attending another conference or meeting on the same subject. Nearly four decades later, work has finally started on Brightline West, though if it ever gets completed is anyone's guess—and another four or five billion dollars

Another memorable interaction occurred during Comdex, the massive computer convention. While dealing, I got into a conversation about new software Microsoft was introducing for developers. Since I dabbled in programming, our chat turned pretty technical. Unexpectedly, he asked for my address and a few weeks later, a package arrived at my door containing the latest version of Visual Basic. There was no name or note, no way to know who to thank, just Microsoft.

The next couple of years were filled with anticipation. Models of the new resort went on display, and the buzz only got louder.

The name? The Mirage.

In 1987, they cleared the stretch of the Strip where it would rise and you could feel the shift happening in real time. Something bigger was coming—bigger than downtown, bigger than anything Vegas had seen before. A new chapter in Las Vegas history was about to begin. And I was already positioned to be part of it.

Chapter 8
Mirage: The Revolution Begins

The $630 Million Gamble That Changed Vegas Forever

From the moment plans for the Mirage were announced, the buzz began to build, reaching a fever pitch over the next two years. The exact details of the property were shrouded in mystery, partly by design to keep intrigue at its peak and partly because planning was still very much a work in progress. After the Castaways casino and neighboring properties were razed, a massive fence went up, sparking a guessing game about what was to come. Wild rumors circulated throughout Las Vegas about what was taking shape behind those barricades—whispers of massive tropical lagoons, elaborate water features, and even Venetian-style canals complete with gondolas that would transport guests through the property. The secrecy only fueled the anticipation, as locals and industry insiders alike traded their theories about Wynn's revolutionary vision.

About six months before the Mirage's grand opening, a scale model of the property was unveiled and put on public display at the Golden Nugget.

The Mirage site, right next to Caesars Palace, had prime real estate—except for one stubborn corner. A two-story walk-up called the Royal Inn Apartments, built in the early '70s, held out during land acquisition. The units were modest, but affordable, and for those who worked at the Mirage, you couldn't beat the location. Some employees joked it offered the shortest commute in Vegas. Rumor had it that if Wynn had secured the property earlier, the lagoon out front might have doubled in size. Eventually, the company acquired the land, and in 1993, Treasure Island opened on that very corner.

At the time, Mirage was the world's most expensive resort, with a staggering price tag of $630 million. Unlike the murky financial arrangements of yesteryear, often involving union funds and "mystery money," the Mirage was the first Las Vegas property built with Wall Street backing. This was made possible through a partnership with Michael Milken.

Milken, an investment banker at Drexel Burnham Lambert, met Steve Wynn in the early '80s when Wynn sought funding for a new casino in Atlantic City. Known for his expertise in high-yield or "junk" bonds, Milken raised the capital Wynn needed, cementing a friendship and business partnership.

Many financial analysts and gaming executives were initially skeptical about the Mirage's chances of success, given that it needed to rake in a million dollars a day just to cover expenses. However, the property would exceed all expectations, proving the naysayers wrong and setting a new standard for the industry.

For Golden Nugget employees, the anticipation was intense and everyone seemed to be on their best behavior, akin to kids hoping to make Santa's "nice" list. If a boss needed you to pull an extra shift, you were more inclined to agree, especially with the not-so-subtle hints that evaluations for potential transfers to the Mirage were underway.

Employees also took extra care to avoid any slip-ups that might land them on the "naughty' list, effectively sentencing them to a lifetime of dealing downtown. But the dirty little secret was that they needed not only the experienced dealers from the Golden Nugget in Las Vegas, but also a substantial number from the Golden Nugget property in Atlantic City.

That's not to downplay that they had more than 100 applicants for every dealer opening. This was the premier job in town and everyone—from downtown dealers to Strip veterans and even international applicants—wanted in. However, they needed a whopping 6,400 employees and we were all a known commodity. Being already acclimated to the company's culture made the training smoother for everyone and eased the transition.

Bringing together seasoned staff from different properties wasn't always seamless and occasionally, old grudges followed the new hires through the doors.

When the Mirage opened, a few supervisors transferred in from the Atlantic City Golden Nugget, including Gordon and Steve, two pit managers with a long-running rivalry. Their tension followed them west like unwelcome cargo.

One busy Saturday night, the dice tables were packed when a woman approached with a handful of $5 chips. The sign clearly said $25 minimum.

"That's okay," she said brightly. "Steve told me I could play the lower limit here."

Gordon, seizing a chance to jab at his old rival, didn't miss a beat. "Well," he snapped, "you can tell Steve he doesn't know what he's talking about. He's an idiot." A solid zinger—if she'd been talking about Gordon's rival. But she wasn't. She walked back across the casino to the bar, where her group was still chatting with their friend—Steve Wynn. Within minutes, the call came down. Gordon's shift was over. Permanently.

It was a quick reminder that at the Mirage, no matter how big your grudge, you'd better know which Steve you're badmouthing.

Despite such growing pains, ultimately, it didn't matter; they took nearly all of us who were interested, which was probably around 99%. This created a bit of a staffing hiccup at the Nugget, but those positions were quickly filled. After all, working at the Nugget suddenly became the gateway to the Mirage, making it an attractive option for new hires.

My first glimpse of the Mirage stopped me in my tracks. The golden windows shimmered in the desert sun like a mirage itself, daring you to believe it was real. Towering palms swayed in the warm breeze and the front lagoon, complete with a smoking volcano, bubbled with promise. But what truly floored me was the deeper realization: This wasn't just a dazzling new property on the Strip. This was *exactly* what Steve Wynn had described to us two years earlier.

Back then, it had sounded like fantasy—lush waterfalls, tropical landscaping, and a resort experience unlike anything Las Vegas had ever seen. Now here it was, standing proud right next to Caesars Palace, not just matching its grandeur, but threatening to upstage it. I felt like I'd stepped into the future of Las Vegas.

Everything about the Mirage felt larger than life, from the roar of the erupting volcano to the faint scent of coconut and chlorine in the air. And yet, beneath the spectacle, there was something personal—a strange kind of pride. I had seen this dream take shape from concept to creation. And now, standing at its doorstep, I knew this wasn't just the start of a new chapter for the Strip. It was the start of a new chapter for me, too.

The training and preparations were top-notch and meticulously organized. In the days leading up to the grand opening, the entire casino staff—dealers, floor personnel, supervisors—rotated through

Mirage: The Revolution Begins

a series of briefing rooms scattered throughout the property. Each room covered a different aspect of operations, including chip handling, shift protocols, high-limit procedures, and surveillance coordination. For those of us moving up from the Nugget, much of this was familiar territory. We'd already dealt with serious action and high-limit players during the Nugget's transformation, so the Mirage felt like a natural next step. But for many of the new hires, it was a crash course in pressure and precision. This was not just another casino. It was the most anticipated opening in years and the stakes were sky high.

Another reason the training had to be so thorough was less glamorous, but just as crucial: security. The first few days of a casino's life are when it's most vulnerable. Word gets out fast in the underground. Scammers, cheats, and advantage players were eagerly waiting for a chance to exploit any hint of confusion or disorganization. A flustered dealer or a poorly understood procedure could cost the house big. The Mirage might have been the crown jewel of the Strip, but we knew it was also a prime target. Management drilled us hard, not just for show, but because they understood exactly what was at stake. Every shift, every rotation, every protocol—it all had to be second nature before that first bet was ever placed.

Play Day served as a dress rehearsal. Half the staff from all departments worked, while the other half played the role of guests. This allowed us to experience the venue from both sides and work out any kinks. We could gamble with play money, dine in the restaurants, and some even had the chance to stay as hotel guests.

As the training period drew to a close and the excitement of Play Day wore off, the final motivational push came from Steve Wynn himself. The man could sell ice to Eskimos and his speech had us all fired up and ready to go. For those of us in the casino, he reassured us not to fret over the $1,000 chips. "They're just plastic," he said. His directive to the bosses was even more comforting: "As long as the game is on the level, don't sweat the money."

That speech landed like a weighted blanket of relief on most of us dealers. I'd been with the company long enough not to flinch when a $1,000 chip hit the felt. They were just high-stakes chips by now, not heart attacks waiting to happen. But it was Wynn's message to the bosses that really lifted the tension in the room. "Don't sweat the money." That was a game-changer. Back downtown, you could feel every loss in the pit. A bad run might earn you grumbles, side-eyes, or outright muttering from some floor supervisors who took every hit to the rack like it was coming out of their paycheck. The pressure was real and not all of it stayed professional. But here at the Mirage, that culture was being scrubbed out. Come to think of it, maybe that's why a few of the old-school bosses didn't make the jump from downtown. They couldn't let go of the anxiety—the constant sweating, second-guessing, and stressing over every payout. For the rest of us, it was clear: The game had changed. And we were more than ready for it.

And then, it was showtime. All the prep work was done; the stage was set. It was November 1989, time to get this party started.

In February 1990, the Mirage unveiled its crown jewel: a $30 million theater custom-built for Siegfried & Roy. This wasn't just a showroom; it was a high-tech temple of spectacle, complete with trapdoors, pyrotechnics, and, of course, tigers. Seating just over 1,500, the space was intimate by Vegas standards, but every inch was engineered to dazzle.

Most nights, I was already into a roulette shift by the time the show let out, but you could feel it. The energy on the floor shifted. Guests spilled out into the casino still buzzing, swapping wide-eyed reactions like they'd just witnessed real magic. In a way, they had.

Mirage: The Revolution Begins

The tigers weren't just part of the show; they were part of the property. Their custom habitat, visible from inside the Mirage, featured a massive glass viewing wall and an open-air section above, allowing natural light and fresh air to enter. It was striking, a quiet pocket of wildness right in the middle of a casino.

One night, that openness nearly turned tragic. Word spread fast: Someone, drunk, disturbed, or just dangerously curious, had climbed into the open-air area above the habitat. He was perched on a narrow ledge, high above the tigers. Security swarmed in. Police arrived, rifles drawn. Fortunately, the handlers moved quickly and secured the animals before anything worse could happen. The man was pulled out unharmed, though probably with fewer brain cells than he started with.

And then there was the elephant.

On more than one early morning drive into work, we spotted her lumbering behind the Mirage—unhurried, serene, making her way back to her enclosure at the edge of the property. No fanfare. No spotlight. Just a living breathing part of the cast, heading home like any other employee after a long night's work.

These weren't just gimmicks; they were reminders that the Mirage wasn't playing by the old Vegas rules. It wasn't just a casino. It was a show, a zoo, a fantasy, all wrapped in one.

But beneath all the spectacle was an invisible army keeping it alive: dealers, engineers, handlers, security, and surveillance. So much of what made the Mirage magical happened out of sight and out of mind. The guests saw the volcano erupting and the dolphins leaping. What they didn't see were the countless people working overnight to make sure everything hummed without a hitch. That was the beauty and the burden of the graveyard shift. We kept the illusion intact, while the rest of the city slept.

As usual, I was dealing roulette for opening night at the Mirage and from the moment I stepped in, it was nonstop. One of those whirlwind shifts where you put your head down, get to work, and before you know it, eight hours have flown by in a blur. Your pulse is still racing from the adrenaline, even as the exhaustion starts to set in.

So thanks to the boxing matches, the holidays, Siegfried & Roy's spellbinding spectacle, and the mesmerizing volcano that erupted nightly out front, the place kept buzzing, showing no signs of slowing down, much like a blockbuster movie that everyone has to see. It seemed like anyone visiting Las Vegas that first year had to get to the Mirage, if only to witness the volcano's fiery display against the desert sky and the 100-foot-tall glass dome towering over the tropical rainforest at the entrance.

The Mirage wasn't just a feast for the senses for our guests; those of us dealing soaked it all in, too. Imagine dealing while the soothing backdrop of a waterfall is just a glance away. Lift your eyes a bit and you're greeted by what appears to be a rainforest canopy. The air itself felt different—humid, tropical, and infused with the sweet aroma of piña coladas. As if that weren't enough, the distant melodies of a calypso band floated over from Kokomo's bar, adding the perfect soundtrack to this paradise.

Now, contrast this sensory experience with my earlier days at the Las Vegas Club downtown. Oh, what a different world that was! Instead of waterfalls, we had buckets strategically placed to catch leaks from the ceiling. The neon lights of Fremont Street did their best to imitate the natural beauty of a rainforest, but let's be honest, they were as far from that as a slot machine is from a lush green fern. And the sounds? Forget calypso rhythms; the cacophony of Fremont Street traffic and the occasional siren were our constant companions.

As for the smells, well, let's say downtown had its own unique "bouquet," a blend of odors that ranged from stale beer to, well, things I'd rather not put into words. Suffice it to say, it was a far cry from the tropical rainforest vibes at the Mirage.

So as I stood there dealing at the Mirage, I couldn't help but marvel at how far I'd come—from dodging rain buckets under neon lights to basking in the ambience of a tropical paradise. It was like going from a black-and-white movie to a full-blown IMAX 3D feature. And let me tell you, I was absolutely loving every minute of it.

Chapter 9
Mirage: Where Art Meets Avarice

*Monet on the Walls, Money on the Tables,
and Turbulence All Around*

Soon after opening, the high-limit salon at the Mirage was temporarily closed for high-tech upgrades. When it reopened, it was nothing short of an art sanctuary. Every wall was adorned with masterpieces by the likes of Vincent Van Gogh, Pierre-Auguste Renoir, Henri Matisse, Pablo Picasso, and Claude Monet.

Back in 1990, that jaw-dropping collection was pegged at $120 million—real money even by Strip standards. Adjusted for inflation today in 2025, it's pushing over $295 million. No wonder the art world and media went gaga over this one-of-a-kind setup; it was like turning the salon into a museum, while we dealers just tried not to bump into a Renoir during our shifts.

Ironically, many of us who worked amidst these treasures all night weren't exactly art connoisseurs. Some of us had a soft spot for kitschy classics like velvet Elvis paintings or my personal favorite, "Dogs Playing Poker." The closest we had to an art aficionado was Kenny, who claimed that watching Bob Ross paint was his go-to sleep aid.

One of the pluses of working in the salon was the comfort level; by that, I mean air quality and temperature, a feature not designed for us or even our guests, but specifically for the priceless art. As I stood at the roulette wheel during the night, if I should innocently take a step back away from my game by a couple of feet, a silent alarm was triggered by one of the laser beams surrounding the Renoir behind me and we got a quick call from surveillance to have me step forward.

That priceless art and the five-star restaurants just steps from the tables weren't just about pampering high rollers. They marked a turning point, a declaration that Las Vegas was done pretending to be a dusty gambling town. The Mirage wasn't just a casino—it was the first real sign that Vegas was becoming a luxury destination, one masterpiece and white truffle at a time. Me? I was just happy for the side perk. That smoke-free atmosphere, pure as mountain air, was cranked up not for the high rollers huffing cigars, but to coddle those million-dollar canvases.

The masterpieces on our walls were just one element of the Mirage's commitment to unparalleled luxury. In addition to its iconic volcano, mesmerizing waterfalls, tiger and dolphin habitats, and the legendary Siegfried and Roy show, the Mirage boasted another jewel in its crown: Shadow Creek Golf Course.

Opened at the same time as the hotel-casino, this wasn't just any golf course; it was one of the most exclusive and expensive in the world, ranking eighth on *Golf Digest's* list of the top 100 golf courses globally. Shadow Creek quickly gained a reputation as a playground for the rich and famous. Its elite roster of golfers included the likes of Michael Jordan, former U.S. presidents, and CEOs from around the globe. The course itself was a spectacle, featuring immaculate grounds, exotic birds and animals, all set against the dazzling backdrop of the Las Vegas Strip.

I remember one particular instance while dealing baccarat to a

Mirage: Where Art Meets Avarice

high-roller betting $100,000 a hand. Intrigued by Shadow Creek, he inquired about playing a round. Given his level of play, I assumed it would be a slam dunk. We called over a host to make arrangements, but hit a snag. To my surprise, the host asked if the player was staying at the Mirage. When he replied that he was staying at Caesars Palace next door, the host regretfully informed him that Shadow Creek was exclusive to Mirage guests.

Today, you might be able to play a round at Shadow Creek for around $500, but back in the day, it was the epitome of exclusivity. And speaking of exclusivity, the groundskeepers had their fair share of challenges maintaining that pristine reputation. One memorable incident involved my favorite Turkish billionaire roulette player, who was offered a tour of the course. Not being a golfer, he took a cart out for a leisurely drive around the beautiful grounds. And that's exactly what he did, getting an up-close view of everything—including driving onto the sacred greens and leaving a trail of torn-up turf in his wake.

With sought-after amenities like Shadow Creek, five-star dining, and museum-worthy art on the walls, the Mirage had claimed its place at the top of the Las Vegas hierarchy. It was the new king of the hill and everyone else was playing catch-up.

While Shadow Creek epitomized the Mirage's commitment to exclusive luxury for our guests, the property's generosity extended to its employees as well, though in decidedly different ways. If the golf course was about pampering high rollers with pristine greens and exotic birds, our perks were more practical, but no less appreciated: free meals that actually tasted good, uniforms that didn't come out of our paychecks, and a buffet that would make some restaurants jealous.

You know, I often ponder the plight of those poor souls who have to pay for parking and their own coffee at work. At the Mirage, we had all that and more: free meals, uniforms provided, and daily dry cleaning. Talk about living the dream.

Our employee haven, the Manga Hall, wasn't just a snack bar. It was a culinary Disneyland. Forget the basic coffee, cookies, and donuts—we had a full-blown sandwich station where a chef crafted your sandwich like it was a work of art. And let's not overlook the omelet station, where you could get an omelet made to order. Dealers, blessed with hourly breaks, could hit this buffet more than once a night. And we certainly made the most of that privilege.

This gastronomic indulgence led us to another Mirage perk: the seamstresses at uniform control. They were always on standby to adjust our uniforms or "upgrade" us to a larger size. I recall a time when Ben, a fellow dealer, was a bit lax in his uniform exchange. We argued it was a public-health issue; as his girth increased, those buttons were a wardrobe malfunction waiting to happen and someone could lose an eye.

But wait, there's more! The high-limit room had its own exclusive buffet. Because, heaven forbid, a player betting $50,000 a hand should have to walk to a restaurant. This buffet was a revolving door of gourmet delights, refreshed every couple of hours.

Initially, the butler offered to save us a filet mignon or crab leg for our break. But as time went on, we snuck into the backroom to feast before our official break time. We had to eat fast, so we wouldn't miss our actual break. Oh, the irony.

The pinnacle of our buffet exploitation was when the floor supervisor started making special requests. "Hey, how about a pizza tonight?" or "Can we get some lox and bagels?" The only time this was ever questioned was when the shift boss raised an eyebrow at a pizza order. Our lone player at the time, a Chinese gentleman, only ate congee.

The butlers didn't mind; they got a 15% cut on every buffet refresh. So everyone was happy, except maybe the house accountants. But hey, it was just a drop in the bucket for those million-dollar

Mirage: Where Art Meets Avarice

players.

These perks kept us well-fed and content, but the real draw of working the high-limit room wasn't the food. It was the front-row seat to a world of international gambling culture, where baccarat reigned supreme.

At the Mirage, I carved out my niche dealing high-limit roulette for those private games, but as our Chinese clientele exploded, baccarat claimed its throne. It was like a custom-tailored Armani suit for the international jet-set crowd. Simple enough to learn on a graveyard shift, exclusive enough to feel like a secret society, it screamed luxury and let our well-heeled guests flex their refined tastes and bottomless pockets without breaking a sweat. Me? I was just along for the tuxedo upgrade, swapping my standard vest for something a bit more James Bond. Though let's be real, I was more like Agent 002.5, licensed to spin wheels and dodge flying chips.

Tommy Renzoni, the father of a fellow Mirage dealer I worked with, brought baccarat to Vegas in 1959 after seeing it thrive in Havana, where he'd run the show at the Capri Hotel Casino. He talked the Sands into trying it, going all-in with a roped-off pit, tuxedoed dealers, the whole nine yards. Opening night was a bloodbath—they reportedly dropped hundreds of thousands. But they hung in there and baccarat became a Strip staple.

Over the years, baccarat lost some of its old-school mystique with the rise of midi baccarat. This stripped-down version featured just one dealer instead of three and the shoe was handled solely by us. No more players dramatically pulling cards. Back in the '70s and '80s, high-end baccarat rooms felt like ultra-exclusive clubs, roped off from the main floor. Dealers pooling their astronomical tokes among maybe 20 people tops—a secret stash that must've been life-changing. But by the Mirage's opening, those tips got funneled into the big pool with all dealers, spreading the wealth, but watering down that elite vibe. Still, it remained a powerhouse, pulling in around

19% of the gaming revenue on the Strip in recent years.

Baccarat had its perks. For one, I got to trade my standard dealer's vest for an Armani tuxedo, which was not a bad upgrade. The game itself was straightforward: just four to six cards per hand for the entire table, even money payouts for bank or player (minus the 5% commission on banker wins), and 8 to 1 on the tie bet. Plus, unlike roulette, you could sit down.

The real challenge came from baccarat's unique ceremony. Players actually handle the shoe themselves, dealing the cards, which adds drama and ritual to each hand. For high rollers, this wasn't just gambling; it was theater and they were the stars, not just spectators. Players drew cards when prompted, but there was always that one guy—drunk, trying to be clever, or genuinely confused, who reached for cards at the wrong time. I became part dealer, part traffic cop, hand extended like I was directing rush hour on the Strip. When cards got exposed out of turn, the high rollers weren't shy about voicing their opinions.

My occasional baccarat dealing had a way of expanding during peak times. Chinese New Year meant 12-hour shifts for 10 days straight as the baccarat room transformed into a high-stakes battlefield. Extra tables appeared wherever we could squeeze them in. The action was incredible—regular $25,000 bets jumped to $50,000 and $100,000 on every table. The air practically crackled with that much money in play.

As word spread that the Mirage was the premier spot for high-stakes action, our clientele went truly global, with Chinese players, riding their country's economic boom, becoming the backbone of the baccarat frenzy. Little did we graveyard grunts know, Steve Wynn was already building bridges with Macau's gaming elite, setting the stage for even bigger things down the line.

At the Mirage, a lot of thought went into designing the high-limit areas and not just the usual luxury stuff. They actually brought in feng shui consultants to help lay everything out in a way that would feel right to our Chinese guests. We're talking about the placement of tables, entrances, even the color schemes and décor. Elements like water features and mirrors were carefully considered, because in Chinese culture, all of that is believed to affect the flow of energy and luck. And when luck is your business, you pay attention to it.

You really saw how important that was during Chinese New Year, one of the busiest times of year for Las Vegas and it's no coincidence. For many Chinese gamblers, the holiday is a chance to test their luck for the year ahead. A win during that time is seen as a sign the whole year might go well. So the casino went all-out with decorations. Red was everywhere, since it's considered the luckiest color, and traditional symbols were placed throughout the space to attract good fortune. It was a cultural celebration, absolutely—but it was also smart business.

And it wasn't just about the look. Many of our Chinese players arrived with lucky charms, wore specific colors, or played at certain times based on their astrological signs. To them, that stuff mattered just as much as the odds on the table. The Mirage made sure to honor it all, not just with decor, but with the whole vibe. It sent a message: "We get it. We respect your traditions."

Eventually, this kind of cultural consideration became standard at high-end casinos around the world. If you wanted to attract serious international players, especially from Asia, you had to go beyond just the games. You had to understand the mindset behind the play, the rituals, the symbolism. It wasn't just gambling; it was something deeper. A mix of luck, belief, and ritual that a lot of players took very seriously.

One of the more infamous examples of what happens when you don't pay attention to this kind of thing? That'd be the MGM Grand back in the early '90s. When they first opened in 1993, they built a giant entrance shaped like the mouth of a lion. The idea was to wow people with something bold—like walking right through the MGM logo.

Except there was one big problem: In Chinese culture, walking into the mouth of an animal is terrible luck. It's like you're being swallowed alive, which is definitely not the vibe you want when you're walking into a casino to gamble. Word spread fast and many Chinese guests started avoiding the place entirely or sneaking in through side entrances.

Eventually, MGM got the message loud and clear. By 1998, they redesigned the whole entrance. Out went the lion's mouth, in came a massive bronze lion statue, much more traditional and respectful. It wasn't just a cosmetic fix either. It cost a fortune. But they knew it had to be done. That's how important cultural sensitivity has become.

Those daily interactions, especially with our Asian players, opened my eyes to customs and cultural nuances I'd never encountered before. From their betting rituals to gestures of respect—and even the exotic dishes they had flown in or prepared in the private salons, like congee (that soothing rice porridge), 1,000-year eggs, and chicken feet—it gave me a deeper appreciation for a world far beyond my own. To them, those were comfort foods, midnight fuel for a hot streak; to a kid from Buffalo like me, they seemed about as appetizing as a dare on a lost bet. I'd have stuck with chicken wings doused in hot sauce or a hearty beef on weck, but hey, in the high-limit room, odd was relative. What's weirder than watching a billionaire slurp congee while dropping $100K a hand?

Not long after the Mirage opened its doors, I got word that I'd be dealing a reserved game in the salon. But this wasn't just any game; it came with a set of rules that were new to all of us. For starters, one of the zeros would be barred and the minimum chip denomination was $1,000. I had seen that before. The new twist was that the player would be making what's known as complete bets.

Unbeknownst to us at the time, complete bets are a staple in French roulette. These are maxed-out progressive bets where the

Mirage: Where Art Meets Avarice

player doesn't just bet the maximum on a single number; they also go all-in on every other possible combination involving that number—splits, corners, streets, you name it. We're talking about a staggering $40,000 on some numbers, with a jaw-dropping payout of $396,000 if Lady Luck smiles their way.

To keep us all on the straight and narrow, we had a cheat sheet of sorts—a chart detailing the various payouts. Trust me, you don't want to make a mistake when you're handling this amount of money.

But let's put things in perspective. Compared to my days downtown, juggling stacks of 10-cent chips, this was a walk in the park. We're talking about eight $5,000 chips or a single $25,000 chip along with three $5,000 chips. The math for the payout was already done for us, double-checked by a usually vigilant floor manager. Once you convinced yourself that you were confident enough to push around $1,000, $5,000, and even $25,000 chips, it was much simpler than the stacks of dime chips from years ago.

Part of the allure of reserved games like these is their unpredictability. Sometimes you waited for days, twiddling your thumbs, wondering if the high roller would ever show. Other times, the action was non-stop, 24/7. But most often, these VIPs had a rhythm all their own—perhaps starting at 2 a.m., playing for four hours, then vanishing into the night. Others opted to play like a marathon for hours on end. The graveyard shift became the VIP shift to dodge the limelight or because their body clocks were tuned to a time zone halfway around the world.

So the table was set and we were ready to roll for our special game. We soon discovered that our high-rolling guest was no ordinary Joe. He was a member of the royal family from the Middle East—a prince, no less. In he strolled, a young man trailed by an entourage of assistants and well-wishers. We didn't exchange a word. It wasn't clear whether it was a language barrier or if he deemed it beneath his royal dignity to converse with the likes of me. He seemed pleasant enough, although he had a bit of a Pillsbury Doughboy vibe.

A young woman stepped forward from his entourage to serve as his gaming proxy. You see, the prince never touched a chip. He pointed and she placed the bets for him. One glance at his hands confirmed his aversion to manual labor. They were as soft and unmarked as a newborn's. Even when nature called and he had to visit the "royal water closet," an aide accompanied him to assist with ... well, most likely a royal flush.

European roulette, also known as French roulette, felt like an exotic import crashing the Vegas party back then. The big hook? Just one zero on the wheel, ditching the American double-zero and slashing the house edge from 5.26% to 2.70%. Sure, that meant less advantage for the casino, but our international crowd demanded it. There was no way we could keep the jet-setters if we stuck to the homegrown version.

To compete globally, single-zero was a must, so I got "volunteered" to master it—reluctantly, after my lukewarm dip into baccarat left me gun shy. We hunkered down in the back of the house for a couple weeks, drilling the nuances: section bets, neighbors, those intricate complete bets, and a slew of other fancy wagers. For extra flair, we even practiced calling out bets and numbers in French, like we were prepping for Monte Carlo instead of the Strip at 4 a.m.. That absurd twist lasted a couple of weeks before we said *au revoir* to it.

Jumping in headfirst post-training was the real teacher. Cheat sheets propped us up at first and we'd already ditched the French lingo for plain English. Those exotic bets were rare beasts, showing up maybe once every six months. But they kept us sharp. Nothing like a surprise wager to remind you why brushing up on payoffs was smarter than winging it with a high roller breathing down your neck.

But hey, mastering those games was one thing—tough enough in a graveyard-shift haze—but the real dealer boot camp came from

Mirage: Where Art Meets Avarice

wrangling the personalities and quirks of our international clientele, where every spin or card flip could turn into a cross-cultural showdown.

At the time of the Mirage's opening, Macau was under Portuguese control; this changed 10 years later, after the 1999 transfer to China. A small group, including Stanley Ho and Yip Hon, held a monopoly on gaming in Macau while still controlled by Portugal. Both were guests at the Mirage.

Yip Hon, known as the "Godfather of Gambling" in Macau, owned the iconic Casino Lisboa. He frequented the Mirage with his entourage of wealthy Chinese gamblers. They played a version of roulette unlike any I'd ever seen. The wheel was divided into four quadrants using colored contact paper applied directly to the wheelhead: bright red, blue, yellow, and green sections that transformed our elegant roulette wheel into something resembling a carnival game. Players bet on which colored section the ball would land in, placing their wagers on the outer edge of the layout using numbered buttons (1-4) to indicate their chosen quadrant.

To make it even more interesting, besides the regular action on the wheel and these quadrants, half of the people in this group also placed side bets amongst themselves on the outside of the layout, essentially cutting out the middleman. I'm not sure how any of this would have gone over with the Gaming Control Board, but it all seemed to work out.

It was obvious to everyone that Yip Hon was in charge and commanded ultimate respect from everyone in the group. I remember one instance when a Chinese couple walked by a baccarat game where Yip Hon was playing. The husband greeted him warmly and made some pleasantries in Chinese. They bowed, but as they walked away, the wife was loudly berated because of some faux pas in their greeting.

When the new Salon Privé was first opened for the highest-stakes play at the Mirage, Yip Hon and his entourage were among the first groups to play in the room. The group of six or seven was playing baccarat, some betting $50,000, and Yip Hon betting $100,000. Everyone played on the same side as Yip Hon, whether banker or player. After they all made their bets, the first cards were revealed, and the dealer announced, "Draw a card for the bank," the lights suddenly and unexpectedly went out. It was completely dark, pitch black in the room. A flashlight was quickly produced from behind the small cashier's cage, but that didn't help much. With close to half a million dollars bet on the table, everyone hoped it would still be there when the lights came back on.

One of the bosses sprang into action and commandeered a table lamp from the other room, holding it up over the table. The hand continued and the house won, but the players all protested that they should get their money back. As I recall, they didn't.

Believe it or not, when something like this happens with a very big player, I've seen casinos give huge amounts back to keep very big players happy. But the squeaky wheel didn't prevail this time.

And the source of the blackout? Was it an electrical problem or a citywide outage? No, it seems that this new room was equipped with all sorts of fancy controls on a panel on the wall that adjusted lights, audio, and temperature with the push of a button. Apparently, a clerk standing next to the wall had leaned back and unknowingly turned out the lights.

While our Chinese guests constituted a significant portion of our top players, the high-limit rooms were a veritable United Nations of gamblers. Take, for instance, a high-profile Japanese baccarat player who strode in precisely at 9 a.m. every day during his visits. Always impeccably dressed in a suit and tie, he was trailed by an entourage of Japanese women donning color-coordinated uniforms. They weren't just there for show; they were his cheerleaders. Literally.

Whenever this Japanese player scored a big win, his personal cheer squad rose to their feet and break into a synchronized cheer. The only thing missing was the pom-poms!

Cultural tensions sometimes required careful choreography in our limited private spaces. Chinese and Korean groups, for instance, had to be seated as far apart as possible. Their mutual animosity could turn a gaming room into a Cold War standoff. It became particularly awkward when one group was boisterously winning, while the other was suffering a losing streak. I witnessed more than a few icy stare-downs and heard grumblings in both Korean and Chinese, likely not the most flattering of words.

But cultural tensions weren't the only memorable episodes I witnessed in these private rooms; some incidents stood out purely due to their sheer audacity.

In the private salons, you witness many things that guests might hesitate to do in public areas. But one incident probably should have been conducted somewhere more private—actually, make that much more private.

Many of our marathon players spent countless hours at a table, completely enthralled in the excitement of the game. As comfortable as the Mirage chairs were, they couldn't always accommodate every player's needs. This became painfully evident one night with one of our high-limit Asian players who, about eight hours into his baccarat session, began showing visible signs of discomfort.

He summoned his private aide/nurse, who was stationed nearby, with the urgency of someone who couldn't wait for proper protocol. The player backed away from the table, retreating to a conveniently placed decorative tree in the corner. Without missing a beat, his trusty assistant produced some sort of magical balm and, with the efficiency of a pit crew member at the Indy 500, applied a handful of the goo to the affected area, while the player's trousers were slightly and strategically lowered. The entire procedure took less than a minute and our newly comfortable player returned to his seat, ready to resume his gaming marathon.

I suppose when you're betting tens of thousands per hand, you get to make your own rules about proper casino etiquette. Still, some things are better left to the privacy of one's villa. Though try telling that to someone who's on a winning streak and doesn't want to leave the table for any reason. At least he had the decorum to use the tree as cover.

Among all the high rollers who graced our tables, two made special marks, not just for their wealth, but for their outsized personalities and the indelible impressions they left on everyone who dealt to them.

Just as Batman had his perennial run-ins with the Joker, I had recurring encounters with Ahmet, my Turkish roulette adversary. As I moved from the Golden Nugget downtown to the Mirage, I was no stranger to high-stakes action. I'd cut my teeth on the roulette tables and found myself frequently stationed in the Mirage's high-limit room. Sure, it was a world away from the bustling energy of the main casino floor, but what it lacked in sheer volume, it more than made up for in high-octane excitement.

Ahmet was one of Turkey's wealthiest men and easily my most unforgettable adversary at the tables. Our relationship spanned two decades. It was an intricate dance of high stakes, quick tempers, and mutual, if grudging, respect. Ahmet was a paradox: short but imposing, hot-tempered but calculated, obscenely wealthy, but tighter than a drum when it came to tipping.

Our first meeting was at the Nugget downtown. That night, Ahmet quickly dropped half a million dollars and was eager to reverse course. When told he'd have to wait until 9 a.m. for additional credit, he didn't argue—he walked to the cage and used an ATM-style phone to wire in $2 million—no red tape. No hesitation. Rumor had it he owned one of Turkey's largest banks and I believed it.

He wasn't just trying to win. He was trying to rattle us. He

Mirage: Where Art Meets Avarice

questioned calls, interrupted procedures, and threw the whole game off balance. Once, he grabbed the roulette ball mid-spin and hurled it at the shift manager. On another occasion, he knocked over the entire chip bank—what we called the "impress"—sending hundreds of chips clattering across the layout, because he could.

Ahmet didn't just play the game, he challenged it.

That first night when he was down half a million, he took a walk to cool off. When he returned, I asked how it went. He said, deadpan, "I was looking for a gun at the pawn shop across the street." Joke or not, I couldn't help but wonder what my fate might have been if this game were happening in his homeland.

Rumor had it he had been banned from a London casino for flipping a table. Given his size, I had my doubts. But with Ahmet, the improbable had a way of becoming inevitable.

At the Mirage, he had a unique strategy: play two roulette tables back to back. This allowed him to place bets on one table, then quickly pivot to the other while the ball was still spinning on the first wheel. This tactic often led to wild swings in his fortunes.

One fateful morning, Ahmet was on a losing streak, down nearly a million dollars. His colorful blend of expletives in two languages had become something of a soundtrack for those of us who regularly dealt with and to him. But this particular morning was a comedy of errors for the incoming day shift.

Just as Ahmet was hitting peak frustration, the day-shift baccarat manager walked in. Oblivious to the tension, he cheerfully greeted Ahmet with a "Good morning!" Big mistake. Ahmet erupted, berating the manager at full volume for a solid five minutes. Those of us at the tables struggled to contain our laughter.

But the comedy didn't end there. Almost on cue, another day-shift executive strolled in, offering a similar cheerful greeting. Ahmet's reaction was even more explosive. Unfortunately, the memo never reached the shift boss, who also walked by with yet another "good morning." Ahmet was convinced it was a conspiracy to make him lose and his tirade—and losing streak—continued.

Ahmet usually played in the main high-limit pit, but on rare occasions, he ventured into the salon. During one of these sessions, I contemplated a delicate issue. Knowing Ahmet's penchant for throwing things when frustrated, I wondered if I should gently remind him of the priceless art surrounding us. On one shoulder, a devilish voice urged me to say it; on the other, an angelic voice warned me against poking the bear. In the end, I chickened out. Ahmet knocked over a few chairs, but, thankfully, didn't launch anything at the masterpieces on the walls.

Over the years, we crossed paths many times. Each meeting felt like a psychological chess match—high-stakes and intense, testing not just the dealers, but the whole management team.

He never tipped. Not once. But he did bring the thrill of elite-level play—and the challenge of holding your ground against one of the most volatile, enigmatic, high rollers I ever dealt to.

It was during those years at the Nugget, dealing with higher action and players at Ahmet's level, that my confidence truly solidified. The dollar amount stopped mattering, whether it was $1 or $25,000 chips, they were all just clay and plastic. You had to stay sharp, of course, but you couldn't let the players rattle you.

Some players, like Ahmet, lived for that. They fed on a dealer's fear like sharks sensing blood in the water. These predators existed at every level of play, not just the high limit. They probe for weakness, test boundaries, and exploit any crack in your composure. A trembling hand, a miscalculated payout, even a moment's hesitation and they pounce.

I remembered an old Vegas Club boss who growl his mantra: "Show no fear."' Like those deodorant commercials, never let them see you sweat. It didn't matter if your heart was hammering or your palms were damp. What mattered was the mask. By then, I'd

Mirage: Where Art Meets Avarice

internalized that lesson. The mask had become real. I was ready for whatever the tables could throw at me.

Just as I had regular run-ins with Ahmet, arguably one of Turkey's wealthiest tycoons, I had the good fortune to occasionally rub elbows with another titan of wealth, Kerry Packer, Australia's richest man at the time.

While my interactions with Ahmet were always up close and personal, dealing to him during each of his visits, my brushes with Kerry Packer were a tad more indirect, as his game of choice was baccarat. I was stationed at a roulette wheel in the same room, a wheel that his entourage frequented. Yet this assignment afforded me a ringside view of Packer's legendary high-roller exploits.

Packer's wealth was more than a number; it was a media empire that dominated Australia's cultural conversation. His company, Consolidated Press Holdings, had its fingers in a multitude of pies, from newspapers and glossy magazines to television networks, all under his influential umbrella.

Yet it was the high-stakes gambling rooms around the world where Packer truly made his mark. He was the high-roller's high roller, placing bets that could make or break fortunes in a single evening. The potential losses for the house could even cause the stock price to temporarily dip after one of Packer's big wins, as I heard the CEO mention in one of his quarterly earnings calls. Without mentioning Packer by name, he just noted that the numbers were down due to some big losses from a few baccarat players. Packer's legendary betting sessions were the kind that spawned tales told with a mix of awe and disbelief.

Regarding temperament, billionaires are a mixed bag, but Packer was in a league of his own. His anticipated visits weren't met with dread, but a palpable buzz among the staff. His reputation for generosity was as vast as his fortune and his presence at the tables could mean a bumper crop in tips for the dealers. It wasn't just the baccarat dealers who benefited; his largesse was felt by the hundreds of dealers working that day, thanks to the pooled nature of the tips.

As I stood by my reserved roulette wheel, I witnessed Kerry Packer in his element at the baccarat table—a spectacle that never failed to captivate. On one notable occasion, I watched as he pushed forward a $100,000 bet, not for himself, but for the dealers. With a nod, he invited them to pick a side: banker or player. The dealers, perhaps feeling the weight of the moment, chose banker. The cards, however, had other plans, and the player won. Packer, unfazed by the outcome, placed another $100,000 bet on the table for the dealers. This extraordinary sequence unfolded nine times, with the tension—and the stakes—mounting with each bet. It was only on the 10th attempt that the dealers' choice came up victorious, much to the collective relief and exhilaration of everyone watching, myself included.

That kind of action wasn't always a thrill to watch, *unless* you had a stake in it. As I stood there, I knew exactly what my slice of each of those $100,000 bets would be. If the toke pool was being split 500 ways that day, every win would mean $200 extra in my pocket. Just one more reason the job never got old.

When the commission reached a staggering $90,000, Packer tossed four $25,000 chips onto the table without hesitation. When the dealer returned the two $5,000 chips as change, Packer quipped, "What am I supposed to do with these?" Just then, a waitress, not even his own, was passing by. Packer, with his characteristic nonchalance, dropped the chips onto her tray as if they were mere crumbs from the high-stakes table I was closely monitoring. And yes, his actual waitress? She was tipped handsomely for every drink she delivered.

Kerry Packer's visits to the Mirage were never short on spectacle or cash flow. On one occasion, after a few intense hours at the baccarat table, Packer and his entourage found themselves in need of a change of scenery. The action at the tables had hit a momentary pause and the group was itching for a bit of diversion. Their destination? Olympic Garden. Despite the name, you wouldn't find any floral displays or athletic competitions there—it was a gentleman's club and a well-known one.

For most visitors to Vegas, a night out at such a place might not raise any eyebrows. But when Packer's crew did it, it was a different story altogether. Packer had one of his associates fetch an envelope from the cashier's cage—a not-so-modest packet stuffed with $50,000 in crisp bills. He split the bounty among the five of them, each pocketing a cool $10,000 for their evening escapades. It's safe to say that the Olympic Garden's performers likely had one of their more lucrative evenings, courtesy of Packer and his high-rolling pals.

Kerry Packer was a high roller on a scale that most casinos didn't dare to accommodate. His appetite for risk and the colossal swings in fortune it could bring meant that a select few establishments would even consider letting him through their doors. Besides the Mirage, the MGM Grand was one of those places, at least initially.

When Packer graced the MGM Grand with his presence one night, he hit the baccarat tables hard, starting at $50,000 a hand. As his winning streak ignited, he upped the ante to $250,000 per hand. By the time the sun peeked over the horizon, Packer had amassed a cool $26 million.

The MGM Grand, however, wasn't too keen on being on the losing side of history. Overnight, they developed a new policy that might as well have been posted at the entrance: "No shirt, no shoes, no winning more than the GDP of a small island nation." Kerry Packer, having swelled his pockets by $26 million in a single night, was banned at the door. When the media quizzed MGM Grand's president & CEO, Frank Fahrenkopf, about the decision, he quipped, "We're in the gambling business. We don't gamble." It was a line that probably sounded better in the boardroom than it did echoing through the now Packer-less casino halls. And as Packer was ushered out of the MGM, the Mirage's dealers couldn't help but smile at their good fortune. Their loss was, quite literally, our gain.

The difference between catering to the two billionaires, Packer and Ahmet, was like night and day. Packer could occasionally be demanding, but those moments were easily overlooked, thanks to his incredible generosity. Ahmet, on the other hand, was difficult from the moment he arrived, with none of the charm or goodwill to soften the impact. While Packer's presence lifted the room, Ahmet's tended to drain it.

Looking back at my time in the Mirage's high-limit salon, I realize I wasn't just dealing cards and spinning wheels. I was witnessing a theater of human nature played out at its most extreme. Surrounded by masterpieces worth more than I'd make in several lifetimes, I watched as fortunes changed hands with the casual flip of a card or the bounce of a ball.

The surreal nature of this world never quite left me. Here I was, a kid from Buffalo who'd started dealing for 10-cent chips downtown, now pushing stacks worth more than most people's houses. The roulette ball didn't care if you were a Turkish billionaire prone to tantrums or an Australian media mogul who tipped waitresses $10,000—it bounced where it wanted, the ultimate equalizer in a room full of inequality.

But Ahmet and Packer weren't the only wild cards in the deck who shaped my Mirage years. Plenty more high-rollers were waiting in the wings, ready to turn the tables on us all.

Chapter 10
Mirage: Madness, Mayhem, and Markers

From Behind the Table: High-Stakes Hijinks and Vegas Absurdities

Amidst the glitz and glamour of the Mirage, some moments reminded us of the human stories behind the flashing lights and high stakes. One particular blackjack scene would have had the old Vegas guard scratching their heads at the growing compassion creeping into the casino world.

The dealer, who happened to be a woman, was presiding over the fate of a chap on a losing streak so epic that it could have inspired a country western song. His reserves had evaporated to the point where he was down to his last stand: nine crisp $100 bills and a scrappy assembly of smaller denominations that looked like they'd seen better days. With defiance and desperation, he declared, "Money plays!" as he planted his last financial soldiers on the battlefield of green felt.

He revealed a 20, and the atmosphere was tense. With a six showing, the dealer flipped a 10 and then, as if fate itself was twisting the knife, drew a 5 for a 21. The shell-shocked player cocooned his bet with his hands, then collapsed his head onto this makeshift pillow of despair. The dealer, embodying the patience of a saint, attempted to delicately lift his fingers one by one, a futile effort to liberate the money from his protective grasp.

And then, the dam broke: The player's eyes became fountains of sorrow. Not to be outdone, the dealer's own eyes mirrored his melancholy. Amidst his sobs, the player confessed that this cash was his golden ticket back to L.A. The floor supervisor, witnessing this emotional spectacle, was at a loss and promptly dialed Al, the shift boss, whose empathy was as scarce as a summer snowflake in the Nevada desert.

Al's directive was as blunt as a sledgehammer. "Put the money in the box," Al barked. Then, after a pause, he repeated, "Just put the money in the box already." And with a gruff nod to benevolence, he added, "If he's strapped for cab fare to the Hoover Dam, we'll spot him the cash." This was in the days before the mandatory sensitivity training from the HR department.

In a twist that could only happen in Sin City, the shift boss secured a hundred for his pilgrimage back to L.A. via Greyhound. But the tale doesn't end there. Like a boomerang, he returned the next day, this time jingling a handful of $5 chips. How he made it back is a mystery for the ages.

While some players left us shaking our heads in sympathy, others tested our patience in entirely different ways. My fellow dealer Angie had perfected the art of handling the latter.

Angie had been dealing cards in Vegas for over two decades and she'd seen it all, from high rollers to penny-pinchers, from lucky streaks to epic meltdowns. But tonight, she was dealing with a special breed of entitled: the "Do you know who I am?" guy.

Angie had been putting up with the guy's nonsense all night, handling the cards with both hands, signaling hits after busting, trying to slip chips in late. You name it, he tried it. Finally, she'd had enough.

"Sir," she said calmly but firmly, "you can't keep doing that.

This is a blackjack table, not a free-for-all."

He straightened in his seat, nostrils flaring like a cartoon rooster about to crow, and bellowed, "Do you know who I am?"

Without missing a beat, Angie glanced around theatrically, then raised her voice so the nearby tables could hear.

"Excuse me, everyone!" she called out, grinning as she gestured toward the table. "We've got a situation—this poor man appears to have no idea who he is!"

Heads turned. A few chuckles rippled out from a table nearby.

"If anyone finds a lost wallet, driver's license, or maybe one of those 'Hi, my name is …' stickers, please bring it up front," she added. "We're trying to help this gentleman remember his identity."

The laughter grew louder, even from a couple of the bosses pretending not to be watching. The guy's chest deflated like a cheap beach ball in August.

Angie gave him a sweet practiced smile. "Now, sir, while we wait for your memory to come back, what would you like to do with that sixteen? Hit? Or stand?"

He hit—and somehow, just like that, remembered every bit of proper player etiquette.

Not all our entertainment came from difficult players. Sometimes, the most memorable moments came just from watching the world around us.

Before I landed a steady spot in the high-limit room, I was dealing roulette on the main floor, a sweet gig in its own right. The place buzzed constantly and even with a packed table, we found ways to stay entertained.

Across from us sat the baccarat bar, prime viewing for eight hours a night. Over time, we began to notice patterns.

Between 4 and 6 a.m., the bar turned into a hotspot for unusually friendly young women, many of them regulars. We couldn't help but wonder if they thought this was *the* place to meet guys at that ungodly hour.

We even made a game of it, guessing how long it would take certain women to return to their barstools after leaving with new "friends." Some came back in twenty minutes, others an hour, a few not for days. The quick returners seemed fickle. And the guys, as the song goes, were looking for love in all the wrong places.

One morning around 9 a.m., a guy wandered into the bar wearing a bathrobe, looking like he'd just lost a fight with a ghost. He was explaining his night to the security personnel. Turns out, he'd brought a woman back to his room and when he woke up, his wallet, his clothes, his Rolex, and the woman were all gone.

He spent a while searching for his "dream girl," but she was probably working at another casino by then. And by that hour, the regulars had already called it a night, tucked in, and were resting up for their next shift.

The summer of 1993 brought both personal recognition and sobering reminders of the real world beyond our casino walls.

In late July 1993, I had the honor of being invited to a luncheon where a select group of us were competing for the title of Employee of the Month. To my astonishment, I was chosen. This accolade came with various gifts, cash prizes, and later, a trip for two to Hawaii at the grand Employee of the Month gala at the end of the year. Admittedly, the recognition was a double-edged sword. My picture seemed everywhere in the back of the house to the point where even I grew tired of my face. The grandeur peaked in the ballroom at the year-end banquet, where they displayed gargantuan photos of all 12 monthly winners, each the size of a garage door. After the event, we were told we could take these photos home. Imagine that—a garage door-sized portrait of me in my driveway? I decided to pass, letting it find its way, presumably, to the dump.

However, that memorable Tuesday afternoon of July 27, 1993, had a shadow cast over it. Steve Wynn, the man everyone expected to present the award and share a congratulatory handshake, was conspicuously absent. In his stead, Bobby Baldwin stepped in. The gravity of Steve's absence became clear soon after.

The day before, Steve Wynn's daughter, Kevyn Wynn, had been kidnapped at gunpoint from her residence in the luxurious Spanish Trail golf course community. The news of this crime not only shook southern Nevada, but also reverberated across the U.S. and internationally.

Following a haunting call from the kidnappers, Mr. Wynn, as per their chilling instructions, went to The Mirage's casino cage to withdraw $1.45 million in cash. After having the ransom delivered to a bar's parking lot on Spring Mountain Road, near the Mirage, he was directed to where he could find his daughter. She was discovered, tied up but unharmed, in the back seat of her car in a long-term parking lot at what is now known as Harry Reid International Airport.

The culprits behind this heinous act weren't free for long. Ray Cuddy, after foolishly attempting to buy a Ferrari in Newport Beach with a substantial cash payment, was arrested, as was his accomplice, Jacob Sherwood. Both were found guilty of kidnapping, extortion, and money laundering by a federal jury. Cuddy served two decades behind bars, gaining his freedom in 2015. A third conspirator, Anthony Watkins, chose to cooperate with the authorities and, as a result, received a reduced sentence of six and a half years.

On Monday morning, January 17, 1994, there was an unusual lull for that time of year. The New Year's revelers had departed and we were still a few weeks away from Chinese New Year and the

Super Bowl. I'd been at my game for only about half an hour when I felt an odd sensation—somewhat dizzy, a bit queasy, as if my knees were about to give out.

Glancing around, I noticed similar expressions of confusion on the faces of those nearby. A woman dealer at the blackjack table across from me abruptly sat down. Within seconds, I saw the chandelier swaying above me in the main baccarat room. Having experienced the slight vibrations from the occasional underground nuclear tests at the Nevada Test Site, just 65 miles away, I immediately knew this was different. Those tests had been halted years ago and this sensation was far more intense. That's when it hit me: We were experiencing an earthquake.

The quake's epicenter was about 250 miles away in Los Angeles. Known as the Northridge Earthquake, it registered a magnitude of 6.7. After the shaking subsided, murmurs filled the room as people tried to understand what had happened. Soon, hotel guests in their robes began descending to the ground floor. The swaying we felt was amplified dramatically for those guests on the higher floors, up to the 30th.

Rushing to the dealer's lounge during my break, I joined everyone in the room to watch the news. The Northridge Earthquake was the costliest natural disaster in U.S. history at the time, with damages totaling $20 billion and 57 lives lost. As we watched the live news coverage from L.A., the anchors suddenly dove under their desks during an aftershock. Oddly enough, we felt the same shaking a few minutes later, although much less intense.

Guests who had come down to the ground floor were accommodated in a ballroom until the building was deemed safe. I'm sure some opted for lower floors and less sway if they were available.

The earthquake served as a wake-up call, prompting the establishment of an emergency training program. We were given instructions that during emergencies, we would lift the lid on our games, wait for the supervisor to lock up the bankroll, and proceed to designated meeting areas.

I've got to be honest, though. If I were to see a fire, hear about a toxic threat, or face an active shooter situation, I'd be inclined to flee the scene rapidly. I imagine the person I'd be waiting on to lock up my game would probably already have bolted ahead of me. While the emergency plan looked good on paper and likely satisfied some lawyers and insurers, one couldn't help but wonder how effective it would be in a real disaster. But hey, some training is better than none.

The Mirage finally grabbed that corner lot with the rundown apartment complex. Still, instead of expanding our upscale oasis, the bosses planned to build something entirely new next door: Treasure Island. This pirate-themed spot was geared toward families and budget travelers—think swashbuckling shows and kid-friendly vibes, a far cry from the high-roller glamor I loved at the Mirage. Construction kicked off in '91, with plans for massive pirate ships and a theater that could host a small army, all set to open in under two years. They even ramped up hiring in '92, scouting for 5,000 new faces.

Me? I stayed put. Why would I want to deal blackjack in some cheesy pirate costume when I could be mingling with high-rollers? Little did I know, TI would soon host one of the wildest characters I'd ever hear about, straight from my buddies who made the move for those ladder-climbing gigs.

It was a sleepy Sunday morning in April of '95 when Patty, a floor supervisor over at Treasure Island, who had recently transferred from the Mirage graveyard shift, rang us up. She had a story too strange not to be true, or at least too good not to retell. A player had walked into TI who didn't exactly match the resort-casual crowd.

Picture this: an octogenarian, barefoot, disheveled, looking like he just rolled out of a cardboard box under an overpass. Word was, people had seen him pushing a shopping cart just off the Strip the night before. Nobody knew where he came from, but he showed up at a blackjack table with $400 in his pocket. Social Security check? Panhandling jackpot? Did he sell his dentures to a pawn shop? Take your pick.

The guy said his name was Joe, though nobody ever got a last name. Dealers quickly gave him a nickname: *Shoeless Joe.* And not in the romantic *Field of Dreams* way. This guy was a grumpy, foul-mouthed, hygiene-optional character who treated the casino like it was his living room.

He kicked things off with a warm greeting to the dealer: "You can wipe that smirk off your face. You're not getting one red nickel from me!"

And he meant it. Joe never tipped. Not a dime. Not even after doubling or tripling his buy-in. Daryl, one of the dealers, said he didn't even crack a grin when Joe hit big hands—just grumbled and asked for another pork chop. That's right, he was literally eating leftover pork chops from the restaurant *at the table.*

Worse yet, he was especially vile to female dealers, so much so that management eventually stopped assigning them to his game altogether. Rob, another dealer, remembered him casually using the most offensive slurs and vulgarities, as if they were punctuation. The guy was, to put it kindly, a walking HR violation.

But here's where it gets truly Vegas: The guy started winning. First, he turned that $400 into $10,000. Then $100,000. By the time our shift ended at the Mirage, we got another call from the folks at Treasure Island. Joe was reportedly sitting on half a million.

Some said he even reached $1.6 million at the peak of his run. Whether that number's real or just got polished up in the retelling, who knows? But everyone agreed it was one of the wildest streaks they'd ever seen. It became the talk of the break room at TI and made its way up and down the Strip like wildfire.

Now, how the story ends depends on who you ask. Some say he lost it all. Others say the casino finally cut him off when he still had about fifty grand left. But one thing's for sure: Joe didn't trust the cage. He refused to let them cut a check. He walked out of there with whatever money he had stuffed into his pockets—likely the only guy in Vegas carrying tens of thousands of dollars while barefoot and smelling like pork chops.

The *Washington Post* even picked up the story, describing it as pieced together from "hushed whispers and boisterous bar conversation by dealers and waitresses and fellow players." Snopes lists the whole thing as "undetermined."

But trust me, it happened. Maybe not every number or detail, but the man, the moment, and the madness? That was real.

He may have been rude, smelly, and vile, but for one chaotic weekend in Vegas, Shoeless Joe ran the table.

Back to the Mirage, what truly set it apart in the '90s was its magnetic pull on celebrities, turning it into the epicenter of a bolder, brasher, Vegas glamor. As a dealer, I quickly learned that stars shine brightest when they're betting big—or behaving badly, whether it was Rodman's wild entourage strutting in like a circus parade or Jackson slipping through the shadows like a ghost.

Vegas was exploding as the world's entertainment capital and the Mirage? It was ground zero for the buzz: athletes letting loose at visible tables with a security guard for that faux-privacy drama, whispers rippling through the crowd, and an electric vibe that made every shift feel like a front-row seat to the show.

It always made me wonder: Do these folks crave anonymity or thrive on attention? I mean, if you're all about privacy, you probably wouldn't be playing roulette or blackjack near the main floor at 10 p.m. on a Saturday, right?

Regardless, their presence was a win for all involved. The atmosphere shifted, whispers circulated, and you could feel the excitement in the air. Something extraordinary was happening and it only added to the allure and mystique of the casino during that golden era.

Celebrities at that time were everywhere at the Mirage; most seemed like everyday regular folks.

But let's talk about Dennis Rodman. Ah, the Worm! This guy was not just one of the most unique and flamboyant athletes of the '90s; he brought that same flair to his gambling and partying. Picture this: Rodman strut into the casino with his eclectic entourage and leading the pack was the man himself—all six feet seven inches of him. His hair was some wild color du jour, tattoos splashed across his skin, and facial jewelry that could rival a pirate's treasure.

Here's the highlight: his sidekick, Verne Troyer, aka Mini-Me from the Austin Powers movies. Standing at a mere two feet eight inches, Troyer rode on Rodman's shoulders as they approached my table. Once there, Mini-Me hopped onto a chair next to Dennis, stood on the seat, and joined the cheering squad. The whole scene was like a surreal painting, where every brushstroke adds another layer of fascination. Rodman knew how to party and he did it like a pro. I was just as entertained dealing to this circus as they were entertained by playing.

Another celebrity who was at the peak of his game in the '90s, fresh off *Die Hard* and a string of blockbuster hits, was Bruce

Mirage: Madness, Mayhem, and Markers 131

Willis. He gambled at the Mirage often, usually strolling up to my roulette table without any fanfare. No entourage, no attitude. Just that trademark smirk and a laid-back swagger.

Unlike Rodman, whose presence screamed lawlessness, Bruce came off like a charismatic everyman—cool, sharp, and genuinely friendly. He chatted about the odds like we were old friends, maybe dropped a few bets, and kept the vibe light.

One night in particular, the table was dead and I was just standing there when Bruce sauntered up and said, "Fire that baby up." I gave the wheel a spin, he tossed a bet on red, and won big. He cracked a grin, gave a little fist pump, tipped me, and moved on. No scene, no ego—just Bruce being Bruce.

Next to Rodman, he looked downright Zen. But then again, anyone would.

One fateful night in 1994, Joe Pesci was engrossed in a game of baccarat in the high-limit room, right next to the roulette table where I was dealing. As he walked by, he noticed that the reader board on my game displayed five consecutive black numbers. Intrigued, he paused and dropped a couple of black chips ($100 each) on red.

He had a minor meltdown after losing a couple of rounds and upping his bet. It was just him and me; no audience, no fanfare. He mumbled something about the game being rigged and questioned the entire play. It was odd, especially considering it was just a couple of bets.

A year later, I saw him in the movie *Casino*, playing a character based on Tony Spilotro. In one scene, he's screaming at the dealer and hurling cards. It made me wonder if that night at the Mirage was some method-acting rehearsal for the film. The timing would have been right, given when *Casino* was shot. We'll never know for sure, but it does add an extra layer of intrigue to an already peculiar encounter. If that was method acting—and I guess that's what you'd call it—he sure committed to the bit. Maybe he wanted to see how it felt to lose it to a dealer in a real casino, just to make it look more authentic on camera.

It's amusing to think about how fame doesn't always travel well. In front of me was a lively group of Chinese players—laughing, betting big, clearly having a great time. No entourage, no spotlight. No one else in the room paid them any mind. Just another group of high rollers doing their thing.

Then the host leaned over and quietly said, "See that guy?" He nodded toward one of the more animated players, who was clapping and singing softly between hands. "That's the Chinese Elton John."

I glanced over. He did have a kind of flamboyant energy—bright blazer, tinted glasses, rings on every finger—but if the host hadn't said anything, I'd have just figured he was another enthusiastic VIP. Turned out he was a pop superstar back home. Stadiums. Fan mobs. Huge record sales. And here? Just another guy trying to beat the banker.

One evening in the salon, right after we'd opened and while no guests were playing, we had an unexpected celebrity drop-in. It was Steve Wynn himself, giving a VIP tour to Donald Trump and his then-wife, Ivana. Wynn proudly showcased the various amenities and said, "These are some of my best people working here," giving us a nice ego boost.

What struck me as odd was the chummy atmosphere between the two men. At that time, they were supposed to be archrivals in the Atlantic City casino scene and the industry at large. This friendly encounter seemed at odds with the public narrative. And sure enough, their rivalry would only intensify in the years that followed, complete with media spats and legal battles.

The Mirage wasn't just a playground for the usual suspects—movie stars, TV icons, and sports legends—it was also a nexus for the affluent and influential from across the globe. One such luminary was Guy Laliberté, who effortlessly straddled the worlds of entrepreneurship and entertainment.

Laliberté, the enterprising co-founder of Cirque du Soleil, had a backstory that read like a fairytale. Starting as a performer on the streets of Canada, he transformed his flair for the dramatic into the foundation of a global entertainment juggernaut. At the Mirage, Cirque du Soleil made its Vegas debut in 1990 with *Nouvelle Experience*. The show was a hit, pivotal in establishing the troupe's reputation as a staple of the Las Vegas entertainment landscape.

At the roulette table, Guy was disarmingly low-key. He confidently placed $1,000 chips across the layout and in a gesture of camaraderie, an occasional $1,000 bet for me as well. It was a grand gesture from someone who, just a few years prior, had been perfecting his craft on the cobblestones of Quebec.

Michael Jackson was one celebrity who was a regular at the Mirage, yet preferred the shadows to the spotlight. He wasn't just a guest; he practically had a long-term lease on one of the villas. But he didn't parade through the casino or show up poolside with a crowd. Instead, he became something of a Vegas legend for how quietly he came and went. Most guests had no clue he was even in the building. He had special arrangements for after-hours access to Siegfried & Roy's Secret Garden and the Dolphin Habitat—places that, for the rest of us, closed at sundown. But for Michael, they stayed open just a little longer ... minus the crowds, minus the cameras.

His route around the Mirage was the stuff of spy movies. He skipped the main floor entirely, gliding through employee entrances, staff hallways, and executive corridors that most of us only saw during fire drills or mandatory HR meetings. It was said that even his villa was outfitted with hidden exits and back-of-house access, allowing him to move from his suite to the dolphins without ever coming into contact with the public. The King of Pop may have lived in the shadows at the Mirage, but that just added to the mystique. For all the lights and noise of the Strip, he was one of the few who could vanish into the back hallways like a magician disappearing behind a curtain—except in this case, the curtain was a fire door labeled "Authorized Personnel Only."

Yet there was a moment when Michael Jackson was the star of a public spectacle. It was when the pirate ship, destined to be the centerpiece of a nightly spectacle at Treasure Island, was paraded down the Strip. Jackson stood proudly on the deck, basking in the cheers of the onlookers—a rare moment of embracing the public gaze.

As I reflect on these moments from the Mirage's golden era, I realize they captured something essential about what made this place special.

These ships later became the backdrop for a nightly spectacle—full-sized galleons battling in mock combat, pirates swinging through the rigging, defeated buccaneers plunging into the lagoon below. At Treasure Island's grand opening, Steve Wynn gave the command and the first cannon thundered to life. But in classic Vegas fashion, one boom wasn't enough. That cannon blast wasn't just the start of a show. It was the cue for the Dunes Hotel, farther down the Strip, to meet its dramatic end in a perfectly timed implosion. Only in Vegas was blowing up a hotel part of the opening act.

This spectacle wasn't just about marking Treasure Island's debut; it was the overture to the next act in Vegas's ever-evolving show, the birth of Bellagio. As the dust settled from the Dunes implosion and the applause for Treasure Island's opening faded, all eyes turned to the future. The Mirage had set a new standard, Treasure Island had broadened the appeal, but Bellagio? That was poised to redefine luxury and sophistication in a city that thought it had seen it all.

Standing there, witnessing this dramatic transition, I couldn't help but reflect on my journey. From the humble beginnings at the break-in joints downtown to the glitz and glamor of the Strip, I'd seen Las Vegas transform. The Mirage had been a turning point, not

Mirage: Madness, Mayhem, and Markers

just for the city, but for me.

But as the saying goes, the only constant in life is change. And in Las Vegas, change is the lifeblood that keeps the city pulsing. With Bellagio on the horizon, I knew my journey was far from over. There were new challenges, new characters to meet, and new tales to be a part of. The Mirage may have been the star of the '90s, but the future? That was an unwritten script, waiting for us to make our mark.

Chapter 11
Bellagio: Welcome to the Show

When Luxury Redefined Las Vegas

Nestled on the Las Vegas Strip is a patch of desert with a wild history, from the dry Las Vegas Wash to the glitzy Dunes Hotel-Casino that rose in 1955, drawing crowds with its entertainment flair. By the '90s, though, it was time for a shake-up. In 1992, Steve Wynn snapped up the Dunes, all 163 acres of it, including a huge golf course that ran nearly all the way down to Tropicana Avenue, for $75 million, not even a half-million an acre compared to today's low of $6 million and high of $40 million per. Unbelievably, the Japanese owner of the Dunes, Masao Nangaku, first approached the owners of Caesars to buy the property, but they turned him down flat, saying, "What could we possibly do with all that land?" Wynn then stepped in, picked it up for a song, and had as big a plan as Caesars had none: to demolish the Dunes in order to construct a luxury landmark inspired by Italy's Bellagio village on Lake Como—a resort poised to redefine the Strip's skyline.

Construction began in 1995 and by 1998, Bellagio had emerged as a $1.6 billion marvel, the most expensive casino ever, hailed as Vegas's new crown jewel. But for us dealers at the Mirage, this wasn't just another shiny addition. It was another game-changer, promising opportunity, while stirring up unexpected rifts among the team.

Working for the Mirage Corporation offered a unique advantage: the chance to transition to new and exciting properties before the onset of job fatigue. No need to resign and start anew elsewhere; we could advance within the company, retaining the comfort of familiar procedures, seniority, colleagues, and even many of our regular players.

However, being selected for the move from the Mirage to Bellagio brought its own set of anxieties. It wasn't as straightforward as the leap from downtown to the Mirage, where nearly all the Golden Nugget staff were essential for the Mirage's opening. Bellagio's staffing situation was different, more selective.

Only about half of the Mirage dealers were chosen. This created intense tension over the ensuing months between those selected and those left behind, even among long-time friends. The workplace became a breeding ground for strained relationships as two opposing teams began forming. Those moving faced subtle and not-so-subtle resentments from colleagues who weren't selected. The selection criteria were unclear and shrouded in mystery, further fueling the division.

At the time, most of us assumed we'd be heading to Bellagio, just like the Nugget crew had moved up to the Mirage when it opened. So when the first acceptance letters started arriving, no one panicked if theirs didn't show up that day. You know how the mail is. I even joked with my buddy Bob when he didn't get his letter right away, saying, "I guess you're staying here," never imagining that would actually be the case. But as the days went by and no more letters arrived, that light-hearted optimism gave way to real anxiety. For those who hadn't been selected, hope slowly faded until it was gone.

The emotional wounds ran deep and the scars lingered long after the transition. Some dealers who were assured a place at Bellagio when needs arose later refused the invitation—the bitterness of being initially passed over still fresh in their minds. The once tight-knit community of dealers was fractured. I found myself caught between survivor's guilt and genuine excitement—grateful to be chosen, but acutely aware of the friends I'd be leaving behind. Every congratulation felt tinged with an unspoken goodbye.

Groups of once-inseparable friends who gathered at birthday parties, backyard barbecues, and post-shift happy hours slowly drifted apart. It was like the high school clique that suddenly splinters before graduation; the camaraderie that once defined their social lives now gave way to awkward silences and guarded conversations. Even simple get-togethers became complicated. Where once there were group invites and shared laughs, there were now side invites and unspoken stress. For some, the sting wasn't just about missing out on Bellagio—it was about feeling left behind by the people they'd shared so many late nights and big moments with.

Interestingly, not all dealers were eager for the change. A few were content with the well-worn familiarity of their current roles, preferring the devil they knew. Adding to the dynamic was a new requirement that hadn't existed for previous openings: mandatory drug testing, which also influenced some dealers' decisions about whether to even pursue the opportunity. One fellow dealer valiantly abstained from his daily marijuana ritual for two grueling months, clinging to the hope of being selected for the Bellagio move, only to face the bitter disappointment of being passed over.

Amidst the buzz, another unspoken truth hung over us: The Mirage was headed for a slowdown. Bellagio's shiny allure would siphon off the top high-rollers, those whales who'd become like fixtures in our pits. I overheard whispers in the break room—"They're pouring everything into the new place"—as the company pivoted to crown it Vegas's ultimate luxury spot. This shift stirred a weird mix of thrill and dread; we were excited for the future, but it meant uncertainty for our jobs and the bonds we'd built with colleagues left behind.

Launching something new always brings its own thrill, but launching a spectacle like Bellagio was a whole different ballgame. This wasn't just another casino; it was the sequel to the Mirage blockbuster and the buzz was that it would outshine its predecessor. Expectations weren't just high—they were stratospheric.

In the run-up to the grand opening, we were swamped with training sessions and meetings. They drilled us on procedures and familiarized us with the property's nooks and crannies. During some of these sessions, I realized they were rehashing procedures I could probably do in my sleep. So I seized the opportunity to sneak away for some reconnaissance around the new kingdom.

On one such covert operation a few days before opening day, I was on a secluded patio overlooking the front lake. It was 4 a.m. midweek, when even the Strip seemed to quiet down a bit. In what felt like a private moment stolen from the frenzy of preparation, the baccarat manager, Paul, was also there, gazing contemplatively over the water. He picked up a phone and, with a touch of drama, requested "Luck Be a Lady Tonight." Suddenly, the night air was filled with Frank Sinatra's unmistakable voice and the lake started to put on a show. As Sinatra's song ended, the mood shifted seamlessly with the opening notes of "Time to Say Goodbye" by Andrea Bocelli and Sarah Brightman. Now swaying and twirling to this poignant duet, the fountains created a mesmerizing spectacle. It was a private show, a majestic fountain transformed into a jukebox with an extremely exclusive playlist. Watching those waters dance to the back-to-back melodies, I knew we were on the brink of something extraordinary.

Before this moment, I'd heard rumors about the fountains being built at the front of the resort, but witnessing them firsthand during this testing period was a revelation. I had no idea how spectacular

Bellagio: Welcome to the Show

these fountains, which would soon become one of Las Vegas's iconic trademarks, would be.

The sparse traffic on the Strip at that hour came to a halt out front, captivated by this phenomenon. This later posed a challenge when we opened, as traffic along the Strip nearly halved with everyone eager to witness the jaw-dropping free spectacle.

That private dawn show revealed the fountains' true genius; they weren't just pretty, they were an engineering beast, built by a massive team for $40 million. With 1,214 jets and 4,792 lights syncing to the music, they crafted everything from dancing sprays to towering water sculptures, blasting garbage-can-sized streams 460 feet skyward. But syncing it all was just the start; maintaining this 22-million-gallon monster meant scuba divers for underwater fixes—way trickier than tending a giant fish tank. And security? Well, that was a whole other headache, with fences around the lake and guards fending off drunks eyeing a free swim.

Despite the fences, guards, and warning signs there was always a supply of drunk and sometimes sober knuckleheads attempting to take a dip in the perilous waters. Perhaps they fancied themselves being launched 460 feet into the air like an amusement-park ride. Security, however, wasn't amused by these reckless antics, nor were the crowds of onlookers anxiously awaiting the fountain show, only to have it delayed while one of these foolhardy daredevils was fished out.

As training wrapped up, we followed the familiar routine of a playday, similar to what we'd experienced with the Mirage. Then, just before the grand opening, came our motivational speech from Steve Wynn. Standing hours away from unveiling this architectural and engineering marvel, he downplayed the architectural grandeur.

Instead, he emphasized that we, the staff, made the place special and brought it to life. While I suspected he didn't mean it literally, it was exactly what we needed to hear. He shifted the focus from the splendor of the building to the significance of the staff.

In an environment where perfection was the expectation and amidst the inevitable imperfections due to the operation's newness and complexities, his words likely offered much-needed reassurance to many of the new employees. The last thing we needed was for staff members to be overwhelmed by the pressure to maintain absolute perfection.

Even with Wynn's pep talk ringing in our ears, a jittery buzz hummed through the staff—we were hours from unleashing the world's priciest resort, a $1.6 billion beast meant to eclipse everything Vegas had seen. Months of rumors had us all on edge: whispers of opulent escapes where guests could ditch the everyday for pure elegance.

Those of us who'd been with the company through this kind of action tried to calm the new crew members, who'd never seen the high-stakes frenzy they'd be dealing to shortly. We did our best, but we had our own butterflies fluttering. Las Vegas, that neon playground of dreams and long shots, was about to flip the script on luxury. And on October 15, 1998, as Bellagio swung open its doors, we stepped into another chapter of the city's wild history.

Opening night was nothing short of a star-studded spectacle. Celebrities from every corner of fame—Michael Jordan, Clint Eastwood, Drew Barrymore, and a host of other A-listers—graced the red carpet, drawing a sea of onlookers that stretched halfway down the Strip. As the doors officially opened, a surge of eager guests poured into the lobby.

Bellagio: Welcome to the Show

You could feel the collective gasp ripple through the crowd as they looked up at the ceiling; 2,000 hand-blown glass blossoms suspended above them in a riot of color. The piece, called *Fiori di Como* by renowned glass artist Dale Chihuly, spanned over 2,000 square feet and for many, it was their first encounter with large-scale museum-quality art in a casino lobby. Cameras flashed. Heads tilted back. Some just stood there, mouths open, trying to take it all in.

Moments later, they were drawn forward again, this time to the front of the property, where the lake came alive with its own performance. The fountains—syncing jets of water with lights and music—danced to Sinatra's "Luck Be a Lady," and then in a dramatic shift, swayed to Andrea Bocelli and Sarah Brightman's "Time to Say Goodbye." Cars on Las Vegas Boulevard came to a halt as people gathered at the edge of the water, transfixed. You could see it in their faces. This wasn't just a casino opening; it was a moment, a memory in the making. Guests even clapped after the fountain show, like they were at a Broadway opening night.

I was in the heart of it all, dealing baccarat on swing shift. The energy in the casino was electric, the air thick with anticipation and excitement. Navigating through the massive crowds, I found my spot in the high-limit area, which offered a little more breathing room amidst the packed casino floor. That night, I had the pleasure of dealing to two notable celebrities: a well-tanned George Hamilton, his signature bronze hue unmistakable, and Don Johnson, riding high on the popularity of his hit TV series, "Miami Vice." Hamilton's deep tan somehow managed to glow even under the casino's carefully calibrated lighting. At the same time, Johnson worked the room with the easy confidence of someone who knew every eye was on him.

I couldn't help but notice the opening-night crowd wasn't just high rollers and stars—it was packed with wide-eyed sightseers who'd never touch a table, drawn in purely by the hype, eager to claim a piece of the spectacle. As a dealer, I watched them flood the floor, dodging between bets to gawk at the Chihuly glass blossoms blooming overhead or rush outside for the fountain's symphony. The place overwhelmed them like a tidal wave of color, light, and sheer opulence. It hit me then: They weren't here for the games; they were witnessing Vegas history unfold, a shift where luxury became the star, not just the stakes.

As stunning as Bellagio was, I couldn't wait to ditch the swing shift frenzy and slide back into my graveyard groove, dealing European roulette under quieter lights. Those overnight hours still drew plenty of high-rollers and celebs, but without the swing-shift circus. It was my routine, steady and familiar. I hadn't chosen swing for opening night; with spots in such demand, even we veterans knew better than to quibble over shifts or days off. Just grab the ticket to the new place and sort it later. Sure enough, after a couple of weeks in the spotlight, I finagled my way back to graveyard, breathing easier amid the calm. It felt like reclaiming a piece of the old Vegas amid this shiny new world.

I soon realized that I was witnessing the exact moment Las Vegas stopped trying to be accessible to everyone.

The Mirage had opened the door to luxury, but Bellagio walked through it and locked it behind them. Those hand-blown glass flowers in the lobby weren't just art; they were a declaration. The days of $1.99 steak dinners and dealers in clip-on bow ties were officially laid to rest under Italian marble and Belgian linen.

I thought about my friends back at the Mirage, dealing the same games to the same limits, but somehow everything had changed. We'd all started together downtown, survivors of the same break-in joints and graveyard shifts. Now there was an invisible line between us, not just the few blocks between properties.

Chapter 12
Bellagio: The Glamorous Circus

An Insider's Take Where Fortune, Fame, and Folly Intersect

Back in my graveyard groove after Bellagio's whirlwind opening, the initial hype had simmered, but the wild ride was just revving up. From my roulette spot, I caught glimpses of Hollywood stars slipping in post-filming or eccentric billionaires treating the floor like their playground—reminders that this wasn't just luxury; it was a circus of fortune and folly. Little did I know, my shifts were about to deliver even more unforgettable craziness.

The announcement was made that director Steven Soderbergh would be remaking a '60s Las Vegas movie originally featuring the Rat Pack. The movie was *Ocean's Eleven*, a classic heist film set in the glitzy world of Las Vegas casinos. People flocked from all over to snag parts as extras and my fellow roulette dealer, Tony, even landed a spot where he had a line as a baccarat player. Much of the filming took place in Las Vegas, with a significant portion at Bellagio.

The cast stayed at Bellagio and could often be found playing blackjack or poker together, usually in the wee hours. This was partly due to their schedules and partly to avoid the crowds. One night at 4 a.m., the whole gang was at a blackjack table around in the high-limit room. I was stationed at the adjacent roulette wheel, observing the action.

A woman from the group walked over and sat at my table. As I spun the roulette ball, she placed two $25 chips on the table. Unfortunately, it was a $1,000 minimum bet table, with $100 chips the smallest denomination accepted. I apologized and informed her of the minimums. She reacted loudly, demanding, "Do you know who I am?" I had to admit I didn't. She claimed to be Matt Damon's girlfriend, though I doubted it, given the high-limit vibe. I apologized again, but reiterated the table's minimum bet.

Apart from this incident, Matt Damon was a frequent and welcome presence at Bellagio during this time. He was often seen in the poker room, learning about high-limit poker. He also played blackjack on the graveyard shift. You couldn't ask for a nicer guy, a joy to deal with, just as he appears in many of his movies.

Much of the filming took place in the casino, and the graveyard shift was the ideal time for it. One scene involved Andy Garcia, playing casino owner Terry Benedict, being filmed right in the middle of the high-limit room between a couple of baccarat tables. The crew probably thought these tables would be quiet by 6 a.m. when they started filming. However, one game was still in full swing, with one of our Chinese guests betting at least $100,000 a hand, his entourage filling the table with cheers. No one dared ask him to move.

The decision was made to proceed with the scene. Garcia walked between the tables, with the camera and dolly tracking down the middle of the room. The high-stakes baccarat game was strategically out of the camera's view, so it wouldn't interfere with the scene. Everything went flawlessly. Garcia looked at a book with some numbers, slammed it closed, and marched down the length of the room, seemingly upset by what he had read. As he passed the baccarat table, the scene ended. At that exact moment, the high-roller won a $100,000 hand, and his group stood up and cheered. Garcia, accustomed to applause, turned to the group, acknowledged them, and moved on.

Everything worked out: The actor was happy with the adulation and the group of Asian players probably had no clue who he was or what was going on in the aisle next to them. A win-win. I just watched the show, a silent observer to this unexpected intersection of Hollywood glamor and the high-stakes world of the casino. It was moments like these that made life in Vegas an experience unlike any other, a place where the extraordinary became ordinary and every night held the potential for something magical. These encounters were uniquely characteristic of my time at Bellagio, a resort that seemed to effortlessly blend the world of entertainment with the excitement of gaming.

As for the Chinese gamblers, the Chan family was a group of international billionaires who were regulars at Bellagio. Hailing from Malaysia and Singapore, they're known for dabbling in just about everything – banking, real estate, hospitality, you name it. Their hotel interests are particularly impressive, with a portfolio that reads like a who's who of luxury hotels around the globe.

For several years, the Chans had a tradition of descending upon Bellagio during Christmas, before jetting off to Vail for a New Year's ski session. It was like watching the migration of extremely wealthy birds, only with private jets instead of wings.

One Christmas morning, I found myself in the reserved room where they were playing baccarat. To them, Christmas morning was probably just another Wednesday, cultural and religious differences and all that. They paused their game for a bite to eat. Now, with their level of play, they could have dined anywhere, from the finest restaurants to the most exclusive rooms in the villas. But no, they chose to dine right at the baccarat table. Why not? Rules, as it turns out, are more like gentle suggestions when you're a multimillionaire or billionaire.

I watched the butler take orders and set up side tables next to the table. My curiosity piqued. What does one of the wealthiest families on the planet eat on Christmas morning? The possibilities were endless, assuming they'd prearranged something exotic. If not, whatever the Bellagio chefs whipped up would no doubt be nothing short of culinary wizardry.

After a short wait, the butlers rolled up with covered serving tables. The big reveal was upon us. I leaned in, expecting caviar, truffles, maybe a gold-leafed something or other. But no, it was hot dogs. Yes, hot dogs with all the fixings. The lifestyles of the rich and famous, indeed.

I couldn't help but chuckle at the irony. Later that day, I'd be sitting down to a traditional Christmas feast with all the trimmings: turkey, ham, stuffing, the works, a meal that would undoubtedly leave me loosening my belt and slipping into a food coma. Meanwhile, these billionaires were scarfing down hot dogs for their Christmas breakfast. It was a stark reminder that money doesn't always equate with extravagance or tradition.

It reminded me of my favorite Turkish billionaire roulette player, who shared that down-to-earth, bordering on stingy, vibe. Win or lose millions, his ritual stayed the same: sending his host for a greasy bag of In-N-Out Burgers, never paying for the run or even offering to cover the food. He barked, "No sodas! We've got drinks in the villa!" And get this. Unlike most whales jetting private, he flew commercial just for the airfare-reimbursement comp post-trip—though I doubt it was coach, even if possible. But the real kicker? He had someone raid the buffet for meats to pack sandwiches for the flight. Apparently, nothing screams high roller quite like DIY airline grub amid all the extravagance.

Not all of us had the luxury of that kind of whimsy during the holidays. For dealers, working through Christmas or New Year's was just part of the job.

Bellagio: The Glamorous Circus

Holidays were celebrated differently from the traditional ways most of us grew up with, partly because many of us were uprooted from our families, but also due to the nature of casino work schedules. Working holidays was part of the job, which created unique challenges. Santa's deliveries had to remain undisturbed until the afternoon for parents with small children working Christmas morning. Single dealers or those without young children often tried to switch days off to help their coworkers with kids.

New Year's Eve, however, offered little flexibility for scheduling switches—it was all hands on deck. Celebrating looked different depending on your age and stamina. For older folks like me, it meant an early dinner around 5:30 p.m. and pushing our limits to stay awake until 9 p.m. The younger more energetic crowd partied until midnight before heading to work. Walking into the casino at 4 a.m. on New Year's Day was always wild, with the celebration still going strong, though it finally began to taper off a few hours later.

As in any workplace, romance sometimes bloomed among casino coworkers. This was especially true among graveyard workers, whose unusual hours created a unique social bubble separate from the rest of the world. Our schedules made meeting people outside the industry challenging, as few could relate to our reversed days and nights. This is how I met my wife, Debbie, in the mid-'80s when she was dealing at the Golden Nugget. Our shared understanding of the casino lifestyle and compatible schedules helped forge a lasting bond. We've been together ever since.

One of our less-than-favorite regulars was a "gentleman" I'll call Mr. X, who owned a gentlemen's club. He was like a character you'd expect to see on "The Sopranos"—gold pinky ring, silk shirt unbuttoned one button too many, and enough cologne to keep vampires and most cocktail servers at bay. Rumor had it that his establishment bore a striking resemblance to the Bada Bing from the TV show.

On one occasion, Mr. X was playing in a secluded game at the back of the private area, in a room all to himself. Accompanying him were a couple of his employees, two young ladies who seemed very friendly and bubbly. I think one was even named Bubbles and the other might have been Tiffany. They were the perfect cheerleaders for our player, full of enthusiasm and quite animated after every winning hand.

My buddy Tim was dealing at Mr. X's table and it was clear to everyone, including Mr. X, that Tim was having the time of his life, probably finding it hard to focus on his job. To make Tim's life even more "challenging," Mr. X, betting $5,000 a hand, started stacking his winnings off to the side. The pile grew to about 15 chips, totaling $75,000. As a form of "motivation" for Tim to keep losing, Mr. X promised that if the stack reached $100,000, the girls would offer a little "show" of their talents, despite their already skimpy attire.

Sure enough, the starry-eyed Tim hit the $100,000 mark and true to his word, the top-heavy duo provided a quick glimpse of their "skills." Usually, I would have looked away, but as a diligent employee, I figured someone had to keep an eye on the chip rack to ensure nothing went amiss during the distraction.

A few months after that memorable night, Mr. X was back, this time at a blackjack table in the regular high-limit area on a reserved game. By the time our shift started, he was already deep in the hole and in a particularly foul mood, even for him. His usual unpleasant demeanor was amplified and he was putting on quite the show, minus his usual entourage of cheerleaders. As his losses mounted, so did his swearing and cursing. He became convinced that the dealers were to blame and demanded they be replaced, one after another.

This cycle of dealer swapping and occasional banishing of a floor supervisor went on for some time. Observing this, I realized we were running low on "non-banned" dealers. Despite my comfortable spot at the European roulette wheel across the room where I'd been enjoying the spectacle, I had a sinking feeling that I might be next.

Sure enough, my number came up. My only hope was that he wouldn't start a winning streak, trapping me with him for the next six hours. Ideally, he'd either burn through his bankroll quickly or I'd manage to get myself dismissed from the table posthaste.

I opted for the latter strategy. Now, there are specific rules to follow when dealing with an irate high roller like Mr. X. So after he lost a couple of hands, he was dealt a pair of aces and upped his bet by another $10,000. Typically, one would assume he intended to split the aces, but to be certain, I asked, "Would you like to split or double?" After all, an eight could come up and he might claim he wanted to double down.

He didn't appreciate my caution. After losing both bets, His following words were like music to my ears: "Get this asshole out of here!" The floor supervisor, Smitty, was just as eager to move on as I was. He wasn't beside me when Mr. X barked his command and mistakenly thought he was the target. I saw him pick up the phone to call for a replacement. Quickly, I caught Smitty's attention and suggested that Mr. X was probably referring to me, not him.

Smitty approached Mr. X and asked, "Which asshole are you talking about?" pointing first to himself and then to me. Mr. X bellowed, "This asshole! Get him outta here!" And just like that, I was happily tossed back into the briar patch of the roulette wheel.

My periodic encounters with the high-profile Turk, Ahmet, continued at Bellagio. We received instructions from upper management that whenever he was playing, a senior manager needed to be present to babysit. The exact reason for this new policy wasn't apparent. Still, it seemed to be either to cater to his demands or, more likely, due to corporate concerns about the increasingly litigious nature of the times.

Despite this mandate, most shift bosses and their backups knew better than to linger too close to the action. They positioned themselves across the room, ready to reluctantly intervene when Ahmet lost his temper, or monitored the game from an office nearby via camera. Engaging in one of his disputes was universally seen as a no-win situation.

For a time, management's solution was to give him a time-out, temporarily barring him from play. The trigger for these time-outs wasn't necessarily any rude comments directed at me or any physical outbursts; it was mainly for instances when he made offensive remarks to women. Consequently, no female dealers were assigned to his table, a decision they were pretty happy with.

One morning at the table, Ahmet leaned in to me and the floor supervisor, boasting how he'd rattled a day-shift dealer into a $10,000 overpay mistake. It wasn't the wins or losses that thrilled him, it was breaking us down, turning errors into his "conquests." He even claimed he regaled Steve Wynn with these tales over lunch, like some twisted bonding ritual. I just nodded, inwardly rolling my eyes at how his real game was psychological warfare, not roulette.

Despite Ahmet mostly playing on the graveyard shift, his antics were a significant concern for the day-shift dealers, who wanted no part of him. The dealers regularly assigned to his table during the day united against his behavior. They collectively informed the casino manager that they would no longer deal to him. This action resolved the issue for them; none of those dealers were assigned to his table again. However, as a consequence, they were also barred from dealing in the high-limit games from then on.

Ahmet's behavior didn't faze me as much as it did others. I attribute this to a combination of factors from my past experiences. As a retail manager, I'd been exposed to my fair share of irate customers. I learned that the calmer I remained, the more ridiculous they appeared in their outbursts. Additionally, my time volunteering at Buffalo State Mental Hospital during college, which felt straight out of *One Flew Over the Cuckoo's Nest*, exposed me to various unpredictable behaviors.

Coupled with my confidence in my dealing skills at the time, I never felt my job was at risk due to Ahmet's antics. I often found myself laughing internally at his outbursts, especially when he was in the process of losing millions. It was a surreal experience, watching someone become unhinged over a game, while I remained composed, secure in my abilities and role. Not all of my memorable Bellagio stories involved high-stakes roulette or tantrum-prone VIPs. Sometimes, it was the little favors and offbeat perks that reminded you how strange and wonderful casino life could be.

In the earlier days of Las Vegas, you could occasionally secure a buffet comp if you knew the right person. While I used this perk from time to time when relatives visited, it wasn't about saving the $20 cost of the buffet, but more about the coolness factor of scoring and using a comp. Once, when my aunt and uncle were visiting, I offered to get them comped at the Bellagio buffet. After arranging this, my aunt called to mention they were traveling with another couple and asked if I could extend the comp to four people. I sheepishly contacted my friend and had it modified. Upon arrival, I told my aunt to ask for the host and he'd take care of everything. When I went to thank him the next day, he laughed and said she'd shown up with a party of eight—now that's chutzpah.

Though I apologized profusely, he assured me it wasn't a problem and had taken care of everyone.

But perks weren't the only fluidities—some nights, the games themselves spun wild tales.

One uneventful night, I was in the salon and in walked an elderly woman named Teresa who said her husband was playing poker and she just wanted to try her luck at roulette.

Teresa sidled up to the single-zero roulette table, armed with a stack of those handy-dandy number layout cards the casino so graciously provides roulette players. Little did she know, she was about to start spinning her wheels faster than the roulette ball.

For two hours, Teresa is laser-focused, scribbling on her cards like she's deciphering the Da Vinci Code. She's placing bets with the confidence of someone who thinks they've cracked the casino's secret algorithm. Meanwhile, the wheel keeps spinning, the ball drops, and Teresa's chip stack shrinks.

Two hours later, Teresa is down $15,000. That's enough to buy a decent used car or a nice pair of shoes at one of the casino shops. Defeated, she calls it a night, leaving behind a small forest's worth of scribbled-on cards.

Now, here's where it gets good. I look at Teresa's discarded "strategy" cards as I clean up. And what do I see? These aren't single-zero roulette cards. Oh no, these are double-zero cards, with a completely different number sequence! Some well-meaning (or perhaps practically joking) soul had filled our single-zero table with double-zero cards. Teresa had spent two hours and $15,000 placing her bets on a wheel that didn't exist before her!

But here's the kicker. As I'm frantically gathering these misleading cards like a squirrel hoarding nuts for winter, a chilling thought hits me: How long have these faulty crutches been out here? How many other players have been using these cards?

Imagine all these players, day in and day out, confidently placing their chips based on a phantom wheel. They're not just spinning the roulette wheel; they're spinning their wheels, going nowhere fast, while their bankrolls race in the opposite direction.

We scramble like we're on a secret CIA mission, gathering all the wrong cards faster than a magician making evidence disappear. Heaven forbid someone realizes this little mix-up and makes a fuss.

Now, let's be real. Would Teresa have won if she'd had the right cards? Probably not. The house always wins, after all. But if she'd found out? Oh boy, you can bet she'd have raised a stink louder than a winner at a bingo hall. And in Vegas, a screaming loser with a legitimate gripe is a squeaky wheel that will get some grease.

The irony of it all? Teresa's random guesses might have been just as good as her "system" based on the wrong wheel. In the end, whether looking at the right wheel, the wrong wheel, or reading tea leaves, the result is usually the same in a casino: The house wins and the player's wallet gets much lighter.

But not all memorable moments at Bellagio involved pranks and celebrity sightings. Sometimes, the house itself reminded us of our vulnerability.

I arrived at work on Easter Sunday, April 11, 2004. Not long into my shift, the lights in the casino flickered and dimmed. It wasn't pitch dark, but the ambience was less bright than usual. Soon, it became apparent that the computers were down. The games continued, as there was sufficient light, and everyone expected the power, including the computers, to be restored momentarily.

Years before, while I was at the Golden Nugget, we experienced a power outage just before my shift ended at noon. Back then, the Las Vegas summer heat began to creep in without air conditioning. The poker players, determined to carry on, illuminated their game with lighters. However, the casino eventually shut down for almost a day until the power was restored. The outage was caused by construction and renovations that interfered with a transformer.

At Bellagio, however, the situation unfolded differently. I don't recall it getting too warm, but it was around 4 a.m. in early April.

The first real challenge we faced in the high-limit area was the absence of computer access. Since most of our players used credit and markers instead of cash, everything depended on the established credit limits or funds deposited at the cage. Accessing or extending a player's credit line became impossible without computers. Initially, we tried to verify transactions directly with the cage, but this proved futile, possibly due to the power outage affecting the cashier's area.

As the outage persisted, some high-stakes players, deeply immersed in their games and losses, grew increasingly anxious. They were eager to continue, convinced their luck was about to turn. Their demands for immediate access to funds or extended credit lines grew more urgent, despite the power outage.

A temporary solution was to call other properties within the company to get the credit information, such as the Beau Rivage in Mississippi. For a brief period that Easter morning, calls were made from the Bellagio high-limit pit to the Mississippi cage to get the OK for credit. Unfortunately, this workaround wasn't enough to solve all of the issues.

The biggest problem wasn't the computers, but the toilets. The restrooms were all no-touch fixtures requiring power to run. After a few hours, due to health reasons, the casino was shut down and we were sent home.

A failure of underground power cables caused the outage, Which significantly impacted operations, causing an estimated $7.5 million in losses. The casino reopened on Wednesday, April 14, 2004, but some operations, such as the dancing fountains, remained closed for several days.

The outage affected not only Bellagio, but several other Strip casinos. It was a bizarre experience, seeing one of the world's most iconic and bustling casinos suddenly grind to a halt due to something as mundane as a power failure. The incident served as a reminder of the complex infrastructure that keeps these massive operations running smoothly and the potential impact when things go awry. For all its backup systems and contingency plans, Bellagio had been brought to its knees by something as basic as plumbing. Even in the most sophisticated casino in the world, when the toilets don't flush, the house doesn't win.

Even in our elegant upscale environment, where we catered to society's elite and donned tuxedos, there were moments when it felt like we were putting lipstick on a pig. Despite the glitz and glamour, the long hours and high-pressure environment could take their toll. To cope, some of us, well into middle age, often indulged in third-grade antics.

One busy Saturday night, a well-dressed gentleman, looking somewhat distressed, approached my table and asked for directions to the nearest restroom. As I guided him, he suddenly let out a loud, unmistakable flatulent sound. My finely tuned ear for such things told me it was a fake. Driven by curiosity, I nudged him to spill the beans on his little secret.

Initially hesitant like a magician guarding his tricks, he eventually gave in. The source was a "Redi-Poot," a small handheld device that replicated the sound to near perfection. He revealed that he owned a novelty company selling these gadgets. While I doubted he was showcasing this in the casino for impromptu sales, I knew I had to have one.

I convinced him to demonstrate his restroom gag for Donna, the dealer across the room, who I knew would be the perfect audience. She was as enthralled by the device as I was. We ended up buying a case of them and splitting it. Donna used hers mainly on the golf course to distract others during putts, while I reserved mine for elevators and crowded spaces, adding a touch of mischief.

I distributed a few to my colleagues, such as floor supervisor Bruce, who I knew would appreciate the humor and add some liveliness to the casino floor. He didn't disappoint. Over the next few months, we were periodically treated to well-timed faux flatulence, usually aimed at the more pompous patrons. The reactions we got were priceless, providing endless amusement and reaffirming that Las Vegas was the entertainment capital, not just for tourists, but for us too.

Another juvenile pastime that helped us get through the night shifts was what we called "tailing." This prank, a favorite among the staff, began with someone discreetly attaching a small piece of tissue, or occasionally a longer strip of bathroom tissue, to the bottom of someone's suit jacket. The unsuspecting victim, oblivious to their new appendage, sometimes paraded around with it for minutes before a kind soul, or our barely contained laughter, gave it away.

As time passed, we refined the prank, adding a twist where the tailed individual was asked to deliver something to another pit, usually across the casino. This extended the joke and shared the fun with our fellow employees. One New Year's Eve, Bruce perhaps took the gag a step too far. He placed a tail on shift boss Rick, who was decked out in his special tuxedo for the occasion. Unfortunately, due to the New Year's Eve bustle, Rick was urgently called away to appease one of our high-rolling international guests, tail and all. Rick maintained his professionalism while handling the crisis, as he was unaware of his new accessory.

Rick was less than thrilled when he discovered the toilet-tissue tail, but Bruce managed to weather the storm, thanks mainly to Rick's sense of humor once he cooled off. After a brief moment of tension, Rick couldn't help but chuckle at the situation's absurdity, realizing that a little lightheartedness was sometimes necessary in their high-stakes world.

With our regular crew, Karen occasionally dealt in the high-limit room on the European roulette game. She was tall and habitually slipped off her shoes while dealing, tucking them discreetly under the table. Smitty, supervising her game, often reminded her to keep

Bellagio: The Glamorous Circus

her shoes on. But when she didn't comply, he stealthily snatched one and hid it a few feet away. I'm reasonably sure Smitty's motive wasn't strictly about rule enforcement; it was more about the entertainment of watching Karen scramble to find her missing shoe during her break.

One day, this shoe heist almost backfired. Karen, as usual, made herself comfortable, shoes off, while Smitty quietly relocated one of them under a chair on the pit's edge. Then, in a twist of fate, Rick, the shift boss, decided to drop by. Unlike his usual brief walkthroughs, he sat and chatted with us for a while.

As luck would have it, he picked the chair concealing Karen's shoe. I watched, half-amused and half-anxious, knowing Karen's break was imminent. If Rick stayed seated, things could get interesting. Would Karen search for her shoe, inadvertently revealing her habit of going shoeless to the boss and implicating Smitty?

When her break time arrived, Karen opted for the most innovative action. She casually slipped her foot into her remaining shoe and, with a poker face that would make any high-stakes gambler proud, gracefully limped her way back to the dealer's lounge. Her poise and quick thinking saved her from an awkward confrontation with Rick and kept her secret safe.

Some might have hinted that I was the mastermind behind many hijinks in our area. I often noticed amusing opportunities around us, lit the fuse, then sat back to watch the fun unfold with an innocent expression.

Carole, one of our fellow dealers, had a peculiar habit. She dashed into the pit, usually just in time to relieve the next dealer, then stopped at the podium behind the game to apply a tiny bottle of Bellagio lotion to her hands. This had become a ritual for her after every break. I couldn't help but notice that the lotion bore a striking resemblance to Elmer's glue.

Half-jokingly, I suggested someone swap the lotion for glue, but no one took the bait. So I took matters into my own hands. I brought in the glue and made the switch. Smitty, always ready for mischief, ensured that Carole picked the right bottle upon her return, even handing it to her to guarantee success. I cautioned him to step back, predicting she might use his suit as a towel once she realized the switch. The plan worked flawlessly, although it took Carole a moment to figure out something was amiss with her "lotion."

The aftermath of this prank was an unexpected bonus. The bottle was tossed into a drawer at the podium and forgotten. About three days later as we prepared for a shift change, I noticed Helga, the day-shift supervisor. Though she was a very nice German woman, her sense of humor was nonexistent. From the corner of my eye, I saw her rummaging through the drawer and picking up the lotion bottle.

Her expression changed as she began to apply the "lotion" and rub her hands together. Somehow, she knew we were involved. I must have given away a tell, because she zeroed in on me and declared, "There's something wrong with you graveyard people." Her stern demeanor and furrowed brow made it clear that she didn't find our antics as amusing as we did. I couldn't argue with her assessment, but I couldn't help but chuckle as she stormed off to wash the glue from her hands.

It was moments like these that reminded me why, despite the pressure and the prima donnas, I loved this job. Where else could you work in a tuxedo while acting like a teenager?

Juvenile? Absolutely. But those pranks were our lifeline—forging team bonds, venting the high-stakes pressure, and reminding us not to take the elite and their whims too seriously. In this glamorous circus, shared laughs kept us sane, proving joy hid in the gravity, turning coworkers into family amid the tuxedos and tantrums.

One morning in early 2000, a peculiar rumor started circulating—Bellagio was being sold to MGM. Initially, we dismissed it as ludicrous, primarily since the rumor originated from a maintenance

Bellagio: The Glamorous Circus

employee rather than any of the higher-ups. Steve Wynn was so closely associated with our casino that it seemed unthinkable he would ever part with his masterpiece. However, a couple of days later, the unbelievable news was confirmed: Kirk Kerkorian's Tracinda Corporation was in the midst of a hostile takeover of the Mirage Corporation. The shock was palpable; no one had envisioned Steve Wynn ever relinquishing his crown jewel.

Once it was confirmed that shareholders had voted in favor of the takeover, with a staggering buyout of approximately $6 billion, we began to grapple with the reality of the situation and what it might mean for our future. The initial shock gave way to a growing sense of unease as we contemplated the potential consequences of this monumental change.

Right around that time, I was offered the position of table games trainer. I'm pretty sure it wasn't because I'd mastered every game in the pit—far from it. More likely, it was because computers were starting to play a bigger role in the casino and I had just enough technical know-how to stand out.

Now, I'd always said I wasn't interested in management. I'd turned down offers over the years and had no plans to cross that line. But this one was different. It was intriguing—part training, part tech—and it felt more like a support role than a traditional management position.

Then reality set in. We were on the verge of a total leadership shake-up, with MGM expected to bring in their people. I took about two seconds to ask myself how long I'd last in a new possibly short-lived position versus the job security I'd have as a 20-plus-year veteran on a familiar game.

I passed. I thanked them, but declined the offer.

Some feared massive layoffs or firings as MGM brought in its own team. Concerns extended even to the property itself. Maintaining Bellagio's high standards was an expensive endeavor, a fact we on the graveyard shift knew all too well, as much of the work to keep the property pristine was carried out overnight.

Rumors swirled, some even speculating about the fate of the famous Bellagio fountains. Whispers suggested that if the high level of maintenance wasn't upheld, the fountains might eventually sputter, with half of their nozzles failing to work.

Most of our initial worries proved to be unfounded; Bellagio continued to operate at its high standard of excellence. However, there was legitimate concern among some employees, as layoffs did occur. Previously, during economic downturns, the company's policy had been to retain as many employees as possible, often opting for giving us an extra day off every other week until business improved.

Fortunately for me, layoffs were based on seniority. Having been with the company for more than 20 years, I had a bit of a safety net. The new management team, however, was quicker to lay off employees following the 9/11 attacks, although most were rehired after a few months. This period of unemployment, while temporary, placed a significant strain on many of my coworkers and their families, highlighting the precarious nature of our industry.

As we adjusted to this new normal, rumors began to circulate about Steve Wynn's next move. It was reported that he had made a personal profit of $500 million from the Mirage Corporation buyout. In April 2000, Steve Wynn had purchased the Desert Inn for $270 million, and it was closed later that year. The first tower of the Desert Inn was imploded in October 2001, marking the beginning of a new era, although details were initially kept confidential.

The plans for the former Desert Inn property were finally unveiled in August 2002, sparking a new wave of speculation among us old Mirage Resorts employees. Many wondered whether this new venture would attempt to replicate the grandeur of Bellagio or carve out its own unique identity. For those of us who had been with Steve Wynn since the early days, there was a certain allure to the idea of being part of this new chapter.

Those with seniority, like myself, faced a tough decision: stay or go? Leaving meant sacrificing accrued benefits, such as vacation time and 401(k) vesting, especially since this was an entirely new company. It also meant leaving behind the familiarity and camaraderie we had built at Bellagio—and for many of us at the Mirage and for a select few Golden Nugget—over the years. Yet the allure of being part of the next big thing on the Strip was tempting. Many wrestled with the fear of the unknown, wondering if the grass would truly be greener on the other side of the Strip.

A few months later as construction on Wynn Las Vegas progressed and recruitment began, I found myself at another crossroads. I was leaning toward staying where I was—after all, I had seniority, established relationships, and knew every inch of the property. It was more than just familiarity; it was home. I could run the game in my sleep. Even after the new management came in, I didn't feel the pressure. I was deep in my comfort zone—and maybe that was the problem.

Then came an unexpected call: Wynn was offering me a pit manager position. Not floor supervisor, but straight to boss.

This was different from the trainer position. It was a chance to be part of something new again, to work for the man who had transformed Las Vegas not once, but twice. I knew that meant leaving behind more than just a job. But I also knew that if Steve Wynn was building something new, the big players would follow. The energy, ambition, magic—they always did. Still, that didn't make the choice easy.

I could have ridden it out at Bellagio, kept the tux, stayed in the groove. But maybe that was exactly why I needed to go. Maybe I needed to shake things up, get out of autopilot. Maybe I needed to prove, if only to myself, that I still had one more reinvention left in me. And I was curious to see what Steve had up his sleeve this time, interested in being part of that spark again.

After much deliberation and more than a few sleepless days wrestling with the decision, I took the leap. Twenty-five years after walking into my first casino job, I was about to climb the casino ladder for the fourth time. In a city built on taking chances, sometimes the biggest gamble is betting on yourself.

Little did I know that my next big decision would test everything I thought I knew about loyalty, ambition, and the price of change.

Chapter 13

The Wynn Blueprint:
Luxury, Loyalty, and a Second Act

Building Another Empire from the Ground Up

Having made my leap to the Wynn, I found myself weeks before opening joining a small group of pit and shift managers with an ambitious goal: to create the entire procedure manual for a property that didn't yet exist.

Most of the information we needed was gleaned from our Bellagio and Mirage experience, with zero help from what were now rival camps. The irony wasn't lost on me—properties that had once been sister casinos were now competitors, their doors firmly closed to us.

The pressure was intense. We had one week to finish these manuals before the floor supervisors arrived for training. A week after that, hundreds of dealers would flood in, expecting comprehensive procedural training and a complete orientation to a property still wrapped in plastic and drywall dust. They'd need to know everything—not just game procedures, but every restaurant, every bar, every amenity we'd offer. Guests would expect them to know the pool hours, menu highlights, spa services, and more.

The catch? Most of these amenities existed only on paper. Walking through the property meant navigating an active construction site, dodging scaffolding, forklifts, and workers in hard hats. Even when we could physically visit a future restaurant or lounge, the bare concrete and exposed wiring didn't exactly paint a picture of the finished product.

The high stress continued right up until the day before opening, when a few other managers and I spent the entire night filling every game's rack with chips. It was late, fatigue was setting in from the process, and I couldn't help but think about how different this felt from the well-oiled machine I'd known at the Mirage and Bellagio.

The challenge wasn't just the new property, it was also the new team. Instead of the tight-knit group I'd worked with for decades, we were now a collection of managers from various casinos across town, each bringing their own ideas about how things should be done. A chasm was already developing between those of us who'd been with the Wynn organization for years and the newcomers who wanted to import their procedures from Caesars, MGM, or wherever they'd come from. Every meeting became a negotiation, every decision a small battle between "how we've always done it" and "how we did it at my place."

Walking through the employee entrance each morning, I caught glimpses of the Desert Inn golf course still intact at the back of the property. It was a daily reminder of the Las Vegas history buried beneath our feet—and the weight of what we were trying to build on top of it.

The land under Wynn Las Vegas carried a storied past, whispering history with every step across the old Desert Inn golf course. For over 50 years, the Desert Inn shaped Vegas—from its mob-tied roots under Moe Dalitz in the '60s, synonymous with high-stakes and shady deals, to Howard Hughes's bold 1966 purchase.

Renting the top floors for a 10-day stay, Hughes stayed put and bought the place outright when asked to leave to make room for New Year's high rollers.

In 1968 alone, he spent $300 million on casinos and land, but the party screeched to a halt when the DOJ filed a monopoly suit against him. He was pulling in a third of the Strip's revenue. His glitzy remodels, marble floors, and a Mayan tower turned heads, but the shine wore off fast once the skimming rumors started and he began disappearing into his own shadow.

By the '80s and '90s, a succession of owners couldn't keep it competitive. In 2000, Steve Wynn acquired it for $270 million as a gift for his wife Elaine, subsequently closing and demolishing it to pursue his and Elaine's dreams. As we worked to open the Wynn on that legendary ground, I felt the weight of history, pushing us to match its legacy with something even grander.

With the Desert Inn now just a memory, Steve Wynn set his sights on creating a new, unparalleled resort that would redefine luxury and sophistication on the Las Vegas Strip once again.

Behind the scenes, navigating the hiring process for a premier Strip property came with its own share of drama, politics, and whispered controversies.

Throughout my early years dealing downtown, the ultimate goal was landing one of the premier jobs on the Strip. While the work itself was similar, or even easier, the real draw was the money to be made. These coveted positions were tough to secure and often came down to who you knew—your connections, or "juice," as we called it. Nepotism and favoritism, being part of human nature, were definitely factors in landing these dealing jobs.

Not only was juice crucial in getting a job, but some people flaunted their connections, sometimes even exaggerating them to keep others at bay and create an aura of being untouchable. While most people with juice kept it discreet, a few did the opposite, sometimes to the point of embarrassing their benefactor. Their brazen attitude occasionally led to their firing, precisely when they thought they were immune to termination.

One dealer who kept his juice quiet was Philip, a young blackjack dealer with a low profile back at the Golden Nugget. One weekday morning around 9 a.m., the pit phone rang. It was for Philip. Fortunately, his table was empty when the pit clerk handed him the phone. After the call, we were all concerned there might have been a family emergency. Vinny, our typically crabby floor person, was quick to scold Philip about taking outside calls in the pit. Philip apologized and explained: Before becoming a dealer, he'd been a hairstylist and one of his regular clients, who had likely helped him get the dealing job, was Steve Wynn himself. The casino owner was calling to schedule a haircut after Philip's shift. Vinny's attitude toward Philip changed dramatically after that revelation.

But not everyone with connections handled them as discreetly or respectfully. In fact, the hunger for a Strip job occasionally led to less savory behavior.

During my years downtown, paying my dues and trying to break into the Strip scene, rumors often circulated about people paying thousands of dollars for these premium jobs. While nothing was ever officially advertised, these stories persistently made the rounds. For many of us, including myself, salvation came with the opening of new properties that needed large numbers of dealers. However, this didn't completely eliminate the possibility of job selling. In fact, before we opened the Wynn, there was a major scandal involving someone who was fired for accepting money in exchange for guaranteed jobs while processing applications, though I don't believe this ever made it to the media.

Even with those tensions and occasional scandals, the excitement around opening day pushed everyone to focus forward.

Amid the noise, dust, and uncertainties, I felt a tug of war—

The Wynn Blueprint

thrilled by glimpses of Wynn's glittering chandeliers and sleek bars, yet skeptical anything could top the Bellagio we'd cut ties with. One night, dodging construction dust, a new dealer's excitement sparked my own, but doubt lingered: Could this really rival our old home? Challenges sharpened our focus, pushing us to build Steve Wynn's next vision. In the end, Wynn Las Vegas rose to the task, matching Bellagio as a dazzling rival.

There was an undeniable sense of excitement and anticipation among the staff. We knew that we were part of something special, a resort that aimed to redefine the very essence of luxury and sophistication in Las Vegas. The challenges we faced only served to sharpen our focus and determination to make Wynn Las Vegas a resounding success, one that would set a new standard for the industry and solidify Steve Wynn's reputation as a visionary in the world of hospitality and gaming.

The Wynn casino was a testament to the power of modern technology, a shining example of how innovation could transform the gaming experience. At the heart of this technological marvel was a cutting-edge software system developed exclusively for the resort. This groundbreaking tool revolutionized the way we tracked guest play and managed markers, setting a new standard that soon became the norm across the industry.

Even the chips themselves were a step ahead of the curve. Each was embedded with state-of-the-art RFID technology, making tracking a breeze. No longer did players have to painstakingly sort their chips at the cage; instead, they could simply present a random stack and the total amount would instantly appear on the screen. It was a marvel of efficiency, a glimpse into the future of casino operations that left us all in awe.

But the technological wonders didn't stop there. Each roulette table was outfitted with an array of sensors, silently recording every number that graced the wheel. This data served a dual purpose. On the surface, it fed the display boards, showcasing the last 20 numbers spun to entice potential players. But beneath this flashy exterior, the data was being meticulously analyzed by sophisticated computers, ever vigilant for the slightest hint of bias or irregularity.

This level of scrutiny was unprecedented. The moment a wheel showed even the faintest sign of favoring certain numbers, it was swiftly replaced and rebalanced. It was evidence of the resort's unwavering commitment to fairness and integrity, a promise to our players that the games they enjoyed were above reproach.

Walking the casino floor, observing the sheer scale of the technology at play, was a marvel. It was like being on the set of a science-fiction movie, surrounded by machines that seemed to have a life of their own. And yet, for all the flashy displays and high-tech gadgets, the true magic of Wynn lay in the people who brought it to life—the dealers, pit bosses, and the countless staff members who worked tirelessly to create an experience like no other.

April 28, 2005, was a date that had been etched in our minds for months. It marked the culmination of our rigorous training, the simulated play days, and of course, the quintessential motivational speech from the man himself. I remember when he was introduced to the assembled staff to thunderous applause, while Heart's "Magic Man" was booming through the auditorium.

We were primed and ready, eager to unveil the most expensive resort ever built at the time, with a staggering price tag of $2.7 billion. Wynn Las Vegas was poised to elevate the standard set by its predecessors, following a successful formula, but cranking everything up to eleven.

The buzz surrounding the opening was electric, an intense energy that had been building for weeks. Steve Wynn's Super Bowl ads had only fanned the flames of anticipation, leaving everyone wondering if reality could possibly live up to the hype. It was a tall order, but one we were confident we could deliver.

The evening before the public opening, the resort played host to a dazzling charity gala for 2,000 lucky guests. It was a night where the stars aligned, quite literally, as A-list celebrities rubbed shoulders with high rollers in an atmosphere dripping with luxury and excitement. Champagne flowed like water and the air was thick with the sense that we were on the cusp of something truly monumental.

As the clock struck midnight, the moment we'd all been waiting for finally arrived. The resort's doors swung open and I found myself standing there, witnessing a scene that could only be described as characteristically Las Vegas. A flood of people, an estimated 10,000 strong, poured into the resort, their faces lit up with wonder and anticipation.

In that moment, it became crystal clear that the Wynn wasn't just opening its doors; it was opening a new chapter in the city's storied history of luxury and entertainment. We'd done it—taken the Wynn brand to new heights and the world was there to witness it.

Watching the sea of people explore every nook and cranny of the resort, I felt a rush of pride. We'd poured our hearts and souls into this place, working tirelessly to create an experience that would leave a lasting impression on every guest. And as I saw the smiles on their faces, heard the gasps of awe as they took in the grandeur of it all, I knew that we'd succeeded.

Less than two years after the Wynn opened, two seismic changes rocked the property—changes that altered not just my career, but the entire culture of the place.

The first bombshell: Management eliminated the pit manager position entirely. Those of us holding the title were offered the option to stay on as floor supervisors. Myself, I was offered to interview for assistant shift manager, essentially a promotion. I surprised everyone by declining. Then I shocked them further: I asked to return to dealing. After some raised eyebrows and hushed conversations, they granted my request. Within a few weeks, I was back behind my single-zero roulette wheel on graveyard, right where I belonged.

But that wasn't the real jolt. The second announcement sent shockwaves through every dealer in the joint: Tips would now be shared not just among dealers, but with floor supervisors too. In 30 years of dealing, I'd never heard of such a thing. Neither had anyone else.

The dealers erupted. This wasn't just about money, though they estimated each dealer would lose about $15,000 annually, with supervisors now called "service team leads" dipping into the toke pool. It was about principle. The company was essentially subsidizing management salaries with dealer tips. The floor supervisors, naturally, were thrilled. The dealers? They were out for blood.

Union organizers materialized faster than chips disappearing from a player's stack. Meetings were held. Cards were signed. When it became clear the vote would be overwhelmingly pro-union, Steve Wynn himself called an all-hands meeting with the dealers.

I'll never forget that day. Wynn stood before hundreds of furious dealers and urged them not to unionize. He promised to make things right, to restore the old way. He talked about family, about the bonds we'd built over decades. But the room had already turned. Dealers jeered. Some shouted. It was ugly—nothing like the reverent atmosphere of his previous pep talks.

My thought, shared quietly with a few old-timers, was simple: Give him a chance to fix it. If he reneged, we could always vote again. But the momentum was unstoppable. The vote came in 3-to-1 for the union.

Watching Steve Wynn, the man who had transformed my career, being jeered by dealers who'd followed him for decades was surreal. These weren't just employees; we were people who'd believed in his vision, who'd moved from property to property based on faith in his leadership. The betrayal cut both ways.

Looking back, trying to piece together how this disaster unfolded, several theories circulated among the dealers. The most common was that Wynn was spending so much time in Macau for the opening there that he was possibly believing bad advice from someone who didn't understand the nature of this level of play at the Las Vegas property. Some of us wondered if these newcomers from other properties saw the tips flowing across our tables, often exceeding their salaries, and simply couldn't stomach it. Were the bean counters finally getting their way? Was it Wall Street's influence after the Bellagio sale? Everyone had their theory, but the truth probably involved a combination of factors we'll never fully understand.

Whatever the catalyst, the damage was done. The family atmosphere Wynn had cultivated for decades evaporated overnight.

The dealers filed a $50 million lawsuit that was dismissed in Clark County court. The policy wasn't overturned until 2018 and in 2021, a settlement of $5.6 million was finally accepted—approximately $2,000 per dealer after legal fees. Cold comfort for years of lost income and a poisoned work environment.

For me, standing at that roulette wheel again, it was bittersweet. I'd given up the headaches of management, but returned to a dealing floor that would never be the same. The trust was broken. The family was fractured. And in a business built on relationships, that mattered more than any amount of money.

The Wynn, though a new property, quickly attracted the same high-end players who frequented the high-limit and private games. My old acquaintance, Ahmet from Turkey, soon became a regular.

In his private room at the back of the high-limit area, Ahmet had the freedom to express himself, especially when his luck was down. During one particularly frustrating session, after losing a few hundred thousand dollars, he picked up a heavy crystal ashtray. For a moment, he considered hurling it through the 10-foot-high glass window, but he redirected his anger toward the roulette wheel, throwing the ashtray into its delicate mechanism and causing significant damage.

Despite this outburst, management's response was a stern timeout—essentially a brief pause, conveniently long enough for the staff to replace and balance a new roulette wheel, allowing Ahmet to continue playing as if nothing had happened.

Ahmet's visits were often accompanied by peculiar requests, such as sending his host out for In-N-Out Burgers. On one occasion, while celebrating his birthday at the Wynn, his gaming session was interrupted by a surprise party arranged by Steve Wynn and several casino executives. They'd set up the celebration in the side dining area of his private room, complete with In-N-Out burgers, cigars, cake, a bottle of rare Scotch, and a special silver-engraved item from Tiffany's. However, as his losses mounted, Ahmet's mood soured and he accused the party of jinxing his luck.

I was routinely scheduled to deal to Ahmet during his visits, but he developed a new tactic of dismissing dealers after a losing streak. This meant I no longer enjoyed complete shifts with him every day. The pool of dealers who could handle Ahmet was limited. Female dealers were avoided due to concerns about sexual-harassment lawsuits, and our Turkish dealers had convinced management that Ahmet preferred not to have them at his table, supposedly to prevent them from understanding his multilingual profanities. After over a decade of dealing to him, however, I'd come to understand the gist of his outbursts, regardless of the language.

The Wynn Blueprint

The Wynn wasn't merely a paradise for gamblers; it also catered to the lavish lifestyles of its patrons with an array of high-end retail shops. For players flush with winnings or those simply looking to indulge, the resort offered about 30 luxury boutiques, including prestigious names like Tiffany, Gucci, Louis Vuitton, Rolex, and Cartier. These shops often came in handy for appeasing neglected partners or significant others with a spontaneous shopping spree.

It wasn't uncommon to see players splurging on extravagant items from these stores after a lucky streak at the tables. Even if they eventually lost their winnings back to the casino, they at least had some tangible mementos from their stay.

One unique retail outlet was the Ferrari dealership. Opened within the resort in April 2005, this was a distinctive venture, the only licensed Ferrari dealer in Nevada and located inside a hotel-casino. The Penske Wynn Ferrari, a joint venture between Wynn Resorts Ltd. and the Penske Automotive Group, was more than just a car showroom.

Housing over 50 high-end vehicles, the showroom charged visitors a $10 entry fee just for the privilege of touring it. The dealership offered an array of new and used luxury Ferrari and Maserati vehicles, each carrying a six-figure price tag. Additionally, it featured a service department with several maintenance bays and a well-stocked parts department, ensuring that every aspect of luxury-car ownership was catered to.

One memorable instance of a player enjoying his temporary winnings involved Omar, a Middle Eastern gentleman who frequented the European roulette table I dealt at. Omar was a guest for a couple of weeks, possibly in town for business, but he made it a point to play for an hour or two each morning. His betting style was bold and aggressive, often reaching the maximum on complete dozens. Each session typically ended with him either up or down by a few hundred thousand dollars.

After a particularly successful session, from which he walked away with about $350,000 in winnings, Omar disappeared for a couple of days. Upon his return, he shared an exciting update. He'd used his winnings to purchase a red Ferrari F430 Spider for around $250,000. He drove it back to Los Angeles. He joked that his new goal was to win enough for a matching blue one.

True to his word, a few days later, Omar had another winning day and bought his coveted blue Ferrari, driving it to Los Angeles to join its red counterpart. However, his luck took a turn after that. He ended up losing $1.2 million in subsequent sessions. Despite this setback, Omar had the consolation of owning about half a million dollars' worth of Ferraris, tangible reminders of his time at the Wynn.

The Wynn was renowned not only as a hub for high-stakes gambling, but also as a sought-after venue for a variety of charity events, drawing celebrities and high society from far and wide. A particularly memorable occasion was a charity gala benefiting The Princess Grace Foundation – USA, a nonprofit dedicated to supporting emerging talent in theater, dance, and film. In a creative twist, Wynn Resorts took the casino experience to the guests, rather than having them travel to Las Vegas.

In the last week of October 2007, an entire casino setup was transported across the country and meticulously reassembled at Sotheby's in downtown Manhattan. This ambitious project aimed to replicate the opulent atmosphere of Wynn Las Vegas right in the heart of New York City. I was fortunate to be selected as one of the dealers for this unique event, which turned out to be more of a lavish party than work. The three-day trip involved only about four hours of actual work, which consisted of dealing roulette and interacting with guests, leaving plenty of time to explore the city's attractions.

The event itself was a relaxed affair, devoid of the usual pressures of a casino environment. Since it was all for charity, there was little concern over money or strict adherence to the rules as in Las Vegas. I even had the opportunity to let one of the guests, a charming elderly lady who was celebrating her birthday, try her hand at spinning the roulette wheel, a gesture that would certainly be frowned upon back in Vegas.

The gala was graced by the presence of various celebrities, including James Earl Jones, Anne Hathaway, Roger Moore, George Lucas, Natalie Cole, Ivana Trump, and Prince Albert of Monaco. These well-known figures mingled with the other attendees, adding to the event's star-studded atmosphere. Alongside them were numerous affluent and influential individuals from high society, all gathered for a night of philanthropy and entertainment.

Settling back into my familiar spot, dealing in the high-limit room at the Wynn, I found myself dealing European roulette on a table reserved for Terrance "Terry" Watanabe.

Terry Watanabe, an Omaha native, transformed his father's modest trading business, Oriental Trading Co., into a lucrative empire. With a sharp eye for marketing and merchandise selection, he propelled the company to staggering heights. Under his leadership, the company achieved annual revenues of $300 million. In 2000, Watanabe sold the company and stepped down as CEO, shifting his focus to philanthropy. His foundation's records highlight his significant contributions to AIDS research and services, among other charitable endeavors.

With ample free time post-retirement, Watanabe began

frequenting Harrah's casino in Iowa in 2003. By 2005, he had started making regular trips to Las Vegas, where his gambling activities and lavish spending escalated dramatically. In the glitzy world of Vegas casinos, Watanabe quickly gained a reputation as both a magnanimous benefactor and a high-stakes gambler, known for his extravagant bets and generous gestures.

Terry, a billionaire with a penchant for flamboyance, was a regular resident in one of the Wynn's villas throughout the early part of 2007. When he reached the maximum duration allowed for a hotel stay, he took a brief hiatus before returning. There were even whispers that he tried to buy the villa he frequented, but the company turned him down.

Each night as I manned his reserved game, I never knew what to expect. The table was even adorned with a foot-tall samurai doll, standing guard until Terry's arrival. One thing was certain: Terry played all the games at the maximum amount allowed on every game, including slot machines.

Terry's unpredictability extended to his gifts. He often brought handfuls of novelty items from Oriental Trading, such as miniature rubber ducks, silly straws, and colorful stickers. Other times, he surprised us with food. One morning he enjoyed his "Moon over My Hammy" breakfast at Denny's so much that he ordered 20 to go, delivering them to us at the table. Another time, he ordered dozens of Danishes from his butler, distributing them among the dealers. We didn't have the heart to tell him we had access to the same treats during our breaks.

While we dealers always appreciated his cash generosity, his other gestures were equally memorable. One morning, he arrived with a porter pushing a cart full of Marie Callender's pies, instructing me to distribute them to all the dealers in the high-limit area.

On another occasion, Terry had breakfast at the roulette table. Normally, eating at the table is frowned upon, but rules tend to bend

The Wynn Blueprint

when you're betting over $100,000 a spin. A butler wheeled over a tray with silver domes and white linen like we were in a five-star dining room instead of the high-limit pit.

As I stood nearby, waiting for him to finish his eggs, Terry casually picked up a slice of toast and held it toward me. "You hungry?" he asked, holding it up like a kid offering a bite to a sibling. "This one's got orange marmalade. Imported."

I froze for a second. "I'm good, thanks," I said with a chuckle, caught between amusement and discomfort. "But I appreciate the offer."

He shrugged and took a big bite himself, crumbs dotting his custom-tailored lapel. It was a strange oddly intimate moment—just me, him, and a slice of toast worth less than a thousandth of his next spin. But it's the kind of surreal detail that stuck with me.

In mid-2007, an incident occurred that marked a turning point in Terry Watanabe's gambling activities at the Wynn. Steve Wynn himself came down to the casino floor for a private discussion with Watanabe. While the exact details of their conversation remain unknown, adding to the intrigue and speculation surrounding the incident, the outcome was evident: Watanabe stormed out and never returned to play at the Wynn again. Speculation was rife about the reasons behind this abrupt departure. Some rumors suggested it was due to Watanabe's delay in settling his debts, while others believed he might have been asked to curtail his gambling. The truth of the matter remained a mystery, known only to Wynn and Watanabe.

Despite the fallout from his encounter with Steve Wynn, Terry Watanabe continued to be welcomed at other Las Vegas properties. Watanabe reportedly wagered over $825 million in 2007, a figure exceeding the GDP of some small nations. As his financial woes deepened, Caesars Palace took legal action against him for trying to settle a $14.7 million debt with a bad check. Watanabe fought back with a countersuit, claiming that Caesars had facilitated his gambling addiction by providing him with alcohol and drugs. The dispute was eventually resolved through an out-of-court settlement, the details of which remain confidential. However, the Nevada Gaming Commission did levy a $225,000 fine against Caesars for allowing Watanabe to gamble while under the influence.

In 2022, Foundation Media Partners secured exclusive rights to Terry Watanabe's story, marking the first time he has publicly addressed his high-stakes casino saga since settling a lawsuit back in 2010. The deal covers book, film, and documentary formats, with Watanabe himself on board to help turn his cautionary tale into multiple projects.

Terry Watanabe's time at the Wynn was a blend of extravagance, generosity, and sheer unpredictability, making each shift an adventure in itself. His larger-than-life personality, coupled with his astronomical bets and quirky behavior, left an indelible mark on those who encountered him during his gambling heyday.

Celebrity sightings were routine at the Wynn, a magnet for the elite, but a few moments stuck with me. Mel Brooks, a regular, sauntered by with that impish grin, tossing a "How ya doin'?" that felt like a scene from *Blazing Saddles*. His comic aura lit up the floor, no bet required.

Then there was Henry Kissinger, his gravelly voice cutting through one quiet morning as he passed the high-limit room on a private tour with a suit—heading, I assumed, to a secluded conference room for talks way above my pay grade. He wasn't there for the tables and neither were the politicians who occasionally glided through: senators, foreign dignitaries, even a rumored cabinet member, more drawn to the villas' privacy for high-power meetings or the spa's serenity than any spin of the wheel. As a dealer, I spotted them en route to exclusive dinners or boardrooms, their folders in hand, turning the Wynn into a discreet hub for global deals.

The property wasn't just a casino; it was a stage for power players. Fortune 500 execs, tech moguls, and heads of state mingled under chandeliers, chasing connections, not jackpots. Half the room wanted action; the other half craved access, proof Vegas had evolved into a glittering nexus of influence and indulgence.

Although I recall seeing many animals while I was dealing downtown, I must say I don't remember seeing many dogs in the casinos back then, other than an occasional service dog. The high-end clientele at the Wynn were sometimes seen passing through with their four-legged companions.

Not long after the Wynn opened, I was admiring the custom-spun carpet that adorned the casino floor, which I had heard rumors was priced in the millions. It was then that an elderly woman, steering a motorized scooter down the casino's main aisle as if she were in some geriatric Grand Prix, caught my attention. She wasn't alone; tethered to her scooter was a dog the size of a small horse and whether you're a dog, horse, or a human, when you gotta go, you gotta *go*. I mean, right there on the multi-million-dollar imported carpet.

Now, I'm no expert in canine gastrointestinal science, but something happened when Fido crouched for his big moment. Either his sudden pause sent a braking signal to Granny's scooter or she looked back and realized she was about to become a YouTube sensation in the worst possible way. So what did she do? She hit the scooter throttle, effectively *dragging* her half-pooping dog down the aisle. Did this solve the problem? No. It merely extended the, er, "mess" into a kind of new abstract design on the carpet.

But get this: A quick-thinking casino employee commandeered some chairs from a blackjack table to act as temporary HazMat barriers. The problem was temporarily resolved until the cleanup crew arrived. Unfortunately, while waiting, some of the guests walking past thought the conveniently placed chairs offered a great spot to stop and enjoy the view from the middle of the aisle. That is, until their olfactory senses told them to move along.

But hang on, we're not done. If you think dogs in casinos were simply there for comic relief and biological warfare, you're wrong. One day, a couple was sitting at a baccarat table with their dog. Not a seeing-eye dog or a certified emotional-support animal. Just a regular dog who was, apparently, consulting on their baccarat strategy. He was sitting there, paws on the table, possibly pondering the odds.

I've seen many things in casinos, including curiosities that probably made the eye in the sky do a double-take. But this was the first time I've seen a dog, not a guy named "Dawg," but a real, tail-wagging man's best friend, involved in the gaming action. In the end, they had a ruff night.

A year after the grand opening of the Wynn, construction began on its sister property, Encore. This $2.3 billion venture was set to open its doors on December 22, 2008, promising to be even more luxurious than the Wynn itself.

As I watched the Encore tower rise, I found myself taking stock. I was 55, had been dealing for nearly three decades, and my body was starting to remind me of every one of those years. The same tuxedo that once made me feel like James Bond now felt more like a straitjacket.

More importantly, I'd done the math. I was comfortable enough to walk away. The thought of waking up without an alarm, of traveling without requesting time off, of never again hearing "no more bets" except in my dreams—it was irresistible.

So as the Encore neared completion, I made my decision. After close to thirty years of dealing to everyone from downtown grinders to Turkish billionaires, sport stars to Kerry Packer, I was ready to hang up the tux. My dealing career had come to an end.

Or so I thought.

Chapter 14
Back for One More Round
A High-Stakes Afterparty

My Retirement Lasted Exactly Eight Months

On March 15, 2008, I walked away from the Wynn, convinced I was done with dealing for good. The Encore project had been moving right along, but I'd decided to step away and begin my retirement. I started traveling almost immediately and even held onto one of my tuxedos, which came in handy for formal nights on cruises. I believed life was good for those seven months, but reality had other plans.

I'd always prided myself on being the calm hand at the tiller during market storms. Corrections? Recessions? No sweat. I'd been around long enough to know the smartest move was usually to pour a drink, mute CNBC, and wait it out. So when I retired at 55, I wasn't expecting to be back in a uniform before I'd be eligible for Social Security. But the 2008 crash? That was no ordinary squall. It was the financial equivalent of finding out your lifeboat has a hole and the Coast Guard's on strike.

This wasn't just a bad quarter or some dot-com fantasy

unraveling. No, this was the entire financial system having a midlife crisis. Lehman vanished, AIG got a taxpayer-funded flotation device, and banks stopped lending to each other, all wondering who was hiding a ticking time bomb under the balance sheet. I wasn't naïve. I knew I was still young and employable enough to go back to work for a few years. It wasn't a panic, but a pragmatic, move. I figured I'd ride out the storm not from a bunker, but from a roulette wheel. And let's face it: Compared to the stock market at that moment, the casino actually felt like the safer bet. Watching my carefully balanced portfolio shed 40% of its value in what felt like minutes had a way of clarifying priorities.

As the news reports grew more ominous—words like "systemic collapse" and "global contagion" being thrown around like confetti—I realized it might be time to stop watching from the sidelines. I'd waited patiently, hoping the markets would come to their senses, but instead, it felt like the entire economy was about to be flushed down the same toilet as Lehman Brothers. I figured if I was going to watch numbers disappear, I might as well do it from behind a roulette wheel where at least the odds were printed on the felt.

I was ready for an encore, both figuratively and literally. So I made a call to a few of the right people now at the helm over at Encore. To my surprise and slight relief, I got a call back the same day. "Yes," they said, "you'd be welcomed back," and oh, by the way, "tomorrow's the last day we're accepting applications and doing auditions." Nothing like a little job-market pressure to add to the global financial panic.

The next morning, I scurried down there, filled out some paperwork, exchanged pleasantries with the hiring manager, and had a brief chat with one of the shift bosses, just long enough to show I still remembered how to hold a conversation and hadn't forgotten how to spin a ball. I gave the wheel a single ceremonious spin like a baptism back into the game. And just like that, I was unretired. Not exactly the grand comeback tour I imagined, but in that moment, it felt like the most stable place to be.

Even as I settled back in, I wondered if Steve Wynn was sleeping easy. In a Charlie Rose interview amid the crash, he admitted the risk he'd taken. Asked if he'd still have built Encore knowing what was coming, he essentially said no-that if he'd known how severe the crisis would be, he wouldn't have gone forward with it if he'd had a choice. Opening a $2.3 billion resort during a financial meltdown wasn't ideal. But like my return, the decision had already been made. The paint was dry, the chandeliers were hung, and the name was on the building. We were all in, crisis or not.

The controversial tip-sharing policy, pooling with supervisors, was implemented at Encore from day one. The crucial difference was transparency: Every dealer who signed on knew they'd be sharing a hefty portion of their tips with management. Unlike at the Wynn, where dealers had the rug pulled out from under them a year into the job, we knew the deal upfront. That transparency made all the difference. While dealers at our sister property still seethed with resentment over what felt like a bait and switch, we'd made our peace with the arrangement before we ever put on the uniform.

The welcome back was genuine—handshakes, nods, and jabs like, "What, eight months off wasn't enough paradise?" Rumors flew that I'd masterminded the perfect sabbatical: retire just long enough to recharge, then slide back into Encore like the prodigal dealer. Ha—not even close; it was pure market panic. One old-timer slapped my back: "Knew you'd miss us too much." He was right, the camaraderie felt like home amid the chaos. And the irony? Had I just toughed it out for another eight months, everything would've probably evened out. But hindsight's got perfect vision and no sense of humor. And besides, I got to witness a couple more years of those wild graveyard stories that make Vegas unforgettable.

As with every major Steve Wynn opening, the Encore came with the now-familiar playbook—orientation meetings, training sessions, and of course, the much-anticipated Play Days. Since the goal was to road test every inch of the new resort, not just the casino floor, I managed to land what I considered one of the more "essential" pre-opening assignments: evaluating the new world-class spa and massage services. Challenging work, but someone had to do it. After a particularly thorough deep-tissue massage, I gave my professional verdict: Our elite guests would not be disappointed.

And the testing didn't stop there. The restaurants needed to be shaken down too—menus tasted, timing fine-tuned, service calibrated. So naturally, we stepped up. Between spa treatments and sampling gourmet meals on the company dime, it started to feel less like prepping for a job and more like retirement with a timecard. It was good to be back.

All of this led up to the customary pre-opening pep rally with Steve Wynn. Despite the proven success of the Wynn resorts, launching a multibillion-dollar property always carries inherent risks. This time, the stakes were even higher, as the opening coincided with the peak of the 2008 Great Recession, a period marked by economic turmoil, particularly challenging for a city like Las Vegas, so dependent on tourism.

Yet against the backdrop of this economic adversity, Encore stood resilient. The resort boasted luxurious accommodations, signature dining experiences, an award-winning spa, and two trendsetting nightclubs. These marked a significant shift in Las Vegas's reputation as "The Entertainment Capital of the World." When Encore opened at the end of 2008, its entertainment focus centered around the 40,000 square-foot XS nightclub, a departure from the city's traditional concert halls, theaters, and themed spectacles.

Nightclubs like XS and Surrender became massive cash cows, with XS alone pulling in over $100 million in its first year, per

Nightclub & Bar magazine—redefining Vegas resorts as party empires. From my graveyard perch, I saw the shift: a younger, dynamic crowd spilling from the clubs into the casino at 4 a.m., buzzing with energy that turned quiet shifts into electric afterparties. It wasn't just gambling anymore; Encore had cranked entertainment to a new level.

A standout feature of the Encore was the Sky Casino, the epitome of high-limit private-gaming luxury. Perched on the 64th floor, it boasted a wall of glass offering a breathtaking view of the Las Vegas Strip. This exclusive venue was truly in a league of its own.

The Sky Casino consisted of two separate areas, each customizable to the preferences of its distinguished guests. Typically, the setup included a baccarat table, blackjack, and a European roulette wheel, with a dice table added upon request. These mini casinos were self-contained, featuring their own cashier's cages and adjacent private dining rooms. Access was streamlined and secure, with a private elevator activated by a special key.

For us dealers, working in the Sky Casino came with its perks. We had our own break room just down the hall and being on the graveyard shift meant we were treated to the dazzling lights of the Strip at night and the awe-inspiring sunrises in the early mornings. It was a unique experience that combined the thrill of high-stakes gaming with some of the most stunning views Las Vegas had to offer.

Celebrity sightings or brief encounters were occasional treats at the Golden Nugget, Mirage, Bellagio, and Wynn. However, at the Encore, rubbing elbows with the stars became more the rule than the exception. Helping to supercharge the star power were XS and Surrender that redefined VIP excess and turned the casino into a post-midnight hotspot for the rich, famous, and just plain rowdy.

The Encore seemed to elevate the celebrity draw, especially among professional athletes. NBA and NFL players, who were already a common sight at other properties, found a new haunt.

Patriots' star tight end Rob Gronkowski was a fixture, known for his lively celebrations. On his birthday, he was presented with a football-shaped cake, which he, true to form, spiked in celebration. It's unclear whether this was a planned stunt or a spontaneous moment of revelry.

The international allure of the Encore also attracted soccer legends. Cristiano Ronaldo, often hailed as one of the greatest players of all time, was someone I had the pleasure of dealing to occasionally. Initially unaware of his fame, I noted his enthusiasm and generosity at the table. It was only during a break that my European colleagues filled me in on the identity of our world-famous guest.

Similarly, when Justin Timberlake and Taylor Swift visited the high-limit room, their presence was pointed out to me. While Timberlake was a familiar face, I embarrassingly admitted to not recognizing Swift at the time, a mistake I wouldn't make today. Ronaldo's visits at least allowed me the excuse of international ignorance. Often, you saw a player on TV and the next day they were partying at the Encore, sometimes even the same night, especially if the game was in L.A. NBA players could hop on a plane and be in the casino in no time.

But celebrities weren't the only ones drawn to Encore's nightclub culture. The tech money from Silicon Valley was equally impressive.

One memorable night, I found myself dealing to a young man who, I believe, was connected to a major tech company in Silicon Valley. He had a somewhat nerdy demeanor, but possessed a substantial line of credit. Accompanying him was an attractive young woman, whose relationship with him seemed either very new or perhaps just temporary.

As he confidently placed $1,000 bets on various numbers and started winning, he requested $25,000 chips with his $35,000 payoffs. Gradually, a neat stack of these high-value chips accumulated. Clearly, he was trying to impress his companion and she appeared suitably awed—who wouldn't be?

At one point, the woman reached out to examine one of the $25,000 chips from his growing pile. While my primary duty was to safeguard the casino's assets, I also had to be vigilant about protecting our players' interests. However, I couldn't outright tell her not to touch his chips—after all, she could have been his wife for all I knew.

To subtly draw his attention to the situation, I commented on the impressive stack he had amassed, now totaling 12 chips. He seemed nonchalant about it, which only encouraged her to start shuffling the chips on the table. I believe he was trying to further downplay the money's significance to impress his date.

Feeling somewhat uneasy, I did my best to alert him discreetly and even mentioned the situation to the relief dealer and floor supervisor during my break. Truth be told, even if his "date" had managed to sneak a chip into her handbag, cashing it out would be nearly impossible for her.

However, as the night progressed, the tide turned, and all the $25,000 chips eventually returned to the rack, leaving none for the player or his companion. The loss didn't seem to faze him or perhaps he was maintaining a facade of nonchalance for his date's benefit.

I wasn't privy to what happened after they left my table, but I suspect the rest of their night wasn't as thrilling as the player had hoped. The next day, the shift boss approached me with a complaint from the customer about allowing the woman to handle his $25,000 chips. I explained the situation, suspecting that the player's complaint might have stemmed more from his disappointment over losing half a million dollars in an attempt to impress a fleeting acquaintance than from any real concern about the chips. Just another typical night in the high-limit room on the graveyard shift.

The graveyard shift kicked off at 4 a.m., right as XS nightclub wrapped, creating an eerie lull while we waited for the party crowd to stumble over. That quiet stretch let us catch our breath before the afterparty wave hit, turning empty tables into buzzing hubs. One regular who owned those post-club arrivals was "Sam" from Dubai (real name Mohamad). Of all the bleary-eyed revelers spilling in, none commanded the scene quite like he did.

Sam's arrival was always a spectacle, accompanied by a large entourage that typically included a couple of bodyguards, a few friends from Dubai, a bevy of beautiful young ladies, and an assortment of eager tag-alongs. These new acquaintances were drawn to Sam's penchant for splurging large sums of money. He relished sharing tales of his extravagant spending at XS, once even flaunting a bar tab exceeding $100,000 for buying a round for the entire bar.

Sam played with abandon at the roulette table, placing large stacks of $100 chips all over the layout. He was also generous with his entourage, occasionally handing out $1,000 or even $5,000 chips. While dealing to Sam could be quite a challenge, the financial rewards for the dealers often made it worth the effort.

Sam loved to regale us with stories about his home city, Dubai, and his polo ponies. He once claimed to have met Queen Elizabeth at a polo match, a story I initially took with a grain of salt. However, my skepticism faded when he showed me a photo on his phone of himself with the Queen, found on a website dedicated to polo. After a night of revelry at XS and a few hours at the gambling tables, Sam and his entire entourage retreated to his villa, where the party likely continued well into the afternoon. What happened in the villas stayed in the villas, even though the next night, he might stop by and imply that the "private party" was wild without getting into any specifics. He left that up to our imaginations.

While Sam represented the fun-loving side of our international clientele, not every cross-cultural encounter at Encore was quite so entertaining. Sometimes, the mix of wealth, ego, and old-world

Encore: Back for One More Round

tensions created situations that required more than just dealing skills to navigate.

Occasionally, players from different backgrounds clashed at the tables. A group of Israelis had been playing for most of one evening and I knew we were expecting a large group of Arabs the following day. Given it was mid-week, the next day's schedule had only one high-limit European roulette wheel open. I raised this concern with my shift boss, but he decided that scheduling an extra dealer for a second wheel wasn't needed.

The next night began with a Canadian player betting stacks of black chips. Soon, the Israeli group arrived, monopolizing all the roulette chips, with one even resorting to playing with $500 chips due to a shortage of available unique chips. Half an hour later, four members of our Arab group arrived, eager to play. One used the remaining $1,000 chips as his color and another opted for $5,000 chips for even-money bets. That was the limit; I couldn't accommodate any more players without risking confusion over chip ownership.

Then, a royal spectator wanted to join and began placing $500 chips on the layout. I had to intervene, explaining that another player was already using that color. He was peeved, insisting that the Israeli player wasn't betting much and that he would wager significantly more.

Tensions escalated quickly, with harsh glances and sharp words exchanged. It seemed as though everyone, except the Canadian, was on the verge of a physical altercation, potentially sparking an international incident. However, the scene quickly turned almost comical as each group's bodyguards intervened, creating a barrier between the disputing parties.

After several minutes of shouting and posturing, the situation calmed down. I'd paused the game, fearing that had I spun the ball, one of the "combatants" who had left the table would claim of course that they would have played that number and would lead to disputes over winnings, of which I had a strong feeling they'd be paid even if they hadn't been playing. This decision, unfortunately, frustrated my Canadian player, who had remained seated and simply wanted to continue the game. Ultimately, management scrambled to open another wheel, effectively separating the groups and restoring peace. The high-limit room breathed a sigh of relief as diplomacy prevailed.

These international dynamics remind me that some relationships transcend the chaos of cultural misunderstandings.

During my time at the Encore, I often caught myself scanning the high-limit room whenever word came down that Ahmet was in town. For close to 20 years, he'd been my most challenging and, in some twisted way, most reliable adversary. The anticipation had become instinctual: a heightened alertness, accompanied by mental preparation for whatever theatrical display might unfold. But at the Encore, those preparation rituals went unused. Ahmet never played on my table there.

When he was in Las Vegas during that period, staying at the Wynn and playing his usual high-stakes roulette, we received the familiar heads-up from management. "Your Turkish 'friend' is in the building," someone whispered and we all unconsciously straightened up, ready for action. But he never made the short walk over to play on our side of the property.

Instead, toward the end of my time at the Encore, something unexpected happened. Ralph, his longtime host, brought him by for what could only be described as a social call.

I spotted them walking through the pit together—Ralph with his usual diplomatic smile and Ahmet looking surprisingly ... relaxed. No entourage of nervous executives. Just two men taking a stroll.

"There's the boy!" Ahmet called out when he saw me, that familiar accent cutting through the ambient casino noise. "My favorite dealer."

Favorite dealer. After all these years of verbal sparring, thrown ashtrays, and not a single tip, I was his *favorite*.

He approached my table with an extended hand, something I'd never seen him do in two decades of encounters. I shook it, still trying to process this surreal moment.

"You know," he said, that trademark grin spreading across his face, "I've been thinking about how much money you've taken from me over the years."

"Well," I replied, "technically, the house took it. I just happened to be the one spinning the wheel."

He laughed—actually laughed. "Funny boy. But seriously, it must be millions by now. Millions!" He seemed almost proud of the figure, like it was an achievement worth celebrating.

"Why don't you play a few hands?" I suggested, gesturing to the pristine roulette layout. "For old times' sake?"

Ralph perked up at this point. But I caught a few supervisors within earshot visibly tense up, their collective sphincters likely tightening at the mere suggestion of Ahmet actually playing. They wanted no part of the potential discord he could unleash. Meanwhile, some of the newer staff looked puzzled, clearly having no idea what kind of legendary drama they might be witnessing.

"No, no. I'm just here to say hello. See how you're doing." He paused, studying the wheel and the room. "This is a nice setup you have here."

What struck me most was the absence of madness around us. In the old days, anytime Ahmet approached a table, you could feel the collective tension ripple through the pit. Supervisors materialized out of nowhere. Dealers at neighboring tables stole glances, waiting for the show to begin.

But now? The pit managers kept their distance and I could see the relief in their body language. Nobody wanted to deal with the potential drama, but nobody wanted to be rude to a player of his caliber either. They were content to let him conduct his social visit and move on.

We chatted for a few more minutes—about Vegas, about changes in the industry, about mutual acquaintances who'd moved on to other properties or other careers. It was the most extended conversation we'd ever had without raised voices or flying objects.

Ralph, who'd been quietly observing this unusually civilized exchange, finally spoke up. "You know, I've got to ask—how long have you two been doing this? I mean, how long have you known each other?"

Ahmet and I exchanged glances. "What do you think?" Ahmet asked me. "Twenty years?"

"Close," I said. "Has to be going back to the late eighties. We first met at the Golden Nugget downtown."

"Ah yes!" Ahmet's eyes lit up with the memory. "My first night at the Golden Nugget. You remember this, Randy?"

"How could I forget? You were down half a million, then walked across the casino to wire in two million more when they said you'd have to wait until morning for additional credit."

Ralph's eyebrows shot up. "Two million? Just like that?"

"Just like that," Ahmet confirmed with obvious pride. "I owned some banks in Turkey. Still do. When you own the bank, the ATM is wherever you are."

We all laughed at that—a genuine moment that would have been impossible during any of our previous encounters.

Finally, Ralph glanced at his watch. "We should probably head back, Ahmet. You have that meeting at ten."

Ahmet nodded and extended his hand again. "Take care of yourself, Randy. Maybe I'll see you around."

"Maybe you will," I replied, knowing somehow that I wouldn't.

As they walked away, I felt a strange mix of emotions. Relief, indeed—my colleagues were visibly relaxed again. But also a kind

Encore: Back for One More Round

of melancholy. For all his theatrics and impossible demands, Ahmet had been a constant in my Vegas story. He'd represented the old Vegas in many ways; the era when personalities mattered more than policies, when individual relationships trumped corporate protocols. This gentle farewell felt like more than just the end of our personal dynamic. It was a goodbye to an entire era of casino culture that was quietly slipping away, one retirement and one policy change at a time.

The whole encounter lasted maybe 10 minutes, but it perfectly encapsulated everything that had changed, and everything that remained, about this strange glittering world we'd both inhabited for so long.

That unexpected handshake with Ahmet reminded me that even the most adversarial relationships could end with mutual respect and that sometimes the person behind the performance was entirely different than the character they played at the tables.

Coming back for one more round had started as a survival move, a way to ride out a financial crisis that was rewriting the rules for everyone. But somewhere between dealing to tech billionaires with their $25,000 chips and managing international incidents at the roulette table, it became something more. I wasn't just earning a paycheck; I was watching Vegas evolve in real time. The nightclub money, the celebrity culture, the global wealth flowing through Encore—was this the same city I'd broken into 35 years earlier?

I'd returned expecting to simply weather the storm. Instead, I'd found myself with another front-row seat to the next chapter of Vegas history.

But the real stories were still waiting to be told—stories hidden in the tools we used, the people we trusted, and the elaborate games of deception that played out around us every night.

PART III
BEHIND THE CURTAIN

The Hidden World Behind the Glamour

The stories they don't want you to know: the elaborate security battles, the dangerous money flowing through the tables, the incredible journey of dealers from around the world, and how it all changed over three decades.

Chapter 15
Behind the Velvet Rope

Eternal Cat-and-Mouse Game

In the late '70s, downtown Las Vegas buzzed with energy, where every spin and hand dealt carried players' dreams of turning a toothpick into a lumber yard. As a newbie dealer, I thought the casino floor was all about the players—dreamers chasing jackpots, drunks chasing luck, and cheats chasing a quick score. Back then at the Las Vegas Club, security meant guys in cheap suits walking catwalks above the games, peering through one-way mirrors and occasionally using a grainy black-and-white camera that could barely make out faces, let alone catch any sleight of hand.

Those primitive cameras were laughably inadequate by today's standards. They used VHS tapes that had been recorded over so many times that the image quality resembled something out of a ghost story. Most of the casino floor wasn't even covered. If you were lucky, there might be one camera per pit and half of those were usually broken. In dim lighting, which described most of the casino, you couldn't make out much more than shadows and vague movement. If something went down, good luck getting any useful evidence from those fuzzy recordings.

It was a stark contrast to the high-definition, multi-angle, surveillance systems I encountered later. Those color cameras could zoom in close enough to read the serial numbers on chips or catch a dealer's nervous twitch. By the time I was dealing high-limit games, I had multiple cameras trained on me from every angle, tracking every move, every gesture. These weren't the fixed grainy relics of downtown—they could pan, tilt, and zoom with crystal clarity even in low light, with everything saved digitally for instant playback.

And today? The eye in the sky has evolved into something Alan Parsons could never have imagined when he sang about reading minds back in '82. Facial-recognition software knows you before you even approach a table. AI algorithms analyze your betting patterns, body language, even the way you stack your chips, literally trying to read your mind and anticipate trouble before it happens. You got used to it after a while, thought nothing of it. Nothing to sweat if you were honest.

But I learned quickly that even with primitive security in those early days, the real threats weren't always the obvious ones. Sometimes the most significant dangers wore the same badge as I did, clocking in with a smile and a scheme. In Vegas, everyone's watching everyone—especially the house—and after 35 years watching this game evolve from mirror-and-catwalk surveillance to systems that can track every chip movement in real time, I saw colleagues turn into con men in ways that'd make your head spin.

From rigged keno under catwalks to elaborate shoe switches at upscale casinos, from chips vanishing into sleeves under the nose of million-dollar camera systems to bathroom blunders that ended careers, these schemes taught me that no matter how sophisticated the technology got, the house still needed to play defense against threats from every direction.

The outside cons were impressive, professional crews who adapted their techniques as security evolved. But the inside jobs?

Behind the Velvet Rope 203

Those cut the deepest, regardless of how many cameras were watching. They shattered the one thing we all counted on in that controlled chaos: trust among the crew.

My education in betrayal started early, in my first week at that old-school Las Vegas Club, with a lesson that resonated through the next three decades. It began with the kind of news that should have made everyone celebrate—a player had just hit the jackpot of a lifetime.

Keno, for the uninitiated, is a game of pure chance: pick up to 20 numbers out of 80, hope they match the 20 drawn, and cash in big if they do. Sounds simple, right? Not when the game is rigged.

I was still wide-eyed, soaking up the casino floor's electric buzz, when the news broke. A player had nailed a $65,000 keno jackpot—a fortune in the late '70s, unheard of for a small joint like ours. The announcement quickly spread through the pit, cutting through the constant din of slot machines and dealer patter. Everyone seemed excited, even though we weren't winning, maybe just proud in some strange way.

But the high didn't last. By morning, whispers spread through the casino, turning joy to doubt. Murmurs hinted that the win wasn't clean. Then the truth dropped like a bad beat: The "lucky" winner was cozy with the graveyard-shift keno manager, the same guy who sat next to me having coffee on a break just that morning. Jaws hit the floor. The pit, once alive with chatter, grew tense, staff swapping stunned looks as suspicion took hold.

Things escalated fast. Mid-shift in front of players and dealers, security swooped in. The manager, eyes glued to the floor, was cuffed and marched out. The casino went dead quiet, the clink of chips replaced by an uneasy hush. It was like watching a house of cards collapse—shocking, sobering, and a little surreal.

Details trickled out slowly. The jackpot wasn't luck; it was a slick fraud orchestrated from the inside. How did they pull it off?

No one shared the full story. The casino locked everything down and the whispers—rigged tickets, possibly a tampered draw—remained just that, whispers. The industry played these things close to the vest, leaving us to piece it together in hushed break-room talks.

The betrayal stung. Trust, already a dicey bet in Vegas, took a hit. We wondered: Who else knew? Could we trust the guy dealing next to us? For me, still green and naive, it was a gut punch. I'd seen the casino as a game of chance, all flashing lights and jackpot bells. That arrest ripped the curtain back, revealing a world where vigilance wasn't optional; it was essential for survival. As a newbie barely breaking in my apron, I learned the house didn't just hold the edge; it had to guard it, even from its own.

That arrest changed how I saw the casino floor. Every smile became suspect, every friendly gesture potentially calculated. The keno manager, whom I knew briefly, had been planning his scam for who knows how long. But if I thought the rigged keno game was bad, I hadn't seen anything yet. At the Golden Nugget, betrayal came wrapped in an Employee of the Month plaque; and this time, the thief was someone we'd all admired.

At the Nugget, they introduced an Employee of the Month program to boost morale. First to win? Eddie, a day-shift blackjack dealer whose easy charm lit up the pit. Players loved him. So did we. The guy was magnetic, always had a joke for fellow dealers, remembered every regular's kids' names, and had this way of schmoozing the bosses that made it look effortless. Even the floor supervisors lingered at his table just to chat. Eddie was the kind of guy who made eight-hour shifts feel like hanging out with your favorite uncle.

Six months after his award, the casino was buzzing, not with cheers, but with shock. New security rules clamped down hard and word spread fast: Eddie, our golden boy, had been arrested. The kicker?

His jealous ex-wife, a cocktail waitress who still worked at the same casino even though they'd been divorced for over a year, tipped off security after spotting his shiny new car and boat. Talk about hell having no fury, especially when you have to see your ex-husband's success up close every shift.

Eddie's scam was slick, relying on his trusted reputation to slip under the radar. When a game ended, he tidied his chip rack as required by the rules, with a floor supervisor supposedly watching. But Eddie's halo blinded them. The supervisor, distracted by another game, barely glanced his way. That was when Eddie pocketed high-value chips, smooth as silk. To cover his tracks, he strolled around the table, adjusting chairs like a model employee. His boldest move was cashing those chips at a satellite cage run by his new girlfriend during breaks. It might have kept working if his ex hadn't ratted him out.

The fallout affected all of us. Dealers were now required to keep their hands beside the chip rack when tables went quiet. The rules felt excessive—until you understood why they were necessary.

What got to me was overhearing colleagues in the break room blaming the ex-wife instead of Eddie. It showed how deeply his charm had fooled us all, leaving a bitter taste. "Poor Eddie," one of them sighed. "If that bitter ex-wife of his had just minded her own business ..." Another chimed in, "She probably set him up. You know how vindictive she was during the divorce." I couldn't believe it. The guy had been stealing and they were still making excuses for him. Eddie's charm was so powerful that even after getting caught red-handed, he had people blaming everyone but him.

Eddie's fall gutted us. His charm had fooled everyone, leaving us side-eyeing every smile in the pit. The Employee of the Month plaque lost its shine and management retooled the program, preaching integrity over popularity. The Nugget's vibe shifted from buddy-buddy to watch-your-back, a cold reminder that camaraderie came second to security.

Eddie's bust woke us up to how small moves hid big crimes. His scam showed that betrayal didn't always come with fanfare—just a quiet dip into the rack. It also taught us that charm could be the most dangerous mask of all. But while we were learning to doubt our closest colleagues, professional crews were operating at a level that made the inside jobs look like amateur hour.

On an otherwise uneventful night, one blackjack table at the Nugget was the center of attention, hosting a full table with players eagerly placing their bets. Among them, those betting the most were riding an unstoppable wave of fortune. As the night progressed, their winning streak seemed to defy the odds. By the time the last card was dealt from the shoe, the biggest winners had cashed out, oddly choosing not to continue through the shuffle. When the dust settled, the table had lost over $150,000.

The next morning brought more than coffee and shift assignments. It ushered in a security crackdown that revealed everything we needed to know about the previous night's so-called lucky streak. As staff members clocked in, we were met not with the usual casual banter, but with a stern directive to tighten adherence to procedural standards. The focus was sharply on the handling of the shoe—a crucial piece of equipment in blackjack games. At the Nugget, the shoe, which held six decks of cards, was always secured to the table with a modest chain and clip for security reasons.

The rules hammered home that morning were specific: maintain physical contact with the shoe at all times and during dead games, pull the shoe to the center of the table directly in front of you. They also stressed watching for players carrying large packages such as shopping bags, gift boxes, or oversized purses, especially those seated at third base on the dealer's left.

Rumors flew among the staff about what really happened. Whispers suggested that the previous night's windfall for the players

Behind the Velvet Rope

might not have been due to luck alone. It was speculated, but never officially confirmed, that the shoe had been tampered with during the game. Such an act would allow the players to know the sequence of the cards, giving them an overwhelming advantage and the ability to predict every hand.

To pull off such a scam, the crew needed the table to themselves, with no outsiders to disrupt the flow of the cards. The method was deceptively simple, but relied on precise timing and misdirection. While the switch took place at third base, the real distraction happened at first base—a spilled drink, a loud argument over a bet, or perhaps a woman's top conveniently falling open. All eyes instinctively turned toward the commotion for just a second or two. That brief moment was all the cheats needed.

Those of us who'd been around figured they'd used a seemingly innocent package with a false bottom, strategically placed to aid in the shoe switch. It took only a split second to do the daring switch.

At first, I had my doubts. How could something like this actually work? Then I pictured it: a nondescript middle-aged woman, maybe wearing a "Birthday Girl" button, carrying a perfectly wrapped gift about the size of a shoe box (pun intended), complete with a fancy bow on top. She'd set it on the table edge, maybe fumble with her chips, and apologize sweetly for being in the way. Meanwhile, that pretty package had a hinged bottom that could drop open in a heartbeat. One smooth motion—old shoe up into the box, new shoe down onto the table. By the time we realized what happened, she'd be long gone, off to celebrate her cut of the winnings at her birthday party.

The beauty of this scam—if you could call it that—was its self-sufficiency. No dealers on the take, no floor supervisors looking the other way. Just a well-rehearsed crew who'd probably pulled this same switch at casinos across the country. They brought their own shoe, created their own distraction, and walked away with house money. Clean, professional, and gone before anyone knew what hit them.

In the aftermath of this incident, the casino's management doubled down on enforcing rules and monitoring games more closely. This vigilance was a clear message that the integrity of the games was paramount. While the stricter enforcement eventually relaxed, as it always did, the memory of that night's elaborate scam stuck with us. Every time I saw a player with an oversized package near third base, I felt my hand instinctively tighten on the shoe.

Tampering with equipment was daring, but some cheats preferred subtler methods that relied on quick hands and sharper timing.

During my shift as a blackjack dealer at the Golden Nugget, the play at the table was relatively calm, with only three players engaged in the game. The scene took an unexpected turn when the player occupying the middle seat excused himself for a restroom break, leaving his pile of chips on the table as a placeholder for his return. It was common among players who intended to return to their game.

Shortly after his departure, an individual with a dubious demeanor approached the table. His direct beeline toward the recently vacated seat caught my attention. Sensing his intentions might not be legitimate, I promptly informed him that the seat was already claimed, though other seats at the table were available. Uninterested in joining the game legitimately, he retreated without a word.

But he wasn't giving up. Minutes later, he was back with a bolder plan—if you could call a grab-and-run "planning." Without hesitation, he reached for the chips left by the absent player and dashed toward the exit. Reacting swiftly, I alerted my supervisor, who in turn notified security. Their quick response led to the would-be thief's apprehension at the casino's entrance, thwarting his escape. The daring of choosing a table situated deep within the casino's labyrinth, far from any quick exit, was a critical misstep in his plan. The stolen chips amounted to approximately $700, a loss prevented by the timely intervention of casino security.

The twist in this tale was the identity of the rightful owner of the chips. The chips belonged to Mike Tyson's sparring partner, a detail that made us all grateful security caught the thief before the owner returned. One could only imagine how that confrontation might have ended. Instead of possible violence, the situation was resolved through the proper channels, leading to the thief's detention at the Clark County Jail.

The following legal proceedings required the floor supervisor, Kay, and me to testify in court about the incident. As we prepared to take the stand, a knot of unease tightened in my chest at the thought of facing the culprit and pointing them out in front of the courtroom. The weight of that moment, publicly identifying the thief under the scrutiny of judge and jury, felt daunting, stirring a mix of nerves and resolve. We traveled the short distance to the courthouse, ready to recount our witness accounts. However, upon arrival, we were informed of an unexpected development. Having already retrieved his stolen chips, the player decided to drop all charges against the individual. This decision brought an end to what could have been a more prolonged legal battle, closing the chapter on an eventful episode that underscored the importance of vigilance and security within the casino environment. Though relieved to avoid the stand, I couldn't shake the lingering tension of what might have been.

Simple theft attempts like this were quickly dealt with, but sometimes the house got its revenge without lifting a finger. Not every cheating attempt ended in arrest or ejection. Occasionally, the best defense was just letting cheaters outsmart themselves.

One prevalent form of cheating in casinos is known as past posting or capping a bet. Past posting involves placing a bet after the outcome is already known, while capping refers to adding chips to a winning bet without being noticed.

I once watched surveillance footage of a past-posting attempt in our high-limit salon that backfired magnificently. A player had $5,000 riding on the bank side in baccarat. For those unfamiliar with the game, it's simple—bet on player or banker, closest to nine wins, and any total over nine drops the first digit (so 18 becomes 8).

The player cards were eight and ten, giving the player side a strong hand, totaling eight. The banker's first card was a five, looking weak. That's when our would-be cheat made his move. In one smooth motion, invisible to everyone but the cameras, he slid his $5,000 chip from banker to player, thinking he'd locked in a winner.

The irony was exquisite. The banker's second card? A four, making nine—the best possible hand in baccarat. His "smart" move had cost him $5,000. Instead of cheating his way to victory, he'd cheated himself out of a legitimate win. All of us watching the tape couldn't help but laugh at the poetic justice.

After 35 years of observing this eternal cat-and-mouse game, I'd seen the scams evolve from sleight-of-hand to sophisticated tech, but the underlying truth never changed: In Vegas, everyone's watching everyone and trust is still the most valuable currency on the floor. The wide-eyed kid who once thought the cameras were just for card counters had learned otherwise. Some of the biggest threats wore uniforms or had charming smiles. Still, I never stopped believing in people. I just learned to believe with both eyes open. Those early days of easy camaraderie gave way to a quieter more practiced vigilance. It wasn't paranoia—just the kind of awareness that comes from witnessing trust occasionally weaponized. The lesson was not to stop trusting, but to trust wisely, while keeping an eye on your rack and a hand on the shoe.

Chapter 16

Dangerous Players

Dealing to Killers, Kingpins, and Crime Bosses

Zhenli Ye Gon tipped like a man who'd never run out of money. At our baccarat tables, he casually tossed $1,000 chips to dealers after wins, betting $100,000 a hand without breaking a sweat. It wasn't until Mexican authorities found $200 million in cash hidden in the walls of his mansion that we understood why.

We thought he was just another pharmaceutical entrepreneur with money to burn. After his arrest made international headlines, we learned about the methamphetamine connections, the money laundering, and the whole twisted empire. Two of the Mexican agents involved in raiding his mansion were murdered months later. It was a chilling reminder that the money flowing across our tables sometimes came with blood on it.

The truth is, you never really knew who was sitting across from you in the high-limit room. Behind the expensive suits and generous tips lurked some of the most dangerous criminals in the world. That well-dressed businessman might be running a cartel. The charming socialite could be laundering mob money. The generous tipper might be trying to lose drug profits as fast as possible.

Over my decades dealing to high rollers, I've encountered characters whose stories would make Hollywood scriptwriters jealous—some merely eccentric, others genuinely dangerous. This chapter delves into my encounters with some of the most notorious individuals to grace our tables. My first real glimpse into this shadow world came through our Japanese high rollers at the Mirage. What started as admiration for their generous tipping gradually revealed something far more sinister.

From flamboyant personalities to shadowy figures whose wealth came from sources we preferred not to think about, these are the players who reminded us that in Vegas, everyone has secrets. Some simply hide them better than others.

At the Mirage, two of our most prominent baccarat players from Japan, known for their generosity with tips, were revealed to have connections to the Yakuza. The Yakuza is a powerful and hierarchical organized-crime syndicate engaged in a variety of illicit enterprises, including drug trafficking, extortion, money laundering, and illegal gambling. They operate with a strict code of conduct and loyalty, including specific rituals.

One of them was Akio Kashiwagi, nicknamed "The Warrior"; he played baccarat for over 12 hours nonstop at $100,000 a hand. Known to us as a real estate investor, the dealers always looked forward to his arrival, as his presence usually meant a nice bump in pay. Despite Kashiwagi's frequent visits to the Mirage, he was known to have also graced numerous top casinos in Las Vegas and around the world. The large bets he placed led to huge financial swings at each property he played at, until a continued string of bad luck led to his downfall. After a huge loss, he returned to Tokyo, where he faced more than just unpaid casino debts; he also owed millions to

Dangerous Players

his Yakuza associates. In early 1992, he was found brutally slain in his luxurious residence at the foot of Mt. Fuji, a victim of a samurai sword attack. His murder remains unsolved, with speculation about its connection to his gambling debts, business dealings, or other aspects of his complex and secretive life.

Another significant Japanese baccarat player I dealt to briefly around the same era as Kashiwagi was Ken Mizuno. Mizuno played even higher stakes than Kashiwagi, sometimes betting up to $200,000 a hand. Over time, he became known for losing a staggering $150 million in Las Vegas, most of it at the Mirage. Still, he was one of our best Georges ever: generous, consistent, and memorable.

But Mizuno's troubles weren't just about the dice failing to roll his way. His downfall came not in a casino, but in court, after over 4,000 angry members of his elite golf club near Tokyo sued him for fraud.

His company had promised exclusivity, limiting memberships to no more than 2,800, but ultimately sold over 52,000, bringing in approximately $850 million. That turned tee times into a fantasy and Mizuno into a fugitive. He faced legal charges in both the United States and Japan for tax evasion and fraud. His U.S. assets were seized, and some funds were returned to creditors and victims.

It was a sobering realization—that some of the most celebrated tippers we dealt to, the players who brought us windfalls and shared laughs, were fueling their generosity through fraud, deception, and mob connections.

And the ties to the Yakuza didn't stop with Kashiwagi. Over the years, as I dealt to more Asian high rollers, I started to notice something even more unsettling.

One astonishing custom I encountered is the Japanese ritual known as *yubitsume*. Occasionally, I noticed Japanese players missing the tips of their pinky fingers. Initially, I assumed these were accidental injuries, but curiosity led me to ask a colleague, who explained the practice known as "finger shortening."

Yubitsume is deeply embedded in Japanese culture, particularly among members of the Yakuza. This act of self-amputation, typically of the little finger, is performed as an apology, punishment, or demonstration of sincere remorse. Traditionally, it also serves to settle debts or signify submission after internal conflicts. The severed portion is wrapped respectfully and presented to the boss, known as the *oyabun*. Losing part of the little finger weakens one's grip on a sword, symbolizing greater dependence and loyalty to the boss for protection. Seeing this practice firsthand reminded me of the complex, often hidden layers of the lives of those who sat at my table.

If the Japanese players earned a quiet respect, even fascination, the Russians inspired something far colder: fear. The entire mood on the floor shifted the moment they appeared, growing noticeably colder and more tense with the rumored presence of individuals with Russian Mafia connections. My colleagues, some fluent in Russian and more acquainted with these factions, hinted as much. In stark contrast to other criminals who might display generosity or a semblance of enjoyment during their games, these individuals embodied the archetype of the formidable outlaw. Their glares alone conveyed a chilling intent, as if they harbored lethal intentions regardless of the game's outcome.

They reminded me of something out of a movie and I don't mean a semi-charming Russian character like John Malkovich in *Rounders*. Instead, their presence was more akin to the menacing figures who dominate the screen with a silent threatening aura. Clearly, a lesson in charm and social graces, perhaps inspired by a Dale Carnegie course, would have been beneficial for them.

Although their visits were infrequent, dealing with these types of players always brought a sense of tension. Their cold piercing stares and intimidating demeanor made it clear they weren't the kind of folks you'd want to mess with. I'd had plenty of experience with players trying to intimidate me with their barking commands and threats, but these folks made my skin crawl like no others.

Their presence always raised an unspoken question: What if things go sideways? With players like these and money stacked sky high, we couldn't help but wonder what kind of backup we really had. Maybe it was hidden out of sight, but always at the ready. You know, like an ace up their sleeve. It seemed like a fairly safe bet that they had more than just tasers and pepper spray to work with, especially given the high stakes and potential dangers that came with the territory. But it wasn't just the Russians that got me thinking about the presence of firearms in the casino.

Guns in casinos has been rare, at least based on my observations. Until the early '80s, security guards at the Golden Nugget were an exception, as they openly carried firearms in holsters. I distinctly remember one guard who even sported a revolver with pearl handles, reminiscent of a cowboy. However, a policy change eventually prohibited guards from carrying guns, leading to a significant departure of security personnel at that time.

One specific incident at Bellagio involved Rick, the shift boss, who hurried after Kerry Packer as he was leaving the casino following an unsuccessful gambling session. Packer was about to depart without signing for a $10 million marker. Given his impeccable reputation for settling debts, it was likely an oversight due to his haste. As Rick approached him while he was getting into his limousine, he was startled by two bodyguards wielding Uzi submachine guns. Rick managed to obtain the necessary signature once he overcame his initial shock.

While Rick's encounter ended with just a signature, not

everyone was so lucky. A memorable incident was shared by a fellow employee, a Native American who was affectionately nicknamed Chief. He had previously worked as a dice dealer at the Aladdin, which frequently hosted junkets from New York that included very intimidating individuals, some with connections to organized-crime families. During one such junket, Chief made a few comments to a player who was losing and didn't appreciate the jests. After the dice rolled yet another loss for this player, Chief's additional remark pushed the player to the edge. The player, evidently connected to powerful figures, possibly even those backing the casino, drew a revolver and pressed it against Chief's side with a chilling threat about silencing him permanently. The authenticity of the threat and whether the gun was loaded remain unknown, but Chief did not utter another word, continuing his duties in silence and fear.

Not all danger wore a scowl or carried a gun. Some of the most suspicious characters looked like regular high-limit players, until the IRS changed the rules with a regulation that turned the spotlight on cash itself. Before 1985, it was common to encounter large sums of cash, often in small bills. We didn't inquire why someone was walking up with $20,000 in $20s and $5s. Maybe they were saving up for their vacation. Maybe they had a small business like a car wash or laundromat. Fortunately, as dealers, it wasn't our concern.

Players strolled in with suspiciously thick wads of bills, dropped them on the table, and we counted them up without batting an eye. Whether that money came from a dry-cleaning empire, a chain of laundromats, or something less savory, we were dealers, not detectives.

A notable group that occasionally visited the Nugget in the early '80s was a crew from Detroit. The most memorable thing about these

Dangerous Players 217

guys was the amount of cash they showed up with. They played craps on one table, while another table was set up for a couple of dealers just to count out the stacks of cash they brought in. At the time, we didn't know what type of business they were in, but they always made a flashy appearance with lots of gold chains, jewelry, and gold teeth. Their gold sparkled under the casino lights, their swagger unmistakable.

Before 1985, cash was king in Vegas. No questions asked. But when the IRS introduced Regulation 6A, requiring ID and reporting for any cash wagers over $10,000, those colorful characters with duffel bags full of small bills vanished overnight.

A few years after the Detroit crew disappeared, I was dealing a quiet Thursday graveyard shift when another dealer showed me a newspaper clipping. "Remember those Detroit guys with the duffel bags?" he asked. The headline made my stomach drop. Their leader, Richard "Maserati Rick" Carter, had been murdered.

But it was the burial that had everyone talking. They'd interred him in a $16,000 coffin shaped like a Mercedes-Benz, complete with spinning tires. Classic Rick. Even in death, he had to make a statement. I remembered watching him at the craps tables, how he'd command the entire pit with that same theatrical energy he apparently brought to everything in life. The craps dealers had counted those endless stacks of bills while we watched from our posts. We had all suspected where the money came from, but seeing it confirmed in black and white—crack kingpin, territorial wars, shot in his hospital bed—made those late-night sessions feel different in retrospect. Those weren't just high-stakes games; we'd all been witnesses to blood money rolling across the felt.

Looking back, Regulation 6A didn't just change our paperwork; it emptied our high-limit rooms of players who couldn't explain where their money came from. The Detroit crew vanished overnight, but the truth about their cash caught up eventually. Every time the craps dealers had counted those bills, separated them into neat stacks for the cage, we'd all witnessed something darker than we'd understood at the time. The money hadn't just been dirty. It was stained by far darker origins.

Regulation 6A might have scared off the big players with their duffel bags of drug money, but it didn't stop every criminal from trying their luck. Some figured if they kept it under $10,000, they'd fly under the radar. They figured wrong, especially when their money was literally marked.

Of course, not all criminals who wandered into our casino were subtle about their intentions. Some practically announced themselves. While dealing at the Golden Nugget, news of a bank robbery a few blocks away stirred the casino floor. Players trickled in, buzzing about the heightened police presence in the vicinity, given our proximity to the crime scene. Roughly 20 minutes post-incident, two jittery individuals entered, approaching a blackjack table with a bag of cash conspicuously stained red, as were their hands. Embedded within the stolen loot, a dye pack had exploded, marking the bills—and the robbers—with a vivid red coloring.

Seemingly under the impression that the bustling casino environment would provide an ideal cover to launder their tainted winnings quickly, they opted to try their luck at the tables. However, their plan was flawed from the start. Our security team, already on high alert due to the nearby robbery, needed no detective skills to connect the dots. The duo was apprehended almost immediately, quite literally caught red-handed in their ill-conceived attempt to blend in.

The incident unfolded in an almost cinematic fashion, adding an unexpected twist to an otherwise ordinary day at the Golden Nugget. As the robbers, cloaked in false confidence, placed their bets, the surrounding patrons couldn't help but cast curious glances at the unmistakable red markings adorning both the money and their hands. It was a stark reminder of how, in the heat of desperation, logic often falls by the wayside.

In the aftermath, the casino handled the situation with a low-key approach, as was common practice for many incidents of this nature. The primary aim was to avoid causing any undue anxiety among the guests. As a result, little was reported in the press about the robbery and capture, at least to my recollection. The casino's security team swiftly and discreetly dealt with the situation, ensuring that the crooks were taken into custody without causing a major disruption to the casino's operations.

While I had the opportunity to explore a variety of global cultures, I also encountered diverse cultures within the United States, some just a four-hour drive away on Interstate 15 to Los Angeles. Throughout the '90s, Las Vegas served as the backdrop for some of the most eagerly anticipated global championship boxing matches.

As dealers, we relished the surge in activity. They attracted high rollers and generous tips alike. However, these events also drew a less-welcome element—disruptive and sometimes violent. There was speculation that at the heart of this were gangs from California, many of whom were avid fight fans.

One of the wildest moments in Las Vegas sports history occurred in 1997 during a boxing match between "Iron" Mike Tyson and Evander Holyfield at the MGM Grand. Tyson, notorious for his aggressive style and headline-making antics, did the unthinkable by biting off a piece of Holyfield's ear during the fight. This jaw-dropping move got Tyson disqualified and kicked off a full-blown riot among the fans. The intensity of the reactions led to a two-hour shutdown of the MGM Grand, marking a first for the venue since its opening four years earlier. Tyson mixing it up with police officers inside the ring turned the crowd into a wild stampede. Outside the arena, the casino was like a scene from a movie, with blackjack tables flipped over, chips scattering like confetti, and drinks making a mess of the floor.

The situation escalated when a false report of gunfire sent the crowd into an even greater frenzy. Despite zero evidence of any shots being fired, the rumor alone was enough to crank the chaos up to eleven. The madness spilled out onto the Las Vegas Boulevard, grinding parts of it to a halt and forcing the cops to shut it down completely.

To give you a taste of how nuts things got, a buddy of mine working at the New York-New York casino, directly across the Strip from the MGM, told me about the crowd storming into their place. This bit of the story really shows how the craziness wasn't just confined to the MGM Grand. Some of the folks from the mob, looking to make a quick buck in the confusion, tried to cash out lammers at the New York-New York cage. These lammers had been grabbed after blackjack tables were overturned at the MGM. If you're scratching your head, wondering what lammers are, they're these little plastic disks casinos use to keep tabs on players' call bets. They're basically worthless outside of the game, which makes trying to cash them out pretty laughable. But that didn't stop people from trying, highlighting just how confused the situation was.

In 2007, the NBA All-Star games were held in Las Vegas, attracting similar crowds. The Wynn was already a hotspot for NBA players, with the Wynn family being big-time supporters of Las Vegas basketball. They even had a knack for bringing in former UNLV players to work in various roles at their casinos. Coaching greats such as Mike Krzyzewski from Duke or John Thompson from Georgetown often visited different Wynn properties when their teams came to the city.

Given the Wynns' love for the NBA and the casino's top-tier nightclub, Tryst, which was a magnet for players and celebs alike, it was no surprise that All-Star Weekend turned the place into party central. However, one promotional event at Tryst spiraled out of

Dangerous Players 221

control. NBA fans and party-goers flipped tables, spilled drinks everywhere, and gave the security team a run for their money. A few folks ended up in handcuffs.

When the SWAT team got called in, things hit another level. That move alone showed just how wild things got and the headaches it caused for everyone trying to keep the peace. Steve Wynn was livid about the mess, saying it was a low point in terms of how people behaved. The damage bill for the night at Tryst alone was over $100,000.

Just walking from my game to the break room, I could feel the tension, passing by bars packed with fans who could explode at any moment. Keeping everyone safe—guests, staff, and the premises themselves—was a top priority, especially with VIPs wandering around decked out in expensive jewelry and carrying substantial amounts of cash. The last thing the Wynn needed was for its high-end brand to take a hit from a wild weekend.

The *Las Vegas Review-Journal* reported over 400 calls related to NBA All-Star Weekend—from brawls to property damage and even a few incidents involving guns near Strip clubs and casinos.

Despite no major catastrophe, it felt like we were walking a tightrope for days. There were constant close calls, angry flare-ups, and the looming threat that something could spiral out of control at any moment. I'd bet most casino employees across the city felt the same. It was, hands down, the most tense and threatening few days I'd ever experienced on the job.

After the dust settled, it was clear the city had to rethink how it handled large events. Hospitality workers, casino execs, and the police realized we needed better crowd management, beefed-up security, and a clearer game plan. The 2007 NBA All-Star event wasn't just another busy Vegas weekend. It was a wake-up call on how thin the line could be between excitement and anarchy.

As I reflect on these encounters during my decades as a dealer in Las Vegas, it's clear that the glitz and glamor of the casino floor often concealed a darker underbelly. From the high rollers with questionable sources of wealth to the notorious figures linked to organized crime, my experiences have provided a glimpse into the rich mosaic of humanity that thrives in Sin City.

I wasn't just dealing cards; I was dealing with the shadows that Vegas tries to keep hidden. For every legitimate businessman at my table, there might have been someone whose money came with a body count. We took their tips, we smiled, we dealt the next hand. Because in Vegas, the house doesn't judge—it just takes its cut.

Chapter 17
The Melting Pot

Stories of Survival, Hustle, and the Long Road to the Table

The break room at the Mirage often felt like the United Nations—only with more coffee, hangovers, and sarcasm. Turkish curses mixed with Tagalog jokes, British complaints about the impossibility of finding "proper tea in this bloody desert" collided with Spanish gossip about last night's high roller, and somewhere in the corner, two dealers from Poland compared notes on which Vegas grocery store carried the closest thing to real kielbasa. I poured myself coffee and realized I was one of the few in the room whose journey to Vegas hadn't required a passport, a prayer, or both.

Throughout my decades as a dealer, I've had the privilege of working alongside individuals from every corner of the globe. From bright-eyed newcomers fresh off the plane to seasoned veterans with stories etched into the lines of their faces, each person brought a unique perspective and background to the table.

Take my friend Manny from Havana. He never dealt in pre-Castro Havana. He was too young. But his father's hardware store stood just blocks from the old casinos. After the revolution, the government confiscated his family's business, along with their rental properties.

During one of our breaks, Manny pulled out his phone, zooming in on Google Maps. "See this corner?" He pointed to a street intersection in Havana. "That was Papa's hardware store. Three stories." His finger traced the street. "And here—this was our house. My mother's roses probably still grow in that garden."

I watched him stare at that screen, his eyes seeing something Google's satellites couldn't capture—a life erased, a childhood stolen. "You ever think about going back?" I asked.

"To visit the buildings that belong to someone else?" He shook his head, closing the map. "No. But I look sometimes. Just to remember it was real."

Manny had recounted his escape before, how his family gathered at a secluded beach under cover of darkness, hearts pounding with fear and anticipation. He was eight years old, clutching his mother's hand as they boarded the small boat that carried them to freedom, his young mind struggling to comprehend why they had to leave everything behind.

Years later, relatives who'd worked in the old Havana casinos helped him find his way to Las Vegas. It was here, dealing cards instead of hardware, that Manny built his new life. But sometimes, during those 4 a.m. breaks, he pulled up that map again, tracing streets he'd never walk again with his finger on a screen.

Among the many international dealers who found their way to Las Vegas was Shela, a woman whose journey from Syria exemplified the casino's role as America's most unlikely melting pot. When she first arrived in Vegas, Shela didn't head straight for the tables. Instead, she performed as a belly dancer, bringing a taste of Middle Eastern culture to the neon-lit stages of the Strip.

By the time we worked together in the early 2000s, Shela had transitioned from dancing to dealing, but she carried the weight of two worlds on her shoulders. During our breaks, she often voiced her worries about relatives back home, where tensions ran perpetually high. The distance between her life in Vegas and her Syrian roots seemed to grow wider with each passing year.

One afternoon, as we chatted about her kids—she had two boys—Shela mentioned something that stopped me cold: She had never learned to ride a bicycle. It was such a small detail, yet it hit me like a sledgehammer. Here was this middle-aged woman who could deal cards with the best of them, had reinvented herself in a new country, but had never experienced something I'd taken for granted since childhood. In that moment, the vast cultural canyon between our upbringings became startlingly clear.

The majority of my fellow dealers who came from abroad were lucky enough to be winners of the green-card lottery. I'll never forget how Dmitri found out he'd won. His mother worked in a government agency back in Moldova and had seen the list of winners before the official notifications went out.

"She called me at three in the morning. I thought someone died," Dmitri told me, his eyes still bright with the memory. "She was crying so hard she couldn't speak. Then she screamed, 'You won! You won! Your name is on the list!'"

He'd jumped out of bed, waking his entire apartment building with his celebration. "My neighbors thought I was crazy—dancing in the hallway in my underwear. But I didn't care. I was going to America." He shook his head, grinning. "Better than winning the real lottery. Money you can lose. This? This was winning a life."

Every winner I knew treated it exactly like that: like they'd hit the jackpot. Because in many ways, they had.

Two groups of people with whom I worked regularly came from Turkey and England. My Turkish colleagues had fled after their government outlawed gambling in the late '90s. Lutfe, a dealer I worked alongside for years, told me about a time he was coming home late from his shift at a casino in Istanbul. He'd just gotten home and was having a beer when he heard a pounding at the door. It was the police. As he opened the door, they pushed him aside, knocking him down, then handcuffed him and hauled him off to jail. It turned out that a bank had been robbed in the vicinity that he had walked by on his way to his apartment and he resembled the description of the actual thief. Luckily, his father had some sort of connection with someone or he might still be in a Turkish prison.

My friends from the UK who dealt single-zero roulette had usually gone through extensive training for the position in a casino back home. The fact that they weren't allowed to accept tips in their home country at the time made their pilgrimage to Las Vegas as much a financial decision as an adventure.

Throughout the '80s and '90s, many of the people I worked with from Southeast Asia had similarly horrific tales of their journeys to the U.S. and, ultimately, to Las Vegas.

Trung, to this day, is claustrophobic. He attributes it to his time as a small boy in the '70s when his family fled Vietnam on a cramped boat. For days, they sat just off the coast, shoulder to shoulder, packed in so tightly there was only a small window for air—they took turns reaching it, gasping for a few precious breaths. He told me how, after drifting for days, excitement rippled through the boat as a vessel approached. Rescue, they thought. But instead, it was pirates, who boarded and stole every last possession the passengers had.

As the situation grew more desperate, another boat was spotted on the horizon. This time, it flew an American flag. That flag, Trung said, was the most beautiful thing he'd ever seen. The rescuers eventually relocated his family to Kansas City, where he went to school before finding his way to Las Vegas. Even now, decades later, tight spaces still send a jolt of panic through him. The trauma never left—it just found quieter places to hide.

Around the same time, Sophal, at the age of 10, was living in Cambodia with her parents during the reign of the Khmer Rouge, led by Pol Pot. She escaped after the tragic loss of her parents to the regime. Alone, she ran through the jungle for days until she was able to cross the border and land at a missionary orphanage, where she was safe. Through the help of the missionaries, she contacted a U.S. charity that she'd written to every week since she was 13, asking to be accepted into a program that relocated refugees to the United States. After a year, she heard back that her prayers had been answered; she was headed to the U.S. She eventually gained citizenship and joined us at the Mirage as a blackjack dealer.

Lena was originally from Poland. I'll never forget standing in line with her at the employee buffet one break, both of us loading our plates with prime rib, shrimp, three kinds of salad.

"You know what's crazy?" she said, adding another spoonful of mashed potatoes. "Growing up in Warsaw, I once stood in line for four hours, because someone said the store might have chicken. Might have." She laughed, but it wasn't amusing. "My mother sent me at five in the morning with my sister. We took turns—one holds the spot, one goes to check the other lines. Maybe butter at one store, meat at another."

I looked down at my overloaded plate, suddenly self-conscious.

"Don't feel bad," she said, reading my face. "This—" she gestured at the endless buffet options, "—this is why I'm here. Well, this and the tips." She grinned, then headed back to her table, leaving me standing there with my mountain of free food, thinking about the different kinds of lines we all stand in.

A few weeks later, I was dealing roulette when Lena was dealing on the table next to mine. During a lull, she casually mentioned she'd dealt in South Africa before Vegas.

"How'd you like that?" I asked.

"The money was good," she nodded. "When we weren't evacuating for bomb threats."

"Bomb threats?"

"Oh yes. Rival casinos called them in, trying to scare away

business." She paused, watching my reaction. "But the worst was the black mamba."

I took a double-take. "The what?"

"Someone threw a black mamba, a very poisonous snake, right onto one of the roulette tables. To clear out the casino." She shrugged like this was normal. "Made those Warsaw bread lines seem safe. At least the bread didn't try to bite you."

These stories of war, upheaval, and survival revealed the quiet strength behind the uniforms we wore.

Many of the casino employees were from the Philippines. My friend Danny embodied something I saw in so many of them—an absolute determination to climb every rung of the ladder, no matter how low they had to start.

"I didn't care if I was cleaning toilets," Danny told me once. "I just needed to get inside the door." He'd started as a porter in Tahoe, mopping floors and hauling trash at 3 a.m. But every break, he watched the dealers, memorizing their moves. He practiced chip and card handling in his apartment, dealing to empty chairs.

Within two years, he was standing behind a blackjack table. Five years later, he was a floor supervisor. By the time I worked at Bellagio, Danny was my boss. "You know why Filipinos succeed in casinos?" he asked me once. "We already know what real hard work looks like. This? This is easy."

Another coworker from the Philippines was Frank. He'd worked in a casino in Israel, but his most memorable story from his dealing journey to Las Vegas happened on a cruise ship in the '90s. The ship was relocating to a new port for the season, carrying only a skeleton crew and a handful of guests.

"Four-thirty in the morning, everything just died," Frank recalled. "No power. No engines. Nothing." The emergency announcement wasn't a drill—the old ship was taking on water. "They're telling us 'abandon ship' in five languages."

The Melting Pot

After everyone was safely in the lifeboats and mayday signals went out, a Russian freighter picked them up. "We watched our ship go down from their deck," Frank said. "All I could think was—there go the new shoes I just bought. They were finally broken in, no more blisters." Frank laughed now at losing his new shoes, but the terror of watching the ship sink lingered in his voice.

He smiled, the way you do at a memory that was terrifying then, but makes a hell of a story now. Then he added, almost as an afterthought, "You know, part of me still wonders if that whole thing wasn't a setup—old ship, light on passengers, probably worth more at the bottom than at the dock." He chuckled. "After that, dealing to drunk high rollers? Easy. At least the casino floor doesn't sink."

While international journeys often involved peril, many of my American-born colleagues brought their own brand of determination, proving that reinvention didn't always require crossing oceans.

But not everyone had to escape regimes or dodge black mambas to end up under the casino lights. Some of us came from right here—Jersey suburbs, Midwest towns, or desert neighborhoods just off the Strip. We didn't have to flee governments, but we still found ourselves side by side with those who had. And somehow, in that break-room stew of accents, attitudes, and backstories, we all found a rhythm that worked.

While the international cast of characters I worked with brought a rich array of cultures and experiences to the Las Vegas casino industry, the diversity within our American-born colleagues was equally remarkable. The casino floor attracted an eclectic mix of personalities, each with their own story to tell.

Some were drawn to the city from far-flung corners of the country, lured by the promise of opportunity, adventure, and the chance to reinvent themselves in a place where anything seemed possible. They came from all walks of life: former teachers, aspiring actors, ex-military personnel, and everything in between. Each brought a unique set of skills, experiences, and perspectives to the table.

Supervisors came from every walk of life. There were guys with thick New York accents, a few cowboys, and plenty of others who made you realize you didn't need to be a rocket scientist to work in a casino. In fact, some of them practically proved you didn't.

But then there was Sal.

He actually *was* a rocket scientist. Before stepping onto the casino floor, Sal had worked at NASA—on the Apollo Lunar Module, no less. It was the ultimate shift in scenery, going from the moon to the Mirage.

Not everyone had a résumé like Sal's. Some people came to the business looking for a fresh start. Others didn't want to talk much about their pasts. But that was the beauty of Las Vegas. Everyone had a story and more often than not, it started over right there on the casino floor.

The women dealers had just as varied backgrounds as the men: single mothers trying to keep a family together, former showgirls who traded their feathered headdresses for a tuxedo and a physically less-taxing profession. Others, just like the men, might have come from fields that they wanted to get away from and start anew.

That was likely the case with Gloria, a blackjack dealer at the Nugget. Since we were splitting our tokes among the entire shift, we were glad to have her on our team; she was a moneymaker. For big events like a fight weekend, she wore this long dress with a slit up the side. She had a Marilyn Monroe look about her and the guys were always very generous with their tips on her games.

The story of her journey to Las Vegas isn't as interesting as the one after she quit. Gloria left the casino business in the early '80s. Without much fanfare, she was gone; rumor had it that she moved to Arizona with her new boyfriend. Her fellow dealers lost touch with Gloria until about two years later, when we saw her on the news and read about her in the papers. It seems Gloria and her boyfriend had been arrested after a string of bank robberies throughout California and Arizona.

We always knew Gloria was sweet and glamorous, though a bit scatterbrained at times and never quite on the same wavelength as the rest of us. But none of us saw *that* coming. When the news broke, we stood around the break room, jaws hanging. It just didn't compute.

We'd worked side by side with her, split our tokes with her, laughed at her quirks. And now we were watching her mugshot on the six o'clock news. Some of us tried to piece together the clues in hindsight, but the truth was simple: Whatever story Gloria was living, we were only part of the first chapter. The rest played out in a plot twist none of us could have predicted.

Many of the dealers I worked with from the U.S. had migrated from other states where they got their start in gaming establishments that weren't exactly legal. Jim told me about his days working in a speakeasy in New Orleans. Besides watching out for the law, he had to provide his own security, a small baseball bat he kept under the table. He claimed he never had to use it, but did need to show it a few times to help solve disputes.

During the '70s, the Alaska pipeline was a gold rush, offering a chance at a hefty paycheck, but life out on the line was brutal and isolated. Pipeline jobs paid significantly more than the national average, with welders pulling in over $100,000 a year during construction (equivalent to over $500,000 today). The work was grueling, with workers battling extreme temperatures, dangerous terrain, and limited amenities.

Some of the dealers I worked with started out dealing in the bars and work camps along the Alaska pipeline, where they found plenty of bored guys with pockets full of money and nowhere else to spend it. After the pipeline was completed in 1977, the big paychecks and work camps disappeared. Some of these dealers, having tasted the gaming life, naturally gravitated toward Las Vegas.

Even though casino gambling was pretty much legal only in Las Vegas and Atlantic City when I started, that didn't stop people from all over the country from frequenting illegal casinos, where some of the old-timers got their experience. The same was true in many countries throughout the world; some of the operations were basic and simple, while others could look similar to a legit casino if the politicians were on the side of the house. I had friends who worked in these types of illegal casinos in the Philippines; they were always given a heads-up about a periodic faux raid.

A bonus for me was the food. I always looked forward to what might turn up in the break room. You could eat your way around the world without ever leaving the casino. One day it might be homemade Chinese dumplings or freshly baked baklava, another day, kimchi or curry or ribs smoked low and slow like someone's uncle had spent all night prepping them. It wasn't a potluck—it was a passport.

We came from everywhere—refugees, dreamers, survivors—but we found the same sanctuary under the casino's neon canopy. In that break room, our stories didn't just pass time; they connected us. Vegas didn't just deal cards, it dealt second chances.

From above, the casino floor looks like choreography—shuffle, pitch, sweep, pay. Different accents, different passports, same games. On break, those same hands come alive, slicing the air to describe storms back home, tracing the curves of mountains left behind, or counting the miles between here and a family they're still supporting.

We didn't all come here chasing the dream. Some were running from things, others just needed a fresh start. But the chips didn't care about your accent, your baggage, or your immigration status. All that mattered was: could you deal clean, handle the pressure, and keep the game moving?

Ultimately, that was the miracle of it all. Not that we came from everywhere, but that for a few hours each night, we came together.

The Melting Pot

And for me? I always knew I was lucky to be there. But hearing the stories of my coworkers—stories of escape, survival, sacrifice—I realized just how easy my path had been. I hadn't crossed oceans or jungles. I didn't flee war or persecution. I just followed a fascination with blackjack and a dream of something different.

They earned their seats the hard way. I got mine with a full tank of gas and a paperback on card counting. I was fortunate. But more than that, I was humbled. Surrounded by people whose journeys would make mine look like a detour, I learned the real meaning of work, grit, and gratitude.

Chapter 18
Ever-Changing Las Vegas

*From Cigar Smoke to Sushi Bars:
Over Three Decades of Sin City Evolution*

As I left the Encore after my final shift and drove down the Strip, the blazing desert sun looked exactly as it had that morning in 1979 when I stumbled out of the Las Vegas Club after my first graveyard shift. But that sun was about the only thing that hadn't changed.

The cigarette smoke that made my clothes reek? Gone. The clatter of coins? Silent digital credits now. The old-school pit bosses with their pinky rings and loud sports coats? Swapped out for MBAs with iPhones. Heck, I'd traded my polyester vest and clip-on tie for an Armani tuxedo somewhere along the way.

The players had evolved just as dramatically. Downtown's grubby tourists in polyester shirts, carrying the eau de desperation scent of stale cigarettes and cheap cologne, had given way to XS nightclub refugees in $1,000 designer outfits, trailing clouds of Tom Ford and Hermès that could perfume an entire pit.

The daily envelope of cash tips was now directly deposited into my bank account. Sometimes I wondered if we'd lost more than we'd gained.

Sure, the air was cleaner, the uniforms sharper, and the payroll system more streamlined, but somewhere along the way, the fun got drained away. The job used to feel like a backstage pass to the wildest show in town. There were nights you couldn't wait to get to work, not just for the action, but for the people. We ribbed one another between spins, swapped stories on break, and celebrated when a dealer dumped the rack to a George and made everyone's night.

Now? It's quieter. Polished. Efficient. But that raw energy—the camaraderie, the mischief, the sense that anything could happen on a Tuesday night—that's harder to find. We used to end shifts with drinks and war stories. Now, most people clock out and check their 401(k). The newer dealers are professional and well-trained. But sometimes I miss the characters.

The differences weren't just on the casino floor, they followed us into the break rooms, too. Even my break activities changed after my return. Despite having hundreds of TV channels in the dealer's lounge, I'd try to get the television switched to the news and politics, while the dice dealers wanted to watch Three Stooges reruns, though I guess those have many similarities to politics.

Instead, I began to gravitate toward the quiet room for a 10-minute nap. Sitting there in the silence, I realized that not all the changes I was seeing were external. The young dealer who once might have stopped by a bar after the graveyard shifts was now sneaking power naps on his break. Maybe the problem wasn't just that Vegas had lost its soul. Maybe I was just getting too old for this all-night party.

I recall the reaction of one of the old-school bosses on a Sunday morning to a woman accompanying her husband at a dice table. The group of rowdy players let the expletives fly as the dealer called seven out with the last roll of the dice, to the horror of the woman spectator. She quickly voiced her discomfort to the pit boss nearby, her face tightening with disapproval as she leaned in with arms crossed.

To her surprise, the boss didn't offer any reassurance. Instead, without missing a beat, he replied, "This ain't no church, lady. St. Joseph's is right down the street."

Her expression shifted instantly. Her eyebrows arched in disbelief, lips parted as if to respond, but no words came out. She looked like she'd just been handed a drink she didn't order. A sharp inhale, a shake of the head, and she turned on her heel, retreating with her husband in tow, in search of a more civilized atmosphere.

That was vintage Vegas management—the kind of boss you just don't see anymore. These were the tough guys with cigars, or at least cigarettes, always with a cup of coffee or possibly something more substantial. Many had looks straight out of central casting, sometimes even sporting the occasional crooked nose that might have been broken in their younger days. Even though they appeared as serious as a heart attack, they could be entertaining and even friendly when you got to know them. Today, that tough-guy image is completely gone. The cigars and cigarettes have disappeared entirely, the cup of coffee replaced by a bottle of Perrier, and the loud sports jackets swapped for custom-tailored suits. While old-school bosses relied on street smarts, today's bosses typically hold college degrees. Characters like the old guard are pretty much extinct today.

Today's bosses would have politely but sternly warned the other players that their language was making other guests uncomfortable, demonstrating a stark contrast in approach and demeanor.

In contrast, today's casino executives bring a more refined and educated approach to the job. Their polish and educated demeanor reflect the increasingly corporate nature of the gaming industry. While they may lack the colorful personalities of their predecessors, they bring a level of professionalism and business acumen that has become essential in navigating the complex modern casino landscape.

As the business evolved, so did the players and their expectations of us. Those old-school bosses with their gruff exteriors and "deal-with-it" attitudes would be considered liabilities today. Back then, their authority was absolute—right out of *Cool Hand Luke*—and a few of them seemed to enjoy flexing it a little too much.

As the bosses traded street smarts for spreadsheets, the floor changed too. The shift didn't just happen at the top—dealers started changing, just in the opposite direction. As management became more corporate and polished, the dealers got a little more outspoken. When I broke in during the late '70s, you kept your mouth shut, did what you were told, and hoped you'd get to come back the next day. Thick skin wasn't optional. It was job security.

Players could blow smoke in your face, wave a cigar near your knuckles, or say things that would get them tossed today. You didn't complain, you adapted. If a red-hot tip from a stogie was hovering near your hand while you paid off a bet, you learned to work around it. That was just part of the gig. Nobody talked about accommodations or comfort. It wasn't even a concept.

Fast-forward to today and the dynamic has shifted dramatically. Dealers now feel empowered to speak up about their comfort and well-being. They'll instruct players on where to place their ashtrays to minimize the impact of second-hand smoke and they're not afraid to voice their concerns to management if a player's behavior or language makes them feel threatened. Some may go as far as complaining to a boss that they don't want to go on a game where a player is smoking or even on a game where the dealer might be distressed by the player or the language they use.

This shift in attitude reflects a broader change in societal expectations and a growing awareness of the importance of workplace health and safety. While some may argue that dealers have become too sensitive or demanding, it's clear that the days of simply grinning and bearing it are long gone.

Ever-Changing Las Vegas

The money was different then, too. We worked for tips, period. The base pay was laughable—maybe $4 an hour—but on a good night, those envelopes could make your month. We received our earnings in cash at the end of each shift, stuffed into white envelopes with our names scribbled on the front. Now it's all digital, automatically divided by some algorithm that ensures everyone gets their "fair share." More equitable? Sure. But something was lost when you stopped feeling the weight of a good night in your pocket.

Having been in the thick of it for decades, I'm struck by the magnitude of change we've experienced. The casino floor may look the same, but the power dynamics and the way we interact with one another have undergone a seismic shift.

Toward the end of my decades-long run dealing high-limit games, the number of mandatory HR meetings shot through the roof. I often wondered how the old-school pit bosses—guys who'd cut their teeth in the mob-run joints of the '70s—would've handled sitting through a PowerPoint presentation on "microaggressions" or "inappropriate workplace humor." Heck, when corporate first banned smoking on the casino floor in the late '80s, these guys practically staged a revolt. Paul, my pit manager who burned through two packs of Marlboros a day, couldn't make it an hour without nicotine. Months after the ban, I'd still catch him ducking between banks of slot machines, frantically sucking down half a cigarette like a teenager hiding from his parents. Vinny, already the surliest boss on the floor, turned into an absolute bear without his constant cloud of smoke—snapping at dealers, pacing the pit like a caged animal, his fingers drumming phantom cigarettes on the rail. These were guys who'd spent decades running the casino with a cigarette dangling from their lips.

The whole process of running a game had changed, too. In the old days, disputes were settled with a look and a nod from the pit boss—no paperwork, no meetings, no review boards. A player got out of line? The boss handled it, end of story. Now, every incident requires forms in triplicate, witness statements, and a follow-up meeting with HR. What used to take 30 seconds and a firm handshake now required three days and a committee.

And they were expected to sit through sensitivity training about appropriate workplace touching? They would have laughed their way right out the door, probably stopping for a smoke break on the way.

The irony hit full force after our first mandatory session on workplace harassment. The HR rep, earnest and professionally dressed, had carefully explained why certain jokes were harmful, using a Mexican stereotype as her prime example of what not to say. Within minutes of the meeting ending, a group of dealers practically sprinted back to our break room—not to discuss the importance of cultural sensitivity, but to gleefully share the forbidden joke with Juan, our Mexican colleague who wasn't at that meeting, but was scheduled for the next day. I wish I could remember the joke itself, but I do recall most of us pinching ourselves to stifle laughter during the meeting.

On paper, these new policies painted a picture of a transformed workplace—zero tolerance for harassment, mandatory respect for all, a safe environment for everyone. The HR rep had guaranteed it would make no difference who violated the rules: zero tolerance, period. But down on the floor, where $100,000 hands played out under crystal chandeliers, the old rules still applied.

The bitter truth? It wasn't the staff who got away with violations—it was the players. The bigger their bets, the more that "zero" in zero tolerance started looking like "zero enforcement." I watched a high roller berate Lisha, our Asian floor supervisor and genuinely the nicest person on staff, telling her to "go back to China" after a losing streak. I had to stand there, unable to defend her, because he was down $200,000, and management didn't want him taking his action elsewhere. Through it all, Lisha maintained her composure. "Go ahead and spin," she told me, her voice steady, as if nothing had happened.

Some of these players didn't just demand dealers of a certain ethnicity, gender, or body type, they made these demands hours after we'd sat through meetings about creating a respectful workplace.

The house always wins, they say. Turns out that applies to workplace culture, too.

Over the years, downtown Las Vegas has had a few makeovers. When the Golden Nugget had its rebirth and expansion in the '80s, an effort was made to clean up the surrounding areas of the pawn shops, adult bookstores, and other shady neighbors. It was a major improvement to the overall area. Then came the Fremont Street Experience. With the rise of the Las Vegas Strip, downtown Las Vegas faced an economic downturn. To counter this, city officials initiated the revitalization of the area in the early '90s. A major part of this effort was the creation of the pedestrian mall and attraction that opened in 1995. This included covering Fremont Street with a canopy and installing millions of lights for a Viva Vision light show, transforming the area into a major tourist destination. As I write this, I'm reminded of how Las Vegas constantly changes. It doesn't seem like we were awaiting the opening of the Mirage all that long ago and now it's gone forever, to become a guitar-shaped Hard Rock hotel. The Tropicana was imploded in 2024 to make way for the A's new stadium, which is scheduled to open in 2028.

These contradictions didn't just change how employees were treated; they reshaped the entire visitor experience. The most noticeable shift? What Las Vegas offers and what it expects in return. Gone are the 49-cent breakfasts and $1.49 steak dinners. Twenty bucks used to be a night out in Vegas. In 1979, that could buy you a prime rib dinner, a couple of drinks, and still leave enough for a few spins at the quarter slots. With any luck, you might even catch a lounge show with your change. Back then, tipping a dealer $20 made you a hero. Today? Twenty dollars might cover the tip for valet parking—if you're not feeling generous. A cocktail at a high-end bar will run you $25, and that's before the "entertainment charge" and automatic 20% service fee.

Today's Strip serves up five-star restaurants with celebrity chefs and entrées priced like car payments. You can still find the occasional gift shop selling used cards and souvenir ashtrays, but you're just as likely to stumble into a Tiffany, Prada, or Rolex store while trying to find the restrooms.

Parking fees, resort fees, and a small-print minefield on your room bill have replaced the bargains and freebies that once defined Vegas. Comps? You'll need to lose a lot more before getting that buffet voucher, if the casino has a buffet any longer. Even the non-gaming parts of the property have been turned into revenue machines, squeezing every square inch for maximum profit.

I'm not saying it's all bad; some of the upgrades really are impressive. And sure, plenty of visitors love the variety, luxury, and Instagram-worthy meals. But let's not pretend the changes haven't come at a price. For those of us who remember when Vegas was a deal-hunter's dream, today's version can feel like being pickpocketed, albeit with style.

After decades in the business, I've had a front-row seat to this transformation. The focus has shifted from creating fun and memories to maximizing margins. It's always been a business, but it used to feel more like it was run by gamblers chasing a big score, not by accountants auditing every napkin.

In the end, the bean counters won. Yet in gaining a global shine, trading grit for gloss, Vegas lost some soul.

Maybe that's how Vegas works—nothing stays the same except the house edge and the desert sun. The city reinvents itself every decade, tearing down yesterday's monuments to build tomorrow's attractions. And those of us who work on the front line? We either

Ever-Changing Las Vegas

adapt or get left behind, like the coins that used to clatter in the slots.

I chose to adapt. Through all the reinventions and renovations, I kept showing up. From the break-in pits downtown to the high-limit salons on the Strip, I carved out a career one spin at a time. Along the way, I dodged some bad beats, bad bosses, and wild players.

Sure, Vegas changed. But so did I. And after 35 years of graveyard shifts and George sightings, I'd earned the right to call it a career.

I left the casino for the last time the same way I entered it all those years ago: squinting into the sun, pockets full of stories, and for the first time in decades, nowhere I had to be at 4 a.m. As I pulled out of the employee lot and turned onto Frank Sinatra Boulevard, it hit me. Frank got a street. I got 35 years of stories. We both did it our way—his just came with better royalties. It felt strange. And perfect.

Epilogue

Now that I'm retired for real, I've traded in my roulette spins for spinning the wheels on my electric bike to the beach here in Florida, with a bit of spinning a pickleball on the side. The Gulf breeze hits differently than that recycled casino air—salt instead of cigarette smoke, seagulls instead of slot machines.

After retiring, I thought I'd finally enjoy being one of those people who sleep as late as they want. Fat chance. My body clock is permanently set to casino time. Even now, I'm wide awake by 6 a.m.—which, granted, is sleeping in compared to those 2 a.m. wake-up calls. But here's the thing: I don't mind it. Those quiet morning hours used to belong to the casino; now they're mine. I make coffee, check the news, and watch the sun come up over the water instead of the desert.

People always say, "I bet you're glad you don't have to go into work anymore," usually with that knowing look, as if I'd been serving a prison sentence. Sure, I'm happy not to have to set an alarm for 2 a.m., but I never really dreaded it. How could I? Every shift was a front-row seat to the most incredible show of human nature. Where else would I have met billionaires and card mechanics, princes and con artists, all in the same night?

What I tell them is this: I miss the people, not the place. I miss that 4 a.m. camaraderie when we were all punch-drunk from the weird hours, sharing stories that no one outside the business would believe. I miss the anticipation of not knowing if tonight would be dead quiet or if some big player would show up and make everyone's night.

I returned for a visit three years after retiring. Flying in at night, I watched the Strip unfold below—a neon snake that had somehow grown another dozen vertebrae since I'd left. The changes hit you harder when you step away and come back. Properties I'd never seen rose where familiar landmarks used to be. The skyline looked like someone had been playing Tetris with billion-dollar blocks.

Walking through Bellagio felt like visiting your childhood home after someone else had remodeled it. Same bones, different soul.

I stopped by the employee entrance at Wynn, half-expecting to see familiar faces. The security guard, maybe 25 years old, looked at me like I was lost. "Can I help you?" I almost said I used to work here, but what was the point? His casino wasn't my casino, even if we'd walked the same halls.

Of all the adventures along the way, the most memorable was the opening of the Mirage. It's not that the other properties weren't spectacular, but that one stands out—maybe because it was my first opening, and because everyone recognized it as a dramatic turning point for Las Vegas. Though it seems like yesterday we were opening it, now it's gone. Just another example of the constant changing of the Las Vegas guard.

Even Steve Wynn, the visionary behind all those magnificent properties, is completely out of the business now, forced out by scandal years after I left—accusations that would have been buried in the old days, but couldn't survive in the #MeToo era. It felt like watching a king toppled by his own excess. The man who'd given me—given all of us—these incredible stages to work on, brought down not by competitors or market forces, but by himself.

The motley crews I worked with over the years are now scattered all over the country and the world, with some returning to their

Epilogue

homelands. I've been fortunate enough to be able to visit some of the parts of the world they described to me during our breaks. From the Grand Bazaar in Istanbul, Turkey, which Lutfe often spoke about, to a visit to London, where my coworker David gave my family a private tour of his hometown. I even made it to Monaco to observe croupiers in another land. And of course, I had to visit Bellagio in Italy—the town that inspired the casino. It was easy to recognize the influence in the restaurants and shops overlooking Lake Como.

Although the players were often entertaining, it was my fellow employees—the cast of characters working the graveyard shift—who truly kept me smiling. These folks, along with the voices in my head that helped pass the time during the more monotonous stretches, made up a truly odd bunch.

Had anyone suggested back in 1979, when I first stumbled onto this career path—never imagining it would become my livelihood—that I would spend 35 years watching fortunes won and lost, I would have said they were crazy. Now that I've lived it, I can honestly say it was a blast. I wouldn't change a thing.

Well, maybe one thing. I'd have bought better shoes from day one.

As I ponder words of wisdom for anyone starting out on a similar path today, two essentials come to mind. First, a thick skin—though it may not be as critical now as it was back when a boss could send you packing just for looking at them the wrong way. Second and most important: Invest in comfortable shoes. Forget about looking sharp; prioritize comfort. Your back and feet will thank you after the first 1,000 miles behind the table.

But here's what I'd really tell them, if they had time to listen: Pay attention, not just to the cards or procedures, but to the people. Every shift is a master class in human nature. You'll see generosity and greed, grace and desperation—sometimes from the same person in the same hour. You'll learn that money doesn't change people. It reveals them.

And one day decades from now, when you're riding your own bike down some sunny street far from the neon, you'll realize you weren't just dealing cards all those years. You were dealing in stories. And brother, what stories they were.

The house always wins, they say. But if you play it right, you can walk away with something even better than money: a lifetime of memories that no casino can ever take back.

Sometimes late at night, when I can't sleep—old habits die hard—I'll close my eyes and hear it all again. The soft click of chips being stacked. The bounce of the ball as it finds a numbered pocket to settle into. Someone calling out, "Winner, winner, chicken dinner," in the distance.

And I smile, knowing I was part of it all. Part of the great, glittering, impossible dream that is Las Vegas.

The ball's still spinning somewhere tonight. It just isn't my wheel anymore.

And that's okay.

Glossary

Action: The play at the casino or the total amount of money put into play. Also, a dealer expression telling a player it is his/her turn to act.

Aggregate Limit: The total amount a casino is liable to pay out in a single round. If this limit is reached, players may have to accept reduced winnings.

All-In: A betting action whereby a player wagers all their remaining chips.

American Roulette: A roulette variant with a wheel that has 38 pockets, one of which is the double zero (00).

Apron: The area of a roulette table where the dealer works to sweep in chips and make payouts. This part of the table is typically located around the betting layout and is used for managing the chips during the game. Also a term used for the lower track of a roulette wheel.

Baccarat: Also called Punto Banco. A card game with several variants in which players bet on whether the player or the dealer (bank) has the winning two-card or three-card hand. Winning hands are determined by achieving a cumulative points total closest to nine. Face cards and 10s don't have any point value.

Bankroll: The money available for participating in casino activities.

Bet Limit: The minimum and maximum amounts a player can bet.

Blackjack or Natural: When the original two-card hand dealt totals 21 points.

Bust: A hand that is worth more than 21 and automatically results in a loss of the bet.

Capping a Bet: Secretly adding extra chips to your wager after the deal has begun.

Checks (cheques): A term for roulette chips, which don't have a set value until established when a player buys into the game.

Chipper Champ: A mechanical device used by the dealer to stack and organize chips efficiently.

Chips: The round colored discs, equivalent to money. They can be purchased in various denominations and used as currency to bet at the casino tables.

Color Up: Changing chips to a higher denomination. When you request that smaller value chips be exchanged for larger value ones.

Column Bet: A bet on one of the three 12-number columns on the roulette layout.

Commission: An added fee that is paid when betting the bank in baccarat, generally 5% when the bank wins.

Complete Bet: A roulette bet that covers all of the various ways a player can bet on a specific number. This includes: straight up, splits, corners, street and line bets for that number.

Comps (short for complimentaries): Free perks and rewards given to players. These can include meals, hotel rooms, show tickets, and other amenities. Casinos offer comps to encourage players to gamble more and to reward their loyalty. The value and type of comps a player receives often depend on how much they gamble and for how long.

Corner Bet: A wager on four numbers made by placing chips on the corner of adjacent numbers, and also known as Carré in French

Glossary

roulette. This wager pays 8 to 1.

Count: The process of tallying up the total amount of money, chips, and vouchers collected by the casino. In card counting, it refers to keeping track of the cards that have been dealt to gain an advantage.

Croupier: A French word for dealer, used to describe the person who operates the roulette wheel and collects and pays bets.

Cut: After a shuffle, to divide the deck of cards into two parts and place the bottom part on top.

Cut Card: A solid-colored card used to cut the deck after shuffling, often placed in the deck to signal the last hand before a reshuffle.

Cutting checks: The process of organizing casino chips into neat uniform stacks, typically of 20 chips each, performed by dealers during gameplay. It also refers to the act of a dealer quickly and accurately determining the value of a stack of chips by removing a portion of the stack to count, often done by feel or sight without fully counting each chip.

Daub: A form of cheating that involves marking cards in a subtle way to identify them later.

Dice Bowl: A small bowl used to hold extra dice on a craps table. It's typically located near the dealer or stickman, who uses it to replace the dice in play if needed. The bowl ensures that there are always backup dice ready in case the current dice need to be swapped out for any reason, such as being damaged or suspected of being tampered with.

Dolly: A marker used by the dealer to indicate the winning number on a roulette table. The dolly is placed on the table in the square of the winning number. It helps players identify the winning number and remains in place until all winning wagers are paid.

Double Down: In blackjack, doubling the original bet and receiving one more card.

Dozen Bet: A bet on one of the three consecutive dozens on the roulette table paying 2 to 1.

Draw (or Hit): When a player requests an additional card.

Drop: The total amount of money and chips taken in by the casino from players' buy-ins at a table.

Drop Percentage (or House Percentage): The portion of a player's cash that the casino wins because of the house edge.

Dumping the Rack: When the dealer is losing frequently to the players.

Edge: Advantage.

EO (Early Out): A dealer can leave before the shift is over if their final break is scheduled to finish at the same time as the shift.

European Roulette: A roulette variant with a wheel that has 37 pockets and no double-zero pocket.

Even-Money Bet: A bet that pays back the same amount that a player wagers.

Eye-in-the-Sky (or Eye): The name given to the cameras and surveillance in a casino.

Face Card: Card with a face (jack, queen, or king) of any suit.

Final: A bet placed on numbers on the roulette wheel that end in the same digit. For example, "final 7" with three chips means betting on 7, 17, and 27.

First Base: The position to the far left of the dealer and the first to be dealt cards in blackjack.

Flat Betting: Betting the same for each hand with no variation in the amount.

George: A generous tipper.

Going South: Taking chips off the table and hiding them.

Handle: The total amount of money wagered by players over a certain period or at a specific game.

Heads Up: When there is only one player playing at a blackjack table.

Glossary 253

High Bet: A bet placed on all of the numbers from 19 to 36 in roulette.

High Roller: A player who plays at high minimum and maximum tables and places large bets.

Hit: A request for an additional card.

Hold: The percentage of the total money wagered that the casino keeps as profit. It's a measure of the casino's earnings from the games.

Hole Card: The facedown cards that a dealer is dealt in blackjack.

Hot Table: When the players at a table are winning frequently.

Hustle: When a dealer becomes somewhat pushy, suggesting that a tip is expected. A soft hustle is a bit more subtle.

Insurance: A side bet that the dealer will have a natural, available when the dealer's up card is an ace.

Junket: A group of players flown in by a casino.

Lammer: A small, usually plastic marker or button used in casinos to track various aspects of gameplay. They're often used to indicate the status of bets, player positions, or game conditions. For example, in baccarat, lammers may be used to mark a commission owed on winning banker bets, while in roulette, they can be used to track call bets or to mark the winning number on the wheel.

Layout: The felt or surface on a gaming table that shows the betting areas and game rules.

Lid: A transparent lockable cover placed over the chip tray on a casino table when the game isn't in use. It serves to secure the chips, prevent unauthorized access, and signal that the table is closed for play.

Limit: A fixed number that a wager can't go over, the table maximum for a bet, and the minimum amount that a player must play, the table minimum.

Low Bet: A bet on the first 18 numbers in roulette.

Martingale: A negative-progression strategy in which says bets are doubled after each loss.

Marker: A form of credit extended to players, allowing them to borrow money from the casino to gamble. It's essentially an IOU that the player signs, agreeing to repay the borrowed amount within a specified timeframe, typically 30 days.

Natural: A two-card blackjack hand that is worth 21 points and is automatically a winning hand, unless the dealer has the same, in which case it is a push or tie. A natural in baccarat occurs when the two cards initially dealt to either the player or the banker total 8 or 9.

Outside Bet: Roulette bets on the periphery of the layout in roulette such as red/black, even/odd, and high/low.

Paint: A face card.

Pencil: The person assigning the dealers to their games.

Press a Bet: To increase the amount bet.

Push: A tie in blackjack, both a player and dealer have the same total and no money is exchanged. A tie between the player and the dealer in a game, resulting in no one winning or losing the bet.

Rack: A tray that holds chips, typically used by dealers to organize and manage chips on the table.

Rainbow Bet: When a player bets a stack of various denomination chips.

Score: A significant win or payout in a game. It can also refer to a good day for a dealer in tips.

Shoe: A device used to hold and dispense playing cards at blackjack and baccarat. It's typically a rectangular box-like contraption made of plastic and can hold multiple decks of cards (usually 4-8 decks). The shoe allows dealers to slide out cards one at a time, enhancing game security by reducing the risk of card manipulation and increasing the speed and efficiency of dealing.

Shill: An individual employed by a casino to encourage gameplay by sitting at tables, placing bets, and creating an atmosphere of activity. Shills use house money to play, helping to attract genuine players to games that might otherwise appear empty or inactive.

Soft Hand: A hand that contains one or more aces that can be worth either 1 or 11.

Spacer: A blank chip or object used to separate stacks of chips.

Split Hand: To split the initial two cards into two separate hands. This is allowed only when the initial two cards are of equal rank. The player adds an additional bet.

Stiff: Someone who doesn't tip.

Straight Bet (or Straight Up): A bet placed on a single number in roulette.

Street Bet: A roulette bet placed on three numbers at once, like 4, 5, 6.

Super George: A player who tips exceptionally well, even more generously than a typical George. The best of the best regarding tips.

Surrender: An option to pay a penalty and throw away a hand. To forfeit a blackjack hand and have half of the bet returned. This action can be taken only before any other action.

Sweep: The action of the dealer collecting losing bets from the table after a game round.

Tapped Out: A player who is totally out of money. Also refers to a dealer being relieved from a game for a break or end of shift.

Third Base: The position nearest to the dealer's right and the last to be played in blackjack before the dealer's hand is played.

Toke: A tip for the dealer.

Whale: A high roller.

Further Reading

The following books provided valuable background information and context for this work. While my book is primarily based on personal experiences from 35 years in the casino industry, these sources have contributed to my understanding of the field and Las Vegas history.

Casino Operations and Gambling
- Brisman, Andrew. *Mensa Guide to Casino Gambling*. Sterling Publishing, 1999. A comprehensive guide to casino games, offering insights into odds and strategies.
- Garcia, Frank. *How To Detect Crooked Gambling*. Arco Publishing, 1977. An intriguing look at the methods used to cheat in casino games.
- Uston, Ken. *Million Dollar Blackjack*. SRS Enterprises, 1981. A detailed exploration of blackjack strategies and techniques.
- Scarne, John. *New Complete Guide to Gambling*. Simon and Schuster, 1961. A classic text offering a broad overview of various gambling activities.
- Scheri, Saverio. *The Casino's Most Valuable Chip*. Institute for the History of Technology, 2005. An examination of the importance of customer service in the casino industry.
- Taucer, Vic & Easley, Steve. *Table Games Management*. Institute for the Study of Gambling, 2003. A practical guide to

managing casino table games operations.
- Thorp, Edward O. *Beat The Dealer*. Random House, 1962. A groundbreaking book on card counting in blackjack that revolutionized the game.
-

Las Vegas History and Personalities
- Binkley, Christina. *Winner Takes All*. Hyperion, 2008. An account of the battle for supremacy on the Las Vegas Strip.
- Castleman, Deke. *Whale Hunt in the Desert*. Huntington Press, 2015. An insider's look at the world of high-stakes gambling and casino marketing to "whales" (top-tier players).
- Smith, John L. *Running Scared*. Da Capo Press, 2001. A biography of Las Vegas casino mogul Steve Wynn.
- Smith, John L. *Sharks in the Desert*. Barricade Books, 2005. An exploration of the colorful characters who shaped Las Vegas.
- Walters, Billy. *Gambler*. Avid Reader Press, 2023. A memoir by one of the most successful sports bettors in Las Vegas history.

About the Author

Randy Rutecki's path to the casino floor wasn't exactly typical. After leaving a vice-president role with Wherehouse Records in California in the late 1970s, he plunged into the world of blackjack card counting and, soon after, dealing on the Las Vegas Strip. A graduate of the University of Buffalo and a native of Buffalo, New York, Randy combined his love of numbers and games into a decades-long career in casinos, where he witnessed—and helped shape—some of the city's biggest changes.

Outside the pit, Randy was a pioneer in sports wagering. In the 1980s, he co-founded the Handicappers Research Group, created software through his company Rutech Software, and wrote a weekly "Computer Gambling" column for *Gaming Today*. He authored *Computing Against the Odds*, a practical guide to developing football handicapping software, and compiled the Handicappers Internet Yellow Pages, a first-of-its-kind resource for bettors in the early days of the web.

Randy's technical skills found their way back into the casinos themselves—developing scheduling software for the Mirage and applications that trained new dealers. Through it all, his eye for detail, wit, and insider knowledge of both gambling and the gamblers make him a natural storyteller of the Las Vegas that tourists rarely see.

Randy lives in Florida with his wife, Debbie, whom he first met in the 1980s when they were both dealers at the Golden Nugget in Las Vegas.

www.ingramcontent.com/pod-product-compliance
Lightning Source LLC
Chambersburg PA
CBHW022058120526
44580CB00017B/123/J